English for Academic C
and Socializing

Adrian Wallwork

English for Academic Correspondence and Socializing

 Springer

Adrian Wallwork
Via Carducci 9
56127 Pisa, Italy
adrian.wallwork@gmail.com

ISBN 978-1-4419-9400-4   e-ISBN 978-1-4419-9401-1
DOI 10.1007/978-1-4419-9401-1
Springer New York Dordrecht Heidelberg London

Library of Congress Control Number: 2011928674

Printed on acid-free paper

Springer is part of Springer Science+Business Media (www.springer.com)

Preface

Who is this book for?

This book is for PhD students, researchers, lecturers, and professors in any discipline whose first language is not English. The book will teach you how to use English to carry out everyday activities in your academic work, such as writing emails, dealing with referees and editors, making phone calls, and socializing at conferences.

What are the three most important things I will learn from this book?

This book is based on three fundamental guidelines.

1 THINK FROM THE POINT OF VIEW OF YOUR INTERLOCUTOR

Whether you are writing an email to a colleague, responding to a referee's report, or interacting face to face over the dinner table at a social event, it pays to put yourself in your interlocutor's shoes. This also means that you always try to be diplomatic and constructive.

2 WRITE CONCISELY WITH NO REDUNDANCY AND NO AMBIGUITY, AND YOU WILL MAKE FEWER MISTAKES IN YOUR ENGLISH

The more you write, the more mistakes in English you will make. If you avoid redundant words and phrases you will significantly increase the readability of whatever document you are writing.

3 RECOGNIZE THAT UNDERSTANDING THE SPOKEN ENGLISH OF NATIVE SPEAKERS DOES NOT NEED TO BE A NIGHTMARE

You will learn from this book that even native speakers sometimes do not completely understand each other. If you don't understand them, it is not necessarily a reflection of the level of your English. Communication is a two-way activity in which both parties are equally responsible for the outcome. You will learn that you simply need to adopt certain strategies when dealing with native speakers and have the confidence to interrupt them as often as you feel is necessary.

What else will I learn?

You will learn how to

- write emails that your recipient will open, read, and respond to
- use standard phrases correctly, and with the right level of formality
- improve your usage of tenses (past, present, future)
- significantly improve your chances of having your paper published by interacting in a constructive way with referees and editors
- talk to key people at conferences and thus improve your chances of having a good career
- understand spoken English over the phone and face to face
- relax when speaking and listening to English
- use Google to translate, and to correct your English

I am a trainer in EAP and EFL. Should I read this book?

If you are a teacher of English for Academic Purposes or English as a Foreign Language you will learn about all the typical problems that non-native researchers have in the world of academia. You will be able to give your students advice on writing effective emails and getting referees and editors to accept their papers and lots of tips on how to network at conferences.

How is this book organized?

The book is divided into seven parts—see the Contents on page xi. The Contents page also acts as a summary of each chapter.

Each chapter begins with a very quick summary of its importance. This is followed either by advice from experts in writing and communication or by interesting factoids. Most of the comments from the experts were commissioned specifically for this book.

A typical chapter then proceeds with a series of important issues to focus on when you are carrying out a particular task (e.g., writing, telephoning, socializing).

Are the emails and other examples in this book genuine? Are they in correct English?

Yes, all the emails apart from one (3.14) are real emails that have only been modified to ensure the accuracy of the English. The same is true for the referees' reports and replies to these reports—although in some cases you might find this difficult to believe! Unless otherwise stated, all the examples are in correct English.

Glossary

The definitions below of how various terms are used in this book are mine and should not be considered as official definitions.

Anglo	I use this term for convenience to refer to a native speaker of English from the following countries: USA, UK, Australia, Canada, New Zealand, the Republic of Ireland, and South Africa
British English	There are many varieties of English. For the sake of brevity I use the terms *British English* and *American English* to refer to the standard English that is also spoken in Australia, Canada, New Zealand, the Republic of Ireland, and South Africa. The English of other English-speaking countries, such as India and Singapore, is very similar to Anglo English, but has its own peculiarities
interlocutor	The person you are speaking to or the recipient of your email
manuscript	An unpublished written work that is going to be submitted for publication
native speaker of English	Someone born in an Anglo (see definition above) country who speaks English as their first language
non-native speaker of English	Someone whose first language is not English
review / report	A report on a manuscript made by a reviewer or referee
reviewer / referee	These two terms are used indifferently to refer to the person who makes a report on your manuscript

Below are some grammatical terms that I have used.

adjective	a word that describes a noun (e.g., *significant, usual*)
adverb	a word that describes a verb or appears before an adjective (e.g., *significantly, usually*)
ambiguity	words and phrases that could be interpreted in more than one way
active	use of a personal pronoun / subject before a verb (e.g., *we found that x = y* rather than *it was found that x = y*)
direct object	in the sentence "I have a book," the book is the direct object
indirect object	in the sentence "I gave the book to Anna," book is the direct object, and Anna is the indirect object
infinitive	the root part of the verb (e.g., *to learn, to analyze*)
-ing form	the part of the verb that ends in *-ing* and that acts like a noun (e.g., *learning, analyzing*)
link word, linker	words and expressions that connect phrases and sentences together (e.g., *and, moreover, although, despite the fact that*)
modal verb	verbs such as *can, may, might, could, would, should*
noun	words such as *a/the paper, a/the result, a/the sample*
paragraph	a series of one or more sentences, the last of which ends with a paragraph symbol (¶)
passive	an impersonal way of using verbs (e.g., *it was found that x = y* rather than *we found that x = y*)
phrase	a series of words that make up part of a sentence
redundancy	words and phrases that could be deleted because they add no value for the reader
sentence	a series of words ending with a period (.)

A note on *he*, *she*, and *their*

A frequent problem for writers is the use of a generic pronoun. Occasionally I have used the pronoun *he* to refer to a generic person, sometimes I have used *he / she*, but most often I have used *they*. In modern English *they*, *them*, and *their* can be used as generic pronouns to refer to just one person even though it requires a plural verb.

Other books in this series

This book is a part of series of books to help non-native English-speaking researchers to communicate in English. The other titles are as follows:

English for Presentations at International Conferences

English for Writing Research Papers

English for Research: Usage, Style, and Grammar

English for Academic Research: Grammar Exercises

English for Academic Research: Vocabulary Exercises

English for Academic Research: Writing Exercises

Contents

Part I
Email

Chapter 1
Subject Lines

You will learn how to write a subject line that will

- be easily recognizable and distinguishable from other emails in your recipient's inbox
- prompt your recipient to want to know more and thus to open your mail
- help establish a personal connection with your recipient
- summarize the content of the email so that your recipient will know what to expect even before reading the contents of the mail

It may seem unusual to have an entire chapter dedicated to subject lines, but more than 250 billion are written every day. They are absolutely crucial in motivating your recipient to open your email and to respond quickly, rather than setting it aside for future reading. The subject line of an email is like the title of the paper. If readers do not find the title of a paper interesting, they are unlikely to read the rest of the paper. Likewise, if your subject line is not relevant in some way to the recipient, they may decide simply to delete your email. British journalist Harold Evans once wrote that *writing good headlines is 50 per cent of text editors' skills*. The same could be said of email.

A. Wallwork, *English for Academic Correspondence and Socializing*,
DOI 10.1007/978-1-4419-9401-1_1, © Springer Science+Business Media, LLC 2011

Factoids

❖ The first email was sent in 1971 by an engineer called Ray Tomlinson. He sent it to himself and it contained the memorable message: qwertyuiop. However, several other people are also claimed to have sent the first message.

❖ If every email that is sent in one day was printed, each on one sheet of A4, two and a half million trees would have to be cut down. If all the printed emails were piled up on top of each other, they would be more than three times the height of Everest and they would weigh more than the entire human population of Canada. If the printed sheets were laid out they would cover a surface area equivalent to two million football pitches. The cost of printing them would be equivalent to Spain's Gross Domestic Product for an entire year—around 1.4 billion dollars.

❖ Although the most common Internet activity is emailing, a "Digital Life" worldwide survey found that people actually spend more time on social media (4.6 hours per week against 4.4 for email).

❖ The term *drailing* was coined in the mid-2000s and means emailing while drunk.

1.1   Write the subject line imagining that you are the recipient

As always when writing emails, you need to think from the recipient's perspective. I lecture in scientific English, and I receive an incredible number of emails from students who use the words *English course* as their subject line. From their point of view, an English course is something very specific in their life—it is only 2 hours a week as opposed to their research and studies which probably take up over 40 hours. So for them, *English course* is very meaningful. But from my point of view, the reverse is true. English courses take up a big part of my week. So the subject line *English course* is not helpful for me at all. A more meaningful subject line would be *Civil Engineers English course* or *English course 10 October*.

So, as with the title of a paper, your subject line needs to be as specific as possible.

It pays to remember that in many cases the recipient is doing you a favor if he / she decides to open your email—your job as the sender is to make this favor worthwhile.

1.2   Combine your subject line with the preview pane

Most email systems display not only the subject line but also make the first few words visible too (either directly as in Gmail or indirectly using a preview pane as in Outlook). It may be useful to use the first words as a means to encourage the recipient to open your email straight away, rather than delaying reading it or deleting it forever.

Using *Dear + title* (e.g., Dr, Professor) + *person's name* as your first words may help to distinguish your email from spam, as spammed mails do not usually incorporate people's titles.

If you adopt this tactic, then it is a good idea to keep your subject line as short as possible. If you can include any key words in the first few words, that too will have a positive influence on the recipient.

1.3   Use the subject line to give your complete message

Some people, me included, use the subject line to give our complete message. This saves the recipient from having to open the email. A typical message to my students might be: *Oct 10 lesson shifted to Oct 17. Usual time and place. EOM.*

EOM stands for *End of message* and signals to the recipient that the complete message is contained within the subject line and that they don't have to open the email.

If you don't write EOM, recipients will not know whether they need or do not need to open the message.

1.4   Consider using a two-part subject line

Some people like to divide their subject line into two parts. The first part contains the context, the second part the details about this context. Here are some examples:

XTC Workshop: postponed till next year

EU project: first draft of review

1.5   Be specific, never vague

A vague subject title such as *Meeting time changed* is guaranteed to annoy most recipients. They want to know which meeting, and when the new time is. Both these details could easily be contained in the subject line.

Project C Kick Off meeting new time 10.30, Tuesday 5 September

This means that a week later when perhaps your recipients have forgotten the revised time of the meeting, they can simply scan their inbox, without actually having to open any mails.

1.6   Include pertinent details for the recipient

If your recipient knows someone who knows you, then it is not a bad idea to put the name of this common acquaintance in the subject line. This alerts the recipient that this is not a spam message. For example, let's imagine you met a certain Professor Huan at a conference. Huan recommended that you write to a colleague of his, Professor Wilkes, for a possible placement in Professor Wilkes lab. Your subject line for your email to Professor Wilkes could be:

Prof Huan. Request for internship by engineering PhD student from University of X

Sometimes it might be useful to include the place where you met the recipient. For example:

XTC Conf. Beijing. Request to receive your paper entitled: *name of paper*

1.7 Examples of subject lines

Here are some more examples of subject lines. The words in italics are words that you would need to change.

Attaching a manuscript for the first time to a journal where you have never published before:

Paper submission: *title of your paper*

Attaching revised manuscript to a journal where your paper has already been accepted subject to revisions:

Manuscript No. *1245/14*: revised version
title of your paper: revised version

Reply to referees' report:

Manuscript No. *5648/AA*—Reply to referees

Request to receive a paper:

Request to receive your paper entitled *title of paper*

Permission to quote from paper / research etc:

Permission to quote your paper entitled *paper title*

Request for placement / internship:

Request for *internship* by *engineering PhD student* from *University of X*

Chapter 2
Beginnings and Endings

You will learn how to

- address someone—whether you know them, don't know them, or don't even know their name
- pay attention to titles (e.g. Mr, Dr, Professor)
- make it clear who your email is intended for
- use standard English phrases rather than translating directly from your own language

First impressions are very important. When you meet someone face to face the first time, you probably take 30 seconds or less to form an impression of this person. After, it will be very difficult for you to change this initial impression. In an email you can form a bad impression within just one second. People's names are incredibly important to them. If you make a mistake in the spelling of someone's name (even by using the wrong accent on a letter), you risk instantly annoying them and they may be less willing to carry out whatever request you are asking them.

If you use standard phrases (see Chapter 22), rather than literal translations, you will ensure that your email looks professional. You will also minimize the number of mistakes you make in English.

A. Wallwork, *English for Academic Correspondence and Socializing*,
DOI 10.1007/978-1-4419-9401-1_2, © Springer Science+Business Media, LLC 2011

Factoids

Indian English tends to be more formal than British and American English. In emails, Indians often use the word *Sir*, even informally, for example, *Hi Sir, how're you doing*. They also use phrases such as *Thanking you, Sincerely yours* and *Respectfully yours*, which are rarely used by British or American academics. Sometimes Indians mix English words with words from their own languages for example, *Yours shubhakankshi*. Young Indians now use phrases such as *C ya soon*; they also adopt SMS lingo: *tc* (take care), *u no* (you know), *4ever* (forever), *4u* (for you), etc.

Chinese students tend to address their professors in this way: Respectful Professor Chang. The word *Respectful* or *Honorable* is the literal translation from a Chinese three-character word (尊敬的). *Dear* is not used as much in mainland Chinese culture as in English / American cultures because it involves intimacy, because to mainland Chinese people "dear" sounds like "darling," "sweetie," or "honey." In mainland China it is generally used between close female friends, girl to girl, and between lovers.

Surnames in Thailand only came into general usage in 1913, when King Rama VI decided that all Thais should have a last name. Every family had to choose their own last name.

2.1   Spell the recipient's name correctly

Make sure your recipient's name is spelt correctly. Think how you feel when you see your own name is misspelled.

Some names include accents. Look at the other's person's signature and cut and paste it into the beginning of your email—that way you will not make any mistakes either in spelling or in use of accents (e.g., è, ö, ñ).

Although their name may contain an accent, they may have decided to abandon accents in emails—so check to see if they use an accent or not.

2.2   Use an appropriate initial salutation and be careful with titles

With Anglos it is generally safe to write any of the following:

Dear Professor Smith,
Your name was given to me by . . .

Dear Dr Smith:
I was wondering whether . . .

Dear John Smith
I am writing to . . . .

Dear John
How are things?

Note that you can follow the person's name by a comma (,), by a colon (:), or with no punctuation at all. Whatever system you adopt, the first word of the next line must begin with a capital letter (*Your, How*).

Dr is an accepted abbreviation for "doctor," that is, someone with a PhD, or a doctor of medicine. It is not used if you only have a normal degree.

The following salutations would generally be considered inappropriate:

Hi Professor Smith—The word *Hi* is very informal and is thus not usually used in association with words such as *Professor* and *Dr*, as these are formal means of address.

Dear Prof Smith—Always use the full form of Professor as the abbreviation Prof might be considered too informal or rude.

Dear Smith—Anglos rarely address each other in emails with just the surname.

If you have had no communication with the person before, then it is always best to use their title. Also, even if Professor Smith replies to your email and signs himself as *John*, it is still best to continue using *Professor Smith* until he says, for instance: *Please feel free to call me John.*

In many other countries people frequently use functional or academic titles instead of names, for example, Mr Engineer, Mrs Lawyer. However, many people in academia tend not to use such titles when writing to each other in English.

2.3   Avoid problems when it is not clear if the recipient is male or female, or which is their surname

It may be difficult to establish someone's gender from their first name. In fact, what perhaps look like female names, may be male names, and vice versa. For example, the Italian names Andrea, Luca, and Nicola; the Russian names Ilya, Nikita, and Foma; and the Finnish names Esa, Pekka, Mika, and Jukka are all male names. The Japanese names Eriko, Yasuko, Aiko, Sachiko, Michiko, and Kanako may look like male names to Western eyes, but are in fact female. Likewise, Kenta, Kota, and Yuta are all male names in Japanese.

If your own name is ambiguous, it is a good idea in first mails to sign yourself in a way that is clear what sex you are, for example, Best regards, Andrea Cavalieri (Mr).

In addition, many English first names seem to have no clear indication of the sex, for example, Saxon, Adair, Chandler, and Chelsea. And some English names can be for both men and women, for example, Jo, Sam, Chris, and Hilary.

In some cases it may not be clear to you which is the person's first and last name, for example, Stewart James. In this particular case, it is useful to remember that Anglos put their first name first, so Stewart will be the first name. However, this is not true of all Europeans. Some Italians, for example, put their surname first (e.g., Ferrari Luigi) and others may have a surname that looks like a first name (e.g., Marco Martina). In the far east, it is usual to put the last name first, for example, Tao Pei Lin (Tao is the surname, Pei Lin is the first name). The best solution is always to write both names, for example, Dear Stewart James, then there can be no mistake. Similarly, avoid Mr, Mrs, Miss, and Ms—they are not frequently used in emails. By not using them you avoid choosing the wrong one.

So, if you are writing to non-academics, be careful how you use the following titles:
Mr—man (not known if married or not)
Ms—woman (not known if married or not)
Mrs—married woman
Miss—unmarried woman

If you receive an email from a Chinese person, you might be surprised to find that they have an English first name. Most young Chinese people have English nicknames, such as university students or even teachers, basically anyone who has to deal with foreign people. They are simply used for convenience (i.e., to help non-Chinese speakers) and they are also used in email addresses.

Thus, a good general rule when replying to someone for the first time is to

- address them using exactly the same name (both first and last name) that they use in their signature
- precede this name with an appropriate title
- adopt their style and tone. If you are making the first contact, then it is safer to be formal in order to be sure not to offend anyone. Then as the relationship develops, you can become less (or more) formal as appropriate. In any case, always take into account the reader's customs and culture, remembering that some cultures are much more formal than others.

2.4 Be as specific as possible when addressing an email to someone whose name you do not know

For important emails it is always best to find out the name of the person to address. This maximizes the chances of your email (i) reaching the right person, (ii) being opened, and (iii) being responded to.

However, on many occasions the exact name of the person is not important, for example, when you are asking for information about products or how to register for a conference. In such cases, the simplest solution is to have no salutation at all, or simply to use *Hi*. Some people like to use the expression *To whom it may concern*, but this expression is really no more useful than having no salutation.

Alternatively, you can write something more specific, such as

> Dear Session Organizers
> Dear Editorial Assistant
> Dear Product Manager

2.5 Remind the recipient who you are when previous contact has only been brief

You can announce your name and where you met.

> My name is Heidi Muller and you may remember that I came up to you after your presentation yesterday. I asked you the question about X. Well, I was wondering . . .

Or without announcing your name you can simply jog their memory

> Thanks for the advice you gave me at dinner last night. With regard to what you said about X, do you happen to have any papers on . . .

2.6 Use standard phrases rather than translations from your own language

Every language has certain phrases that cannot be translated literally into another language. A high percentage of the content of emails is made up of such standard phrases. You need to be very aware of what these standard phrases are, and what their equivalents are in English—see Chapter 22. You could create your own personal collection of useful phrases, which you can cut and paste from emails written by native English speakers (which hopefully will be correct!).

If you make literal translations into English, the result may sound strange or even comical and thus sound unprofessional. Here are some examples:

GERMAN	JAPANESE	RUSSIAN
Beautiful greetings.	To omit the greetings.	Healthy.
I feel pleasure for myself from you to hear.	Thank you for supporting us always.	Wish a success.
Say you a greeting to your wife.	Please kindly look after this.	Calm night.

Using standard phrases enables you to be sure that at least the beginnings and ends of your emails are correct! Then in the body of the email it is advisable not to experiment too much with your English.

Note that the use of English varies from one English-speaking country to another. If you are a researcher from India, Pakistan, Bangladesh, and other countries (e.g., in Africa) with strong historical ties to England, then your standard English usage may be considerably more formal than, for instance, in the UK and the US.

English-speaking researchers in the West tend to be less deferential to their professors and use considerably less salutations at the end of an email. An expression such as *Sincerely yours* that might be considered perfectly acceptable by Indian speakers of English sounds much too formal or even rather archaic to someone in the UK or US, where even *Yours sincerely* tends to be reserved for very formal letters. A much more typical salutation is *Best regards*, which works both in formal and more neutral situations.

2.7   Begin with a greeting + recipient's name

If you begin an email simply with "hi" or "good morning" or with no greeting at all, it will not help the recipient know if the message really was intended for them. Given that your recipient will be able to see the beginning of your email without actually opening the email, if they do not see their name they may think either that the message is not for them or that it is spam, and thus they may delete it without reading it.

A greeting provides a friendly opening, in the same way as saying "hello" on the phone. A greeting only requires a couple of words, and on the recipient's part will take less than a second to read so you will not be wasting their time.

However, if you exchange messages regularly with someone and that person does not make use of greetings, then you can drop these greetings too.

2.8   If there has been no previous contact, give reason for your email immediately

Begin by explaining your reason for writing rather than giving your name, which the recipient will have already seen before even opening your email. Here are two examples.

> I would like to have permission to quote part of the experimental from the following paper. I am planning to use the extract in my PhD thesis. I will of course acknowledge the journal, the author...

> I attended your presentation last week. Could you kindly give the link to the online version—thank you. By the way I really enjoyed your talk—it was very interesting and also very pertinent to my field of research which is ...

Note how the key information is given immediately. Even if the recipient reads nothing after the second line, it does not matter because all the key information is contained within the first line.

However, if the recipients read only the first two lines of the following two emails, the senders would not get the result desired:

> I attended your presentation last week. I really enjoyed your talk—it was very interesting and also very pertinent to my field of research, which is hydro-energy robotics, i.e. water-powered robots. What I found particularly relevant, and which I think our two lines of research have in common, is ... Anyway, the reason I am writing is to ask if you could kindly give me the link to the online version.

> My name is Ibrahim Ahmed Saleh and I am a second-year PhD student at the University of Phoenix. My current research activity can be divided into two broad areas. My first line research investigates a question of global governance...

2.9   Indicate to multiple recipients who actually needs to read the mail

If someone is on a mailing list, they may receive hundreds of emails that are not specifically for them. It is thus good practice to begin your email by saying who exactly the email is for and why they should read it, then those who may not be interested can stop reading.

2.10   Make it clear who should read your email and what it is you are requesting

The email below is written in good clear English. But it has a major problem.

Dear Sirs,

I am an enthusiastic and motivated 24 year-old Electronics Engineer with a special interest in RF. I have spent the last six months doing an internship at XTX Semiconductors Inc in Richmond. This internship was part of my Master's and regarded the characterization and modeling of a linear power amplifier for UMTS mobile handsets. While at XTX I studied linear power amplifier architectures and worked on RF measurements. I will be getting my Master's diploma in March next year. Thank you for your time and consideration.

Best regards

Kim Nyugen

Kim uses a concise style and gives clear details of his activities. But it is not clear

- who the email is addressed to
- what Kim wants

Does Kim want a job—if so, is he writing to the human resources manager? Is he applying to a summer school—if so, is he writing to the course organizer? The recipient has no idea.

When you write an email, you should always address it to someone in particular. Recipients feel much more motivated to reply if they have been addressed in person. It makes them feel personally responsible. If you simply write *Dear Sirs*, you are severely limiting your chances of a response. Find out the exact name of the person to write to—from the website or by telephoning directly.

The reason for your email should be clearly stated as early as possible in the email. So Kim could have begun his email like this:

> I am interested in applying for the post of junior scientist advertised on your website.

Or:

> I would like to apply for a placement in your summer school.

Finally, don't assume that your email will be opened and read. Given that getting an internship is an important step in your career, it is worth following up your email with a phone call if you don't get a reply within 10 days or so.

2.11   Avoid templates for beginnings and endings

While preparing this book I analyzed a collection of around 1,000 emails that had been kindly supplied to me by PhD students, researchers, and professors. One thing I noticed was that the emails often began and / or ended in exactly the same way. This was irrespectively of the recipient and the reason for the email, as if the first lines and final salutations belonged to a template. The advantage of this method is that, provided the template is written in correct English, it is quick and easy for the writer. But the recipient may be forced to read information that has no relevance for them.

Here is an email from a student who has booked hotel accommodation for a congress.

I'm Carla Giorgi, a PhD student from the University of Pisa, Italy.

I'm the author of a paper at ISXC16.

Yesterday, I booked my hotel room using the forms on ISXC16 website.

I'm waiting to be contacted, as specified in the message after sending the form.

Please could you tell me if there are some problems with my reservation, if it was not successful, and when I'll be contacted.

I apologize for my scholastic English, I hope to clearly have explained my problem.

Thanking you in advance, I look forward to hearing from you soon.

Best regards,

Carla Giorgi

What I noticed was that the parts shown in italics were a cut and paste from several other emails that Carla had sent (including a request for the source code of some software, a request for a copy of a paper, and a request to go to a summer school). The problem of doing this is that the recipient has to scan the mail to decide what is and is not relevant to them. It would have actually been quicker for Carla if she had begun from the third line of her email and ended at the fifth line.

Only write what the recipient needs to know. This will save time for both you and them.

Another problem with templates is that they are totally impersonal. Here are extracts from two emails that I received on the same day from the same person.

> Good morning Adrian
>
> Thank you for your email.
>
> We can confirm that we are happy for you to quote as suggested in your email and also to provide a link to the XXX website.
>
> We look forward to receiving a copy of your publication in due course.
>
> If you have any further questions, please do not hesitate to contact us.
>
> Kind regards

> Good afternoon Adrian
>
> Thank you for your email.
>
> Please find the verification that you have requested.
>
> If you have any further questions, please do not hesitate to contact us.
>
> Kind regards

This kind of semi-automatic email is unlikely to create much of a relationship with the recipient. However, I recognize that it is fast and efficient, and thus may be useful if you have to reply to hundreds of emails every day.

2.12   If in doubt how to end your email, use *Best regards*

There are many ways of ending an email in English, but the simplest is *Best regards*. You can use this with practically anyone—whether you have met them before or not, whether they are a Nobel prize winner or a fellow PhD student.

Best regards is often preceded with another standard phrase, for example, *Thank you in advance*, or *I look forward to hearing from you*. For more standard phrases, see Part 8.

Note the punctuation. Each sentence ends with a full stop, apart from the final salutation (Best regards) where you can put either a comma (,) or no punctuation.

. . . very helpful.	. . . very helpful.
I look forward to hearing from you.	Thanks in advance.
Best regards,	Best regards
Adrian Wallwork	Adrian Wallwork

2.13   Don't use a sequence of standard phrases in your final salutation

When writing emails in your own language, you may be accustomed to using a sequence of standard phrases at the end of your emails.

Imagine you need to ask your professor for a favor. When writing to North Americans, British people, Australians, etc., normally two phrases would be enough in your final salutation. For example:

Thank you very much in advance.
Best regards
Syed Haque

The above ending is polite and quick to read. The following ending contains too many salutations and is also rather too formal.

I would like to take this opportunity to express my sincere appreciation of any help you may be able to give me.

I thank you in advance.

I remain most respectfully yours,

Your student, Syed Haque

Bear in mind that many people in academia receive up to 100 emails a day; thus, they do not have time to read such a long series of salutations.

2.14   Ensure your signature contains everything that your recipient may need to know

What you include in your signature has some effect on the recipient's perception of who you are and what you do. It is generally a good idea to include most or all of the following.

- Your name
- Your position
- Your department (both in English and your mother tongue) and university/institute
- Your phone number
- The switchboard phone number of your department

Make sure your address is spelt correctly and that you have correctly translated the name of your department.

2.15   Avoid PSs and anything under your signature

When recipients see your salutation (e.g., *Best regards*) or name, it is a signal for them to stop reading. If you write a PS (i.e., a phrase that is detached from the main body of the mail and which appears under your name) or anything under your signature, there is a very good chance it will not be read.

Chapter 3
Structuring the Content of an Email

You will learn how to

- plan your email
- organize the information in the clearest and most logical (and grammatical) order
- be concise and use short sentences
- avoid ambiguity

People in the world of business (and perhaps in the work of academia too) spend up to 40% of their day emailing. Given that emails take up such a huge amount of our time, a clearly laid out email which gives the recipient information in its most accessible way is sure to be read more willingly than one long paragraph full of long sentences. Putting yourself in your recipient's shoes is key to getting your email read. This chapter teaches you how to write from the recipient's point of view.

A. Wallwork, *English for Academic Correspondence and Socializing*,
DOI 10.1007/978-1-4419-9401-1_3, © Springer Science+Business Media, LLC 2011

What the experts say

The longer the message, the greater the chance of misinterpretation.

Ricardo Semler, CEO, Semco SA

The fact that someone sends me a message does not automatically impose an obligation on my part to respond. So I've started to delete messages without reading them. . . . It's your job to make it interesting enough to get a response. You have to remember that you are not the only human being on earth writing e-mail messages.

Stewart Alsop, Alsop Louie Partners, columnist Fortune magazine

Executives at every level are prisoners of the notion that a simple style reflects a simple mind.

William Zinsser, communication trainer and Life magazine writer

The great enemy of clear language is insincerity. When there is a gap between one's real and one's declared aims, one turns instinctively to long words and exhausted idioms.

George Orwell, English writer

3.1   Plan your email and be sensitive to the recipient's point of view

Think about the following.

- What is the goal of my email?
- Who is my recipient?
- What is their position in the academic hierarchy? How formal do I need to be?
- How busy will my recipient be? How can I get his / her attention?
- What does my recipient already know about the topic of my email?
- What is the minimum amount of information that my recipient needs in order to give me the response I want?
- Why should my recipient do what I want him / her to do?
- What is my recipient's response likely to be?

Write in a way that shows you understand the recipient's position and feelings. Even though you may be requesting something from them, you are at least doing so by trying to address their needs and interests as well.

Think about how your recipient will interpret your message—can the message be interpreted in more than one way, is there any chance it might irritate or offend the recipient, will they be 100% clear about what its purpose is?

Also, if possible try to think of a benefit for the recipient of fulfilling your request.

Even if you contact someone frequently, you cannot assume that they will know the reason for your message.

3.2   Organize the information in your email in the most logical order and only include what is necessary

The email below is to the session organizers of a congress. The sender is requesting a delay in the submission.

Dear Session Organizers

At the moment we are not able to submit the draft manuscript within the deadline of 10 October for the SAE Magnets Congress.

The paper is the following:

Manuscript #: 08SFL-00975

Paper Title: Rejection System Auto-Control for a Hybrid BX Motor

Authors: Kai Sim, Angel Sito, Freidrich Sommer - University of Place; Gertrude Simrac, Kaiser Ko - Mangeti Industries S.p.a.

We are very sorry but we underestimated the overall effort necessary in order to collect the results to include in the paper.

We would be very grateful to you if we could obtain a delay of a couple of weeks for the draft submission.

We are confident that we will be able to complete and submit the draft manuscript by 21 October.

Best regards

Conference organizers receive hundreds of emails in the weeks up to the conference that they are organizing. Given that the success of the conference depends to a large extent on the numbers of people who attend and participate, the organizers are likely to read every email they receive. However, they clearly have to be very selective with regard to which manuscripts they accept. When writing to them (or journal editors) to ask for deadline extensions, tell them immediately exactly when you think you will be able to submit your manuscript. It is also a good idea not to force the recipient to read a mass of non-essential information before you finally tell them your request. The above email could thus be rewritten as:

> I would like to request a delay in submission of manuscript #: 08SFL-00975 until 21 October. I hope this does not cause any inconvenience. Best regards.

You may think the above is rather direct, but the recipient will appreciate the fact that he / she only needs to spend three seconds on reading your email.

Here is another example of a short email which makes its point immediately and clearly.

> I inadvertently submitted my manuscript #08CV-0069 for the SAE Magnets Congress, as an "Oral only Presentation" instead of "Written and Oral Presentation." Please could you let me know how I can change the status of my paper. I apologize for any inconvenience this may cause.

3.3   Minimize mistakes in your English by writing short and simple emails

Keep your emails short and simple.

The following are two versions of an email from a French student who wishes to do an internship at another institute.

ORIGINAL VERSION (OV)

Dear Professor Gugenheimer,

I am Melanie Duchenne, the french student who Holger Schmidt told you about few days ago.

Firstly, I would like to thank you for the opportunity you afford me to spend with your staff a short period, which would be extremely useful for me in order to obtain the master degree.

I have been adviced by Holger to communicate to you my preference as soon as possible, and I beg your pardon for not having done it earlier, due to familiar problems. Then, if possible, the best option for me would be a two-months period, from the beginning of june to the end of july. Waiting for your reply, I wish to thank you in advance for your kindness.

Best regards,

Melanie Duchenne

REVISED VERSION (RV)

Dear Professor Gugenheimer,

I am the French student who Holger Schmidt told you about.

Firstly, I would like to thank very much you for the opportunity to work with your team.

If possible, the best option for me would be June 1 - July 31.

I apologize for not letting you know the dates sooner.

Best regards,

Melanie Duchenne

The RV is much more concise and precise. All non-essential information (from the recipient's point of view) has been removed. Reducing the amount of text reduces the number of mistakes. Below are the mistakes in the OV, with the correct version on the right.

few days ago = a few days ago

the opportunity you afford me = the opportunity you are giving me

obtain the master degree = to get my Master's [degree]

I have been adviced = I have been advised by Holger *or* Holger advised me

familiar problems = family problems

a two-months period = a two-month period

All of the above mistakes have been removed, simply by reducing the amount of the text.

Note also the correct capitalization (*Prof*, *French*, *Best*) in the RV.

3.4   Be concise and precise

Below are some examples of words and phrases that are typically used to introduce new concepts or link sentences together. For example, the following phrases could all be replaced with *because*:

because of the fact that

due to the fact that

in consequence of

in the light of the fact that

in view of the fact that

And these could be replaced with either *although* or *even though*:

in spite of the fact that

regardless of the fact that

However, do not confuse conciseness with brevity (i.e., using the minimum number of words). Brevity may have two major disadvantages:

- lack of precision and clarity
- it may sound rude and suggest that you couldn't find the time to make yourself polite and clear

For guidelines on how to be concise, see Chapter 5 in the companion volume *English for Writing Research Papers*.

3.5   Use short sentences and choose the best grammatical subject

A lot of research has shown that when native English speakers read, their eyes tend to focus at the beginning and end of the sentence, whereas the middle part of the sentence tends to be read more quickly.

The way we read today is also very different from the way we read until the mid-1990s. The Internet encourages us to read very quickly—this is known as browsing, scanning, or skimming. Because we want information fast in order to help us decide whether to respond to an email and what action to take, we tend not to read every word. Instead we skip from word to word, sentence to sentence, and paragraph to paragraph until we find information that we consider useful or important. If we don't find anything of value, we stop reading.

Essentially, you need to

- select the most important item to put as the grammatical subject of the sentence
- put the verb and object as close as possible to the subject
- limit yourself to a sentence with two parts—so that there is only a beginning part and an end part. If you have three parts (or more), the middle parts will be read with less attention

The sentence below is a 48-word sentence written by a female PhD student. It contains three parts. It is not hard to read.

> I am a PhD student in psycholinguistics and one of the professors in my department, Stavros Panageas, kindly gave my your name as he thought you might be able to provide me with some data on the use of the genitive in Greek dialects of the 17th century.

Nevertheless it requires more effort than this alternative:

> Your name was given to me by Professor Stavros Panageas. I am doing a PhD on the use of the genitive in Greek. Prof Panageas told me you have a database on 17th century Greek dialects and I was wondering if I might have access to it.

The first sentence of the alternative version now has *your name* as the subject rather than *I am*. This means that the recipient sees himself / herself as the most important topic, and the sender thus takes second place. The second sentence then explains who the sender is and indicates her research area (which coincides with that of Prof Panageas). In the third sentence Prof Panageas is the subject of the sentence, not because he is the most important element in the sentence, but only because it would be unnatural to make *17th century Greek dialects* the subject. Thus, the three parts of the original sentence have become three separate sentences in the revised version.

Having short sentences

- helps your recipients locate the key information in your sentence with the minimal mental or visual effort
- makes it much easier for you to delete parts of your email or add parts to it. For example, if the sender realizes that her email is too long, she could easily delete the phrase *I am doing a PhD on the use of the genitive in Greek* in the alternative version. Deleting *I am a PhD student in psycholinguistics* in the original version would mean that the rest of the sentence would also have to be modified for it to make sense

3.6   Use the correct word order

This subsection only outlines some very general rules. For full details of English word order, see Chapter 2 in the companion volume *English for Writing Research Papers*.

SUBJECT + VERB + OBJECT

The standard word order in English is: (1) subject, (2) verb, (3) direct object, (4) indirect object

> I am attaching a file.

> We are meeting at the bar at six o'clock.

If there are two objects and one is a pronoun, with verbs like *send*, *give*, *email*, *forward*, and *write*, there are two possible orders:

> Please forward this message to her / Please forward her this message

But in other cases, that is, with two nouns, the direct object usually comes first:

> Please send my regards to Professor Smith.

> Did you send the attachment in your last email?

INVERSION OF SUBJECT AND MAIN VERB/AUXILIARY VERB

Note the inversions (highlighted in italics) of the normal word order in these cases:

> (1) In questions and requests.

>> *Are you* sure?

>> *Have you* done it yet?

Can you help me?

Will you let me know how you want me to proceed—thanks.

If possible, *could you* do this before tomorrow.

(2) After *so* and *neither / nor*.

I am afraid I don't have any clear data yet, *nor do I* expect to have any before the end of the month.

I expect to be able to meet the deadline and *so does* my co-author.

(3) In sentences that begin with *only* or a negation.

Only when / Not until we receive these corrections, *will we* be able to proceed with the publication.

(4) After *should* in formal expressions.

Should you need any further clarifications, please do not hesitate to contact me.

ADJECTIVES

Adjectives are normally placed before the nouns that they describe:

We hope we will be able to find a satisfactory solution.

If there are a lot of adjectives, use this order: quantity, size, color, origin, material, use.

A large white Russian plastic bag.

The department is offering ten 3-year full-time contracts.

If you put an adjective or description after the noun, then you need to use a relative clause, that is, a phrase that begins with *who*, *that*, or *which*.

I sent the paper, which had been revised by the proofreader, to the editor.

PAST PARTICIPLES

Most past participles can be placed after the noun they refer to, although some can come before or after. I suggest that you always place them after, then you are less likely to make a mistake.

The results obtained prove that...

The method described is ...

ADVERBS

Adverbs of frequency and *also*, *only*, and *just* go after (i) *am / is / are / was / were* (ii) between the subject and the verb, and (iii) between the auxiliary and the main verb.

(i) I am *occasionally* late with deadlines.   I am *also* an expert chemist.

(ii) I *sometimes* arrive late for work.   I *only* speak English and German.

(iii) I have *often* given presentations.   I have *just* seen her presentation.

Adverbs of manner go at the end of the phrase.

She speaks English *quickly / fluently*.

Adverbs that indicate times of the day, week, year, etc. can always be located at the end of the sentence.

I can send you the package by courier *today / tomorrow morning / at 09.00*.

Note the position of *above*:

As mentioned *above*, this method only works if. . .

The *above*-mentioned method only works if. . .

LINK WORDS

Most link words can go either at the beginning or in the middle of the sentence.

We have lost most of our government funding. *As a result*, we will have to make some drastic cuts.

The paper was presented at an international conference. *In addition*, it is going to be published in. . .

I will, *however*, still require another two months to finish the work.

I have *thus* decided to withdraw my paper.

too and *as well* are generally found at the end of the sentence.

She has a degree in Physics and a Master's in analytical chemistry *too / as well*.

although, *though*, and *even though* can be placed in two positions.

Although he has worked here for years, he has never been given a contract.

He has never been given a contract *even though* he has worked here for years.

AVOID PARENTHETICAL PHRASES

The examples sentences below are not written following the natural word order of English.

Your paper, which was sent to me by Wolfgang Froese, a colleague of mine at the XTC lab in Munich, was extremely useful and I would like. . .

Our manuscript, owing to some difficulties with our equipment due an electrical black out caused by the last hurricane, will be delayed.

The two sentences above both contain parenthetical phrases, that is, a phrase which separates the subject (*paper*, *manuscript*) from its verb (i.e., *was*, *will be delayed*). When someone reads an email, they want to be able to absorb the information as quickly and as easily as possible. Recipients are generally not prepared to devote the same attention to reading an email as they might to a paper. Here are possible rewritten versions of the two sentence above:

> Your paper was sent to me by Wolfgang Froese, a colleague of mine at the XTC lab in Munich. I found it extremely useful and I would like...

> I am writing to inform you that unfortunately our manuscript will be delayed. The delay is due to...

Using the same word order as you would if you were speaking does not mean that your email should sound like someone is talking—it still has to be well organized and all redundancy removed. It means writing in a way that is "recipient friendly": short, simple sentences with minimal need for punctuation (i.e., no parenthetical phrases divided off by commas).

PLEASE

Be careful of the location of the word *please* as it can give a very different tone to the sentence.

> Please can you let me know as soon as possible. (neutral)

> Hugo please note that... (neutral)

> Please Hugo, note that... (irritated)

Please is not usually followed by a comma.

3.7   Bear in mind that long emails will be scrolled

In long emails it is imperative to gain the recipient's interest quickly so that they will be encouraged to continue. Ensure that there is a topic sentence showing what the email is about, and what response or action you require from the recipient.

If you have written a long email, it is generally a good idea to have a bulletted summary at the beginning of the email, so that if your recipient is in a hurry he / she can quickly see the important points.

Everything you say must add value for the recipient so that they will read each detail rather than quickly scroll down to the end. However, you should also allow for the fact that they might scroll your email. Make it easy for them to do so by using

- bullets
- bold to highlight important words or requests
- white space to separate items

The email below is impossible to decipher because it is one long paragraph, the punctuation is poor and doesn't help the recipient, there is no white space, and the English is chaotic. It is also poorly organized and sounds like a stream of loosely connected thoughts.

Dear Kai

Yesterday, I talked to Hans and James who said maybe its ok to move the instrument for a few days but he didn't know the setting of the instrument etc that would be better to talk to other people first: Rikki and Kim. For Kim, its clear to her for us to measure using a different concentration I think she meant that "for measuring in interval of hours is possible so why we don't do this", but its clear now, that we need the first step to confirm the sensitivity of the polymer film, in any case, I can try to manage to put the film inside the multi-well and with longer cable so that sterile environment will preserved. In this way, it is possible as well moving the multi well box inside if the PQS measurement need (if the moving the PQS is so complicated). I'll keep you uptodate. Regards.

When you have finished writing an email, show your recipient some respect by checking that it is comprehensible. Most people would get a headache trying to decipher the email above.

3.8   Use link words in long emails to show connections and to draw attention to important points

If you have long explanations in your emails, you may find it helpful to use words that link your sentences together in order to show logical connections.

Below are some words that you can use; the first line of examples contains words that are perhaps a little less formal than the examples in the second line.

ORDERING AND SEQUENCING
first, then, next, at the same time, finally, in the end
firstly, secondly, simultaneously, subsequently, lastly

ADDING INFORMATION AND/OR MARKING A CHANGE IN TOPIC
another thing, while I'm at it, by the way, and, also
moreover, in addition, furthermore

DRAWING ATTENTION
note that, what is really important to note is
NB, please note that

CONTRASTING
although, though, even though, however, instead, on the other hand, even so
despite this, by contrast, nevertheless, on the contrary, nonetheless, conversely

CORRECTING OR GIVING DIFFERENT EMPHASIS TO PREVIOUS STATEMENT
actually, in fact
as a matter of fact, in reality

GIVING A PARALLEL
in the same way, similarly
by the same token, likewise, equally

GIVING EXAMPLES AND SPECIFYING
e.g., i.e., such as, like, this means that, in other words
for example, for instance, that is to say

INDICATING A RESULT
so
consequently, as a result therefore, thus, hence, thereby, accordingly

CONCLUDING
in sum
to conclude, in conclusion, in summary

For an explanation of the difference in meaning between these words and phrases, see the companion volume *English for Research: Usage, Style, and Grammar.*

3.9   Avoid ambiguity

You should make sure that you give an email the same attention as any other important written document by making it 100% clear and unambiguous. If you don't, it can be annoying for the recipient, who is often forced to ask for clarifications.

Ambiguity arises when a phrase can be interpreted in more than one way, as highlighted by these examples:

The student gave her dog food. Does "her" refer to the student (i.e., it is the student's dog), or is "her" another person to whom the student gave dog food?

You can't do that. Does *can't* mean that it would be impossible for you to do that, or that you don't have permission to do that?

Our department is looking for teachers of English, Spanish, and Chinese. Is the department looking for three different teachers (one for each language), or one teacher who can teach all three languages?

The older professors and students left the lecture hall. It is not clear if "older" just refers to the professors or to the students as well.

I like teaching students who respect their professors who don't smoke. Who are the non-smokers, the professors or the students?

Each subscriber to a journal in Europe must pay an additional $10. Is the journal a European journal, or do the subscribers live in Europe?

For more on this topic, see Chapter 6 Avoiding Ambiguity and Vagueness in the companion volume *English for Writing Research Papers.*

3.10   When using pronouns ensure that it is 100% clear to the recipient what noun the pronoun refers to

A common problem in emails is the use of a pronoun (e.g., *it, them, her, which, one*) that could refer to more than one noun. The sentences in the first column below have been disambiguated in the third column.

AMBIGUOUS SENTENCE	REASON FOR AMBIGUITY	POSSIBLE DISAMBIGUATION
Thank you for your email and the attachment *which* I have forwarded to my colleagues.	*which*—email? attachment? or both?	Thank you for your email. I have forwarded the *attachment* to my colleagues.
To download the paper, you will need a user name and password. If you don't have *one,* then please contact. . .	*one*—user name? password? or both?	To download the paper, you will need a user name and password. If you don't have a *password*, then please contact. . .
Yesterday I spoke to Prof Jones, and on Tuesday I saw Prof Smith and one of his PhD students, Vu Quach. If you want, you can write to *them* directly. You will find their emails on the website.	*them*—Smith and Vu? all three people (Jones, Smith, and Vu)?	Yesterday I spoke to Prof Jones, and on Tuesday I saw Prof Smith and one of his PhD students, Vu Quach. If you want you can write to *all three of them* directly.
After a student has been assigned a tutor, *he / she* shall. . .	*he / she*—the student? the tutor?	After a student has been assigned a tutor, the student shall. . .

As highlighted in the third column you can avoid ambiguity if you replace pronouns with the nouns that they refer to.

3.11   Ensure that recipients in different time zones will interpret dates and times correctly

Researchers work in an international environment over many time zones. In the sentence below, it is not clear exactly when the server will and will not be available.

> For maintenance reasons, the server will be not available tomorrow for all the day.

The problem words are *tomorrow* and *for all the day*. As I write this section I am in Italy and it is 17.00 local time. In Australia it is already *tomorrow*. What does *day* mean? Is it my day in Italy or my colleague's day in Australia?

Thus, if your project involves researchers from different parts of the world, you need to be much more specific:

> The server will not be available from 09.00 (London time) until 18.00 on Saturday 17 October.

To avoid misunderstandings due to differences between the ways various people write dates, I suggest you always write dates as follows:

> 12 March 2024

So: number of the day, then month as a word, then the year. If you write 12.03.2024, then this could be interpreted as 3 December or 12 March. Some people also write: March 12, 2024, but I find this less clear as the two numbers are together and a comma is also required.

3.12   Be aware of the importance of an email—not just for you or your recipient, but also for a third party

It is crucial to judge the importance of an email when you write it. Some emails are considerably more important than others.

Avoid sending messages from mobile phones. They tend to be written outside of the office and generally in a hurry while in the middle of doing something else. I strongly suggest that if you have something important to say, wait till you are in front of your computer.

The email below is extremely important, not really for the sender himself or for the recipient, but for the student who is the subject of the email. However, the email was probably written in less than a minute and sent without being re-read or revised (there are many mistakes in the English and in the punctuation).

Dear Professor Howard

I'm Pierre Boulanger, and Iím a University of X professor. Our research interests include power electronics, energy conversion and electric motor drives design and diagnosis.

I see on your web site that you research team is interested to receive foreign students. One of my best student, Celine Aguillon, is available to come in Boston to do research activity in the fields stated above. I will sent you a short biography and a C.V. of Celine. She will be happy to work in your laboratory and finally to prepare her PhD thesis.

Im waiting for your reply.

Like the other example emails in this book, the email above is real: just the names have been changed and the name of the university has been replaced with X. Pierre received no reply. The thoughts of Professor Howard were probably:

- This person has spent 30 seconds writing this request, why should I spend my own valuable time in replying, or organizing anything for his student?
- The fact that the email is full of grammar and spelling mistakes tells me that Professor Boulanger is not interested in detail and he may show the same lack of interest in his research. OK, he is not a native speaker, but he could at least have used the spell checker.
- Finally, I am not at all clear about the benefits of having Celine in my lab. What exactly will she be able to help my team with? I get the impression that the benefit is really for Celine and not for me.

The result was that Celine missed a wonderful opportunity to work with a top professor at a top university in Boston. And just because her professor could not take the time to write a decent email. Obviously, there may have been other reasons why Professor Jackson did not reply, but the more effort you put in to writing an important email the more likely you are to get the outcome desired.

Give yourself plenty of time to write an important email. Do a draft version and then leave it for a couple of hours. Then delete anything not absolutely essential. Leave it again just in case you remember any other info that you need to add or to ask for.

3.13 Check your spelling and grammar

The email below is a request for an internship.

Dear Prof Caroline Smiht,

I am student at the department of biology who is working with Professor Ihsan (Vibravoid Project). How You probably remember, I asked to You to have the opportunity of spending a period at the Your lab in Toronto. What I'd know is if I can still came to Your lab, in order to confirm the acomodation I have found in Toronto.

Waiting for Your replyThank you in advance,

Boris Grgurevic

PS I have booked my flights to get cheap ones

The above email is a disaster. First, the sender misspells the professor's name (*Smiht* instead of *Smith*). This will instantly put the professor in a negative frame of mind and will not help her to be receptive to the request. Second, it contains many mistakes in English, spelling, capitalization (e.g., *You* instead of *you*) and layout.

It is essential that you check your English and particularly your spelling. Mistakes create a very poor impression on your recipient who may think "if this person cannot take the time to check their spelling then they might have the same approach to not checking their data."

A more acceptable version would be:

Dear Professor Smith,

We met last month when you were doing a seminar at the Department of Biology in *name of town*. I am a student of Professor Ihsan (Vibravoid Project). You mentioned it might be possible for me to work at your lab for two months this summer.

I was wondering if the invitation is still open, if so would June to July fit in with your plans? My department will, of course, cover all my costs.

I would be grateful if you could let me know within the next ten days so that I will still be in time to book cheap flights and get my accommodation organized.

I look forward to hearing from you.

3.14   Don't rely 100% on your spell checker

As you can see from the poem below, spell checkers will only find words, or rather, combinations of letters, that do not exist.

Eye halve a spelling chequer	I have a spelling checker
It came with my pea sea	It came with my PC
It plainly marques four my revue	It plainly marks for my review
Miss steaks eye kin knot sea.	Mistakes I cannot see.
As soon as a mist ache is maid	As soon as a mistake is made
It nose bee fore two long	It knows before too long
And eye can put the error rite	And I can put the error right
Its rarely ever wrong.	It's rarely ever wrong.

This means that your spell checker would not find any of the mistakes in the following email.

> Tanks for your male, it was nice to here form you. I was glad to no that you are steel whit the Instituted of Engineering and that they still sue that tool that I made for them, do they need any spare prats for it? I am filling quite tried, tough fortunately tomorrow I'm going a way for tow weeks—I have reversed a residents in the Bahamas!
> That's all fro now, sea you soon.

Of course, even if your email is full of spelling mistakes, most people will be able to read it, as the extract below proves. However, you will give a poor image of yourself.

> The phaonmneal pweor of the hmuan mnid. Aoccdrnig to rscheearch at Cmabrigde Uinervtisy, it deosn't mttaer in waht oredr the ltteers in a wrod are, the olny iprmoatnt tihng is taht the frist and lsat ltteer be in the rghit pclae. The rset can be a taotl mses and you can sitll raed it wouthit a porbelm. Tihs is bcuseae the huamn mnid deos not raed ervey lteter by istlef, but the wrod as a wlohe. Amzanig huh? yaeh and I awlyas thought slpeling was ipmorantt!

3.15   If the mail is very important, have it checked by an expert

If your career in some way depends on the email, then ensure you have it revised by a native English speaker.

Chapter 4
Requests and Replies

You will learn that

- how you structure and specify your request is a strong determinant of whether your request will be met
- intelligent use of numbering and white space can increase the chances of your recipient replying with the correct information
- you should avoid focusing just on your own needs but also try to understand the recipient's viewpoint
- you can avoid mistakes in English by inserting your replies within the sender's original text

The two most common types of emails that academics send are (1) requests, and (2) apologies for not having answered a previous email. Many of your requests as an academic may have a big impact on your career—for example, requests for an internship, for a summer school, or for someone to revise your paper. It is thus essential to make your requests clear and concise, as well as quick and easy for your recipient to answer. Equally, when replying to a request your answers should be precise and easy to understand.

A. Wallwork, *English for Academic Correspondence and Socializing*,
DOI 10.1007/978-1-4419-9401-1_4, © Springer Science+Business Media, LLC 2011

Factoids

❖ According to Wikipedia, typographical emoticons have been around for more than 150 years. But the first time in emails was obviously more recent. Here is what Wikipedia says:

> *The first person documented to have used the emoticons :-) and :-(, with a specific suggestion that they be used to express emotion, was Scott Fahlman; the text of his original proposal, posted to the Carnegie Mellon University computer science general board on 19 September 1982 (11:44), was thought to have been lost, but was recovered 20 years later by Jeff Baird from old backup tapes.*

```
19-Sep-82 11:44 Scott E Fahlman
:-)
From: Scott E Fahlman <Fahlman at Cmu-20c>
I propose that the following character sequence for joke markers:
:-)
Read it sideways. Actually, it is probably more economical to mark
things that are NOT jokes, given current trends. For this, use
:-(
```

❖ To understand a Western smiley, you have to tilt your head: <> Amazed, %-) Confused and / or Drunk, :'-(Crying, :") Embarrassed, :-) Happy, (:-* Here's kissing you, :-D Laughing, :o Ooooh!!" shocked, :-(Sad, :-P Tongue in cheek, (:-(Very Unhappy, '-) Winking, l-O Yawning,

❖ Japanese emoticons, *kaomoji*, are written horizontally and are consequently quicker and easier to understand:

(^_^) or (^o^) Happy
(>_<)> In trouble or a bit embarrassed
(*^_^*) Embarrassed but happy
m(_ _)m Apologetic
(#^.^°) Shy
(-_-#) Angry
(@_@) Surprised

4.1   Decide whether it might be better just to make one request rather than several

If you have one particular important thing to ask, only ask that one thing. If you have only one request in your email, the recipient will have fewer options—he or she will either ignore your email, or will reply with a response to your request. The fewer options you give your recipient, the more likely you are to achieve what you want.

Do not add other requests within the same email. Generally speaking, when we receive several requests within the same email, we tend to respond to the request or requests that is / are easiest to deal with, and ignore the others.

For multiple requests see 4.5.

4.2   Give the recipient all the information they need

When you are asking for a placement in someone's lab, you need to provide your recipient with all the information they need to assess whether there would be benefits for them in having you in their team. The email below is a good example that is likely to motivate the recipient in helping the student to get a placement.

Subject: Laboratory placement - Prof Shankar's student

Dear Professor Janson

I am a PhD student at the University of X. I attended the ACE-Y conference last week and I found your seminar very interesting, the part about the finite element formulation was particularly useful.

I saw on your webpage is it possible to have a placement period in your lab. It would be a real pleasure for me to join your research group and do some further research into the formulation of an efficient finite element for the adhesive layer.

My research covers almost exactly the same topics:

1. FE calculations of complex bonded structures
2. Efficient techniques to reduce d.o.f
3. Enhancing adhesive strength

The area where I think **I could really add value would be in enhancing adhesive strength**. I have attached a paper and some recent results, which I hope you will find both interesting and useful. I believe my approach could work in conjunction with yours and really improve efficiency.

If it would suit you, I could come from April next year, for a 3–6-month period. I would be able to get funding from my university to cover the costs of a placement period, so I need no grant or scholarship.

Please find attached my CV with the complete list of my publications and a letter of recommendation from my tutor, Professor Shankar.

Thank you in advance for any help you may be able to give me.

Mercedes Sanchez Tirana

Mercedes structures her email as follows; she

- explains who is she and how she knows of Janson
- makes a compliment on Janson's seminar
- states why she is writing to Janson
- gives a short summary of her research area highlighting its similarities with Janson's
- highlights where she could add value—she uses bold to attract Janson's attention (he may just be scanning the email to see whether it is worth him reading it)
- says when she is available and that she already has funding
- attaches her CV and other information that provides evidence that she would be a useful addition to Janson's team
- mentions the name of her tutor (who through the literature may be known to Janson)

She also uses a clear subject line which should motivate Janson to open the email.

4.3 Consider not sending an attachment to someone with whom you have had no previous contact

Some people do not appreciate

- receiving attachments from people with whom they have had no previous contact
- long introductory emails

If Mercedes (4.2) wanted to avoid sending an attachment, she could use the same beginning as in her original email up to where she says *really improve efficiency*. Then she could then proceed as follows:

> In addition, I could send you my CV with the complete list of my publications and a letter of recommendation from my tutor, Professor Shankar.
>
> If it would suit you, I could come from April next year, for a 3–6-month period. I would be able to get funding from my university to cover the costs of a placement period, so I need no grant or scholarship.
>
> I look forward to hearing whether you think a collaboration would also be of benefit to you and your team.
>
> Mercedes Sanchez Tirana

With respect to her initial draft, Mercedes has

- removed all references to attachments and simply suggested that she could send him such information
- retained the reference to when she could come and the fact that she needs no funding from Janson
- referred to the possible benefit for Janson and his team

4.4   Include all the relevant information that the recipient needs to assess your request

If you have an important request to make, for example, the one outlined in 4.3, then it is imperative to supply the recipient with all the information that they need in order to assess your request.

An internship could lead to a considerable enhancement in your career possibilities. It is thus wise to give the following information to the person who might be hosting you:

- some details about what you are proposing in terms of scientific content. Also, give the professor other possible areas that you could work on together
- your ideal dates and other dates that you could come
- an indication of whether or not you will be financially autonomous
- a letter of recommendation from your professor
- references from other people

The idea is that it really seems that you want to work with them and that you are trying to make their life easier by providing them with all the information they may want to know.

4.5   Make all your requests 100% clear

Sometimes you do need to make multiple requests in the same email. This is often the case when asking for details about conferences, summer schools, products, etc. In this case, you are not asking someone for something important such as an internship in a top professor's lab, but simply for information which your recipient should be able to provide without too much effort. Thus, it is perfectly legitimate to ask multiple questions. However, unless you lay out and structure your email very carefully, you are unlikely to get answers to all your questions, but probably only to those questions that your recipients can see the most quickly or which require the least effort on their part.

Make your requests absolutely clear.

Here is an email I received from the permissions department of a publisher:

> Please let me know how many copies of the book are being printed, where they will be sold (what territories), and what is the term of license under section 4779.09 of the Revised Code for this book.

There are two problems with this request. First, there are three requests in one sentence. For recipients this is a problem, because they cannot quickly identify the requests when replying to them. Second, it includes the phrase "term of license under section 4779.09 of the Revised Code." This phrase was probably very clear for the sender (i.e., the publisher) because it relates to their field of business, but it meant nothing to me—it was too technical. My choices were (i) try and find out the meaning on the web, (ii) ask for clarification by writing another email, or (iii) just ignore it completely and simply answer the other two questions.

Basically, most recipients will opt for what seems to the easiest solution, which would be the third solution—ignore the request. So if you are making a request, ensure that you phrase it in such a way that your recipient will have no problem understanding it and will thus

- not need to ask for or look for clarification (and thus not waste further time)
- respond to your request, hopefully with the information you wanted

As always, think in terms of your recipient and not of yourself.

A clearer version of the above email could be:

> Please could you kindly answer these three questions:
>
> 1. how many copies of the book are likely to be printed per year?
> 2. what territories will they be sold in?
> 3. what is the term of license for this book (i.e., when will the contract for the book expire)?

The revised version alerts the recipient that there are three requests to answer, and underlines this by using numbered bullets. The first question is also more precise (*per year*), and the third question now includes an explanation of part of the technical phrase and has simply deleted the reference to the section of the Revised Code as being unnecessary.

Clearly, the revised version would take more time to write than the original version, but the benefit is that the writer is more likely to get replies to all three questions.

To ensure that all your requests get answered, it is generally wise to number them and keep them as short as possible.

4.6   Lay out your request clearly

Below is a request to register for a conference. Unfortunately, it forces the recipient to read the mail carefully in order to understand exactly what the request is.

> Dear Secretariat of the 5th XTC Ph.D. Symposium,
>
> My Supervisor and I would like to register for the XTC Symposium but we couldn't find any registration form in your website. I would be very grateful to you if you could suggest me the best way to register for the event. Moreover, would it be possible to pay the registration fee by credit card? Finally, is the preliminary program available for download?
>
> Thank you very much in advance for you kind cooperation.
>
> Best regards

Here is a better organized version of the above:

> Dear Secretariat
>
> Please can you answer the following questions:
>
> 1. how can I register for the 5th XTC Ph.D. Symposium?
> 2. can I pay by credit card?
> 3. where can I download the preliminary program?
>
> Best regards

Or alternatively, given that you have probably simply been unable to locate the right link and that all your questions could be answered by having access to that link, you could write:

Please can send you me the link for registering for the 5th XTC Ph.D. Symposium. Thanks.

4.7   Avoid blocks of text and don't force your reader to make sense of everything

In the case below the sender is requesting some product information. However, she is seriously jeopardizing the chances of receiving an answer. In fact, she has written one long block of text containing a considerable amount of information that is of little or no interest to the recipient. The recipient only needs to know the exact details of the sender's request.

Dear Inlt Pipes Inc,

I'm Dr Maria Masqueredo and I work as a researcher at the Department of Engineering of the University of *name of place*. I am currently working on a project that entails the use of shape memory alloy tubes and a colleague of mine referred me to your website where I found a few examples that might satisfy my requirements. Essentially, I need shape memory alloy tubes (not superelastic alloys). The transformation temperature is not a critical parameter (Af $= 70 \infty$C or more would be adequate). What is really important is that the ratio between the internal diameter, di, and the external diameter, de, must be near the value of 0.7–0.8. The external diameter can be 1.5 mm or more (not exceeding 12 mm). Do you have any product able to satisfy my constraints? Can you send me an estimate for 5 m of your products? By the way I found a mistake in one your product descriptions, under "steel tubes" I think it should say "alloy" rather than "allay."

Thank you in advance for any help you may be able to give me.

Best regards

A better version would be:

Hi

Do you have a shape memory alloy tube with the following characteristics?

1. transformation temperature of $Af = 70\infty C$ or more
2. ratio between the internal diameter and the external diameter must be 0.7–0.8
3. external diameter in a range from 1.5 mm to 12 mm

If so, please could send me an estimate for a 5-m tube.

Thanks in advance.

Maria Masqueredo

In the original example above Maria has not thought about the recipient. She has simply written down her thoughts as they came into her head, thus leaving it to the recipient to make sense of everything. If the recipient has the time to deal with the email he / she might answer it, but there is a good chance that he / she will leave it till later or simply delete it on the basis that it is not time-efficient or cost-effective to deal with it.

4.8   For multiple requests, include a mini summary at the end of the email

Many recipients only read the email once. This means that by the end of the email they may have already forgotten any requests that were made at the beginning of the email. Thus, they may respond to only the request/s that they remember or simply the ones that are easiest for them to deal with. This happens even if you have used bullets and used lots of white space to indicate a clear division between your requests.

Two techniques may help you to increase your chances of getting a reply. These techniques are illustrated in the email below.

Dear Dr Suzuki

I hope you had a good summer. I have three short requests that I hope you might be able to help me with.

REQUEST 1

Do you have any openings for PhD students in your laboratory? I have one truly excellent candidate whose CV I have attached. She has a lot of experience in your field and she also speaks some Japanese.

REQUEST 2

When we met before the summer vacation you told me that you were getting some interesting results in your experiments. I was wondering if you had now completed testing and whether you would be willing to share those results with me.

REQUEST 3

At my department we are planning a series of workshops on XYZ in November this year. Given your international reputation and your expertise in the field, I was wondering whether you might be interested in giving a series of seminars. Your travel and accommodation expenses would of course be paid for by my department.

Summary:

1) Internship for PhD student?
2) Your results
3) Seminars in November

I look forward to hearing from you.

The two techniques are as follows:

- precede each request with a number (Request 1, Request 2, etc.) and put the word request in capital letters so it clearly stands out
- provide a summary of all the requests at the end

Generally speaking, you would only need to use one of the two techniques, particularly if the email is reasonably short as in the example above. But if an email is long and requires scrolling by the recipient, then a summary at the end will certainly increase the chances of your recipient answering all your requests. The summary also helps the recipients as they can simply insert their answers under each point of the summary.

4.9   Ensure that your layout and organization give the recipient a positive impression

The writer of the email below is a student who has already organized an internship in a university in the USA. He is now dealing with the secretary who is helping him with various bureaucratic procedures in preparation for his visit.

Dear Ms Jackson,

I apologize for my late reply, at the moment I am still waiting for the funding letter. Please find attached to this e-mail the DS 20-19 form, duly filled in with all my personal details. As far as the copy of my passport is concerned, I am sending you a copy of my old one, but please note that I need to apply for a new electronic passport complying with the US foreign passport requirements. I will send the application for my new passport this week and start with the visa procedure as soon as I can. I will keep you up to date with the progress of my visa application.

I would be grateful if you could provide me some advice on accommodation, since I am now also trying to look for somewhere preferably within walking distance of the department. I hope you have completed the XTC poster, sorry again for my late reply to your last e-mail. I hope this hasn't caused you any problems.

Best regards

The above email is very confused and poor Ms Jackson must be wondering why her boss accepted the student's application for an internship! A more helpful version would be:

Dear Ms Jackson,

I just wanted to update you on my progress with getting all the documents ready.

- DS 20-19 form: see attached.
- Passport: I am attaching a jpg of my passport; however, tomorrow I will apply for a new electronic passport in order to comply with the US foreign passport requirements.
- Visa: I made the application three weeks ago, I hope to have some news by the end of this week.
- Funding letter: I should have this ready early next week - thanks for your patience.

Just a couple of other things: 1) Do you have any suggestions for finding accommodation within walking distance of the department? 2) Did you manage to complete the XTC poster? Thank you.

I am very sorry it has taken me so long to get back to you, but bureaucracy in my country is a nightmare!

Best regards

The revised version would certainly take the writer about twice as long to write. But in taking this extra time he will impress Ms Jackson with his efficiency and clarity, and he is far more likely to get Ms Jackson's help in his search for accommodation. People are always more willing to help you, if you have clearly shown that you have tried to help them too—in this case the student has helped Ms Jackson perform her work by laying out everything very clearly in his email to her.

4.10   In replies to requests consider inserting your answers within the body of the sender's email

There are basically two ways of replying to an email:

- write your reply under the sender's text
- insert your replies within the sender's text

Let's imagine that you are Raul, a Spanish researcher, and that you have a collaboration with Peter, a British researcher. Peter sends you the email below.

Hi Raul

I hope all is well with you. I was wondering if you could do me a couple of favors. Attached are two documents. The first is an Abstract that I would like you to read and hear your comments on. It is actually 50 words over the limit required by the conference organizers, so if you could find any way to remove a few words that would be great. Also attached is the proposal for the request for funding - for some reason I can't find the email addresses of the people in the Research Unit in Madrid, so could you possibly forward it to them? Thanks. Then finally, you mentioned last time we met that you said that you had a useful bibliographical reference that you thought I should look up, do you think you could send it to me. Thanks very much and sorry to bother you with all this.

If we don't speak before, I hope you have a Happy Christmas!

Best regards

Peter

You could decide to write your reply under Peter's text as follows:

VERSION 1

Hi Pete

Good to hear from you. Yes, I am happy to read your Abstract and I will try to reduce the word count. I have forwarded the request for funding proposal to the members of the Madrid RU and I put you in cc. Please find below the references I mentioned:

Sweitzer BJ, Cullen DJ, How well does a journal's peer review process function? A survey of authors' opinions (JAMA1994; 272:152–3)

Let me express my warmest wishes to you and your family for a very happy Christmas and a New Year full of both personal and professional gratifications.

Best regards

Raul

Alternatively you could insert your replies into Peter's text:

VERSION 2

>The first is an Abstract that I would like you to read and hear your comments on. It is actually 50 words
>over the limit required by the conference organizers, so if you could find any way to remove a few
>words that would be great.

OK.

>Also attached is the proposal for the request for funding - for some reason I can't find the email
>addresses of the people in the Research Unit in Madrid, so could you possibly forward it to them?

Done.

>Then finally, you mentioned last time we met that you said that you had a useful bibliographic
>references that you thought I should look up, do you think you could send me them. Thanks very much
>and sorry to bother you with all this.

Sweitzer BJ, Cullen DJ, How well does a journal's peer review process function? A survey of authors' opinions (JAMA 1994; 272:152–3)

>If we don't speak before, I hope you have a Happy Christmas!

Happy Christmas to you too!

Note that the word *Done* means that Raul has already forwarded the proposal to the RU in Madrid—it means *I have done what you asked me to do*. If he hasn't done so yet, he could write *Will do*.

The advantages of Version 2 are as follows:

1. You can considerably reduce the amount you write and thus the number of potential mistakes. Raul has written only 7 words compared to the 77 words of the first version.
2. You save yourself time in writing and the recipient time in reading.
3. You are more likely to remember to answer all the requests. Also your recipient can see your replies in direct relation to his / her requests.

The only possible disadvantage is that because you write much less it may seem to the recipient that you are in a hurry and want to deal with his / her email as fast as possible—Version 1 is more friendly. However, given the number of emails that people receive and send every day, this is in my opinion a minor consideration.

4.11   Don't experiment with your English, instead copy / adapt the English of the sender

The less you write, the fewer chances you have of making mistakes with your English. In Version 1 (4.10), Raul writes:

Let me express my warmest wishes to you and your family for a very happy Christmas and a New Year full of both personal and professional gratifications.

Raul's Christmas greeting is four times longer than Pete's Christmas greeting—the potential for making mistakes in English is thus substantially higher. Raul's greeting has two problems:

- It is extremely formal compared to the rest of the email and thus sounds a little out of place
- It is probably a literal translation of what Raul would have said if he had been writing in his own language—however, the last part of the sentence (*full of both personal and professional gratifications*) does not exist in English (a Google search does not give any hits)

In Version 2 Raul limits the number of mistakes he could potentially make by repeating part of Peter's greeting:

Happy Christmas to you too!

Copying the phrase of the sender and / or adding *too* is a good tactic for repeating a greeting, as the following examples highlight (the sender's greeting is on the left, the recipient's reply on the right):

I hope you have a great weekend.	I hope you have a great weekend too.
Have a great weekend.	You too.
Enjoy your holiday.	I hope you enjoy your holiday too.

Obviously, you cannot say *You too* in the Version 1 style of reply. It can only be used if you insert your reply directly under the sender's sentence (i.e., Version 2). Also, not all phrases can be replied to simply by adding *too*. For example, if the sender writes *See you next week at the meeting*, you cannot reply with *See you next week too*. Instead, if you are using Version 1 style, you could write *I am looking forward to seeing you at the meeting*. Or in Version 2 style: *Yes, I am looking forward to it* or *I am looking forward to seeing you again*.

4.12   Insert friendly comments within the body of the sender's text

You can use the same technique as illustrated in Version 2 (4.10) to insert friendly remarks within the body of an email you have received. Let's imagine that you are a researcher who lives and works in Pisa, Italy. You have just been to Prague to give some seminars. The email below is from the Czech person who organized the seminars for you. You have inserted your comments within her email.

>Hi Paolo
>I hope you had a good trip back to Pisa.

Unfortunately there was a three hour delay due to fog, but anyway I got home safely.

>I just wanted to say that it was good to meet you last week. I thought your seminars were very productive.

Thank you. Yes, I was very pleased by the way they went and I was very impressed by the level of knowledge of your students.

>Say hello to Luigi.

I will do. And please send my regards to Professor Blazkova.

Thank you once again for organizing the seminars and I hope to see you again in the not too distant future.

>Best regards
>Hanka

4.13   Give deadlines

You will increase your chances of people responding to your requests if you give them a specific deadline. This is much more effective than saying *as soon as possible* or *at your earliest convenience*, as these two phrases give no idea of the urgency of the sender.

However, it pays to give them a reasonably short deadline and not too many options. The longer the deadline you give them, the greater the chance that they will simply not remember to fulfill your request. Typical phrases you can use are as follows:

> I need it *within* the next two days.

> He wants it *by* 11 tomorrow morning at the latest.

> I don't actually need it *until* next week, Tuesday would be fine.

> I need it some time *before* the end of next week.

Note how the words in italics are used in the context of deadlines.

> *within*   to mention a period of time, which is always indicated by a plural noun (hours, weeks, months).

by	to indicate a specific moment in the future which is the end point of a period of time during which something must be done
until	with negative verb (*I don't need*) to mean "not before"
before	the same as *by*, but *by* can also mean *at*, whereas *before* can only mean "at any point during a period of time"

The difference between *within* and *by* is the same difference as between *for* and *since* with the present perfect. Examples:

> He has been here *for* two days.

> He has been here *since* yesterday morning.

If you are the receiver of a deadline or if you simply wish to establish your own deadline, then you can use similar phrases. For example, if someone writes to you saying *Could you revise the section as soon as possible.* You can say:

> I should be able to get the revisions back to you *by* the end of this month / *within* the next 10 days.

> I am sorry but I won't be able to start work on it *until* Monday / *before* next week at the earliest.

4.14   Motivate the recipient to reply by empathizing with their situation or by paying them a compliment

Most recipients are more likely to meet your requests if you seem to show some understanding of their situation or if you appreciate their skills in some way. Here are some typical phrases that senders use to motivate their recipients to reply.

> I know that you are very busy but . . .

> Sorry to bother you but . . .

> I have heard that you have a mountain of work at the moment but . . .

> Any feedback you may have, would be very much appreciated.

> I have an urgent problem that requires your expertise.

> I really need your help to . . .

> I cannot sort this out by myself . . .

Chapter 5
Building a Relationship and Deciding the Level of Formality

You will learn that

- establishing a good relationship can lead to useful meetings and collaborations
- although English uses *you* in both formal and informal relationships, it adopts other devices to show respect toward the recipient of an email
- you should adopt an appropriate level of formality when dealing with people of different cultures

In most areas of language you can make fairly literal translations from one language to another and produce something that is reasonably comprehensible in the target language. This is not the case with proverbs and idioms and is certainly not the case with typical salutations and standard phrases in email. If you make a literal translation, you will either confuse or amuse your recipient.

A. Wallwork, *English for Academic Correspondence and Socializing*,
DOI 10.1007/978-1-4419-9401-1_5, © Springer Science+Business Media, LLC 2011

What the experts say

Within the academic world, and even in an informal society such as that in North America, addressing academics using titles such as Dr and Professor, may make the recipient more willing to help you. Using titles may also help to differentiate you from those students whose emails resemble text messages to friends rather than requests to top academics. You may also get a more successful outcome to an email request if you use some apologetic or slightly deferential language such as "Sorry to bother you but ...", "I wonder if you could ...", "I know you must be very busy but ...".

David Morand, Professor of Management, School of Business Administration Pennsylvania State University—Harrisburg

In Senegal salutations are very important, we always begin an email with salutations asking about the family, and how life is going. If it's a person you've never talked before, you'll try to find some links (parents or friends). And we always finish by formulating wishes (praying to Allah). If someone goes directly to talk about business, he or she is seen as a materialist or an opportunist.

Ibrahima Diagne, IT specialist, Senegal

We tend to ascribe other people's behavior to their personality, instead of looking at the situation and the context in which their behavior occurs. We might excuse our own actions more easily ("I was tired; I felt a cold coming on."). ... Behavior is oftentimes more because of reaction to a context than because of fundamental personality traits.

Andy Hunt, author, Pragmatic Thinking and Learning: Refactor Your "Wetware"

In my younger days as a researcher I made the mistake of being rather arrogant in my communication, which I believe cost me a few interesting projects that I could have been part of. I am now very conscious that good relationships are part of the key to having a successful career in academia. I try very hard to be both constructive and sincere—not an easy thing to do in a foreign language (i.e., English) but which I have learned from some of the emails I have received from native-speaking colleagues.

Anonymous

5.1   Use common interests to establish and cement a relationship

When you call someone on the phone, you probably begin by asking *how are you?*. You are not necessarily interested in the answer, but it is just a formality at the beginning of a phone call. Some people also ask this question at the start of an email—again they may not be expecting an answer, but it just acts as a friendly start rather than being too direct.

If you have a good relationship with your recipient, then they are more likely to carry out your requests and do so more quickly than they might if you are totally anonymous to them. My tactic after a few email exchanges is to reveal / announce some personal information.

This could be at the beginning of the email, for instance:

> Hope you had a good weekend. I spent most of mine cooking.

> So how was your weekend? We went swimming—we were the only ones in the sea!

> How's it going? I am completely overloaded with work at the moment.

Or it could be the end of the email:

> Ciao from a very hot and sunny Pisa.

> Hope you have a great weekend—I am going to the beach.

These little exchanges only take a few seconds to write (and to be read, i.e., by the recipient). Also, by making comments such as these, you might discover that you have something in common (cooking, swimming), and this will give you something to "talk" about in your emails.

I have found that such exchanges "oil" the relationship. Also, if in the future there are any misunderstandings, then these are likely to be resolved more quickly and with a better outcome than there might be with an anonymous interlocutor.

However, it is really important not to take this to extremes. One of my colleagues complained that a student, who she hardly knew, began his email to her saying:

> I saw your status on Facebook. It seems you had a nice time in Venice!

Although Facebook is public and was specifically designed to let people into your private life (or at least that part of your private life that you want them to have access to), some users of Facebook find the idea of people who they hardly know looking at their pages and then commenting on them as being quite distasteful. It is a bit like being stalked. So, be careful to respect people's privacy and not be invasive.

5.2   Maintain a friendly relationship

Whenever you write an email, always be aware that there is probably more than one way to interpret what you have written and that this other way may cause offence. So, before you send your email, check for potential misinterpretations, and rewrite the offending phrase.

For example, here is what appears to be an inoffensive reminder.

> For your reference I remind you that it is VERY important to always specify your current workstation IP address.

However, this sentence has various problems:

- *For your reference* could be interpreted as sounding like someone who has been contradicted and is now giving their point of view in quite an aggressive way
- *I remind you*—the present tense in English is sometimes used to give a sense of authority or formality. It thus sounds very cold and unfriendly
- *VERY*—rather than using capitals, consider using bold. Also, it sounds rather like a teacher talking to a naughty (badly behaved) child

Here are two different ways of rewriting the sentence:

> Just a quick reminder—don't forget to specify your current workstation IP address. Thanks!

> I'd just like to remind you that the IP address of a workstation must always be specified.

The first alternative is informal and friendly. The second is more formal, but uses three tricks to make it soft:

1. a contracted form (*I'd* rather *than I would*) which gives the phrase a less authoritarian tone
2. the passive form—this then makes the *IP address* the subject of *specified* (rather than the implicit *you must specify*)
3. *a workstation* rather than *your workstation*—this makes the message sound that it is not directed personally at the recipient

5.3   Adopt a non-aggressive approach

If you have something negative to say, it is advisable not to adopt an aggressive approach. Aggression is more likely to aggravate the situation than solve it. Compare:

AGGRESSIVE	NON-AGGRESSIVE
You have sent us the wrong manuscript.	You appear to have sent us the wrong manuscript. It seems we've been sent the wrong manuscript.
I need it now.	I appreciate that this is a busy time of year for you but I really do need it now.
I have not received a reply to my email dated ...	I was wondering whether you had had a chance to look at the email I sent you dated ... (see below)

When you revise your email before hitting the "send" button, make sure you remove anything that is not strictly necessary, particularly phrases that might annoy the recipient. Recipients do not like to be treated like schoolchildren or be made to feel guilty; thus, in most contexts the phrases below should be deleted:

This is the second time I have written to request ...

I am still awaiting a response to my previous email ...

As explained in my first email,

As clearly stated in my previous email,

In summary: Use a more roundabout, softer approach and include an introductory phrase that in some way tones down any aggression. If possible empathize with your reader's situation.

5.4   Be careful of your tone when asking people to do something for you

One of the most common reasons for writing an email is to get someone to do something for you. You are more likely to achieve your aims if you adopt a friendly and positive approach and if you don't sound too direct (i.e., as if you were giving someone an order). Here is an example of a request written in various ways from very direct (using an imperative) to overly cautious and extremely polite. You can choose the one you feel is the most appropriate:

Revise the manuscript for me.

Will you revise the manuscript for me?

Can you revise the manuscript for me?

Could you revise the manuscript for me?

Would you mind revising the manuscript for me?

Do you think you could revise the manuscript for me?

Would you mind very much revising the manuscript for me?

If it's not a problem for you could you revise the manuscript for me?

If you happen to have the time could you revise the manuscript for me?

When you translate from your own language into English, you may lose the sense of politeness that the version in your own language had. Thus, it is possible that an email that sounds courteous in your language might sound quite rude when translated into English.

Another problem is that when you write in English, you may be less worried about how your email might be interpreted than you would if you were writing to a colleague of your own nationality. For many non-native speakers, writing in English is like writing through a filter: the way you write seems to have much less importance than it would if you were writing in your own language.

Below is an email from one co-author of a paper to another co-author.

Here is a first version of the manuscript. Read and check everything: in particular, you have to work on the introduction and prepare Fig 1.

You should send it back to me by the end of this month at the latest.

I ask you to suggest also some referees that would be suitable for reviewing the paper.

The above email was written by an Italian researcher to her Canadian co-author. If this email were translated into Italian, it would sound absolutely fine, and the recipient would have no reason to be offended. But in English it sounds like a series of orders given by someone very high in a hierarchy. Thus, the Canadian co-author might have been a little surprised or offended by the tone. The problems are due to the use of

the imperative (*read and check*)—this gives the impression that the sender is not a co-author on a equal level to the recipient, but rather quite an aggressive professor giving instructions to a student

have to—this sounds like a strong obligation rather than a request

should—again, this sounds like an order

The email could be improved as follows:

Here is a first version of the manuscript. Please could you read and check everything. In particular, it would be great if you could complete / revise the introduction and also prepare Figure 1.

Given that our deadline is the first week of next month, I would be grateful to receive your revisions by the end of this month.

The editor might ask us to suggest some referees to review our paper, so if you have any ideas please let me know.

However, when you are giving a formal list of instructions these will generally be quicker and easier to follow in the form of imperatives (i.e., the infinitive form of the verb without *to*). So the first rather than the second sentence below would be more appropriate in a list of instructions:

Attach your application form to your email.

The application form should be attached to the email.

This approach will not be rude

- if you have a friendly introductory phrase before a list of commands
- if the rest of the mail is friendly

If in doubt, use *please.*

5.5   Use appropriate language and don't mix levels of formality

Below is an email written by a PhD student to a professor. Much of the email is formal, as is appropriate given the student / professor relationship. However, the parts in italics are very informal, and are thus inappropriate.

Dear Professor Anastasijevic,

I hope you *have been having a really good time* since our meeting in Belgrade. I have started to prepare for my period in your *lab* and first of all I'm trying to get the visa*!*

I would be very grateful if you could kindly tell me how to obtain the DS2019 document in order to request the visa.

I would like to thank you in advance and *have a great Xmas.*

Cheers,

Lamia Abouchabkis

The following email from one of my PhD students sounds very strange with its incredible mixture of polite English mixed with chatroom / text message style.

Dear Professor Adrian

I am pleased that you enjoyed my presentation. Dunno how much it is useful and meaningful.

I am happy if u r ok wid it.

Best regards

It is always worth remembering who you are writing to, and that not all people of every generation write in the same way.

5.6   Show your recipient respect and motivate them to reply

Poor spelling and text message writing may not be acceptable to many recipients. They tell the recipient "I am sorry but I could not be bothered to find 30 seconds to check my spelling or to write words in their full form because I have more important things in my life." Below is an email I received from a student I had taught the previous year.

Subject: hlep with cv

Hi pfof Wallwoark

how r u? do u remember me? u said in your lessons that we could send u r cvs for correction. in attachment is mine. pls I need it for tommorow nigth if poss. thankx u.

You need to change your email writing style depending on who you are writing to (their age, position, nationality). Also, just because a professor may have been informal and friendly, it does not mean that you should write to him / her in a casual way. A more suitable version would be:

Subject: help with CV

Dear Professor Wallwork

I attended your scientific papers course last year. I am the student from Russia who told you about Russian writing style. I was wondering whether you might have time to correct my CV (see attached). Unfortunately, I need it for tomorrow - my professor only told me about it today. I know it is asking a lot but if you could find 10 minutes to correct it, I would really appreciate it.

Please let me know if you need any further information about how Russian academics write.

Best wishes

The revised request is better because:

- it reminds me who he is and that he once did a favor for me
- the student acknowledges that his request may be asking me "a lot" but he shows his appreciation of what I might be able to do for him
- he offers to return the favor

Clearly, there does not need to be an exchange of favors. The email could have been written as follows:

Subject: help with CV

Dear Professor Wallwork

I attended your scientific papers course last year - it was really useful and since then I have had two papers published. Thank you!

I seem to remember that during your course you offered to correct our CVs for us.

So although it is a year later, I was wondering whether you might have time to correct my CV (see attached). Unfortunately, I need it for tomorrow - my professor only told me about it today. I know it is asking a lot but if you could find 10 minutes to correct it, I would really appreciate it and I am sure it would make a significant difference to my chances of getting the post.

Thank you very much in advance.

5.7   Be careful how you use pronouns

Unlike most languages, English uses the same word *you* for everyone. It is not possible to show more respect by capitalizing the *y* (i.e., *You, Your*)—this form does not exist in English. Thus, the phrase below is incorrect:

> I believe Your paper would help me in my research. Thank You in advance for any help You may be able to give me.

Christopher Robin, a character in A. A. Milnes' famous stories about Winnie the Pooh, said:

> If the English language had been properly organized ... then there would be a word which meant both "he" and "she," and I could write, "If John or Mary comes, heesh will want to play tennis," which would save a lot of time.

In modern English this problem has been resolved by using "they." In Anglo countries there are some rules regarding the use of politically correct language which help to make the communication more neutral and avoid the likelihood of offending anyone.

The masculine pronoun should not be used to refer to a generic person who is not necessarily or specifically a man.

GENERALLY INCORRECT	CORRECT
Someone called for you but *he* didn't leave *his* name.	Someone called but *they* didn't leave *their* name.
This should enable the user to locate *his* files more easily.	This should enable *the user* to locate *his / her* files more easily.
	This should enable *users* to locate *their* files more easily.

As can be seen from the examples:

- *they / their* can be used with reference to singular subjects (e.g., *someone, a person, some guy*)
- *he / she* and *his / her* can be used as an alternative to *he* and *his*

The simplest solution is often to make the subject plural and then use *they* and *their*.

5.8   Note any differences in style and level of formality between English and your language

The English language has increasingly become more and more informal. Below are three examples of salutations from letters written by Benjamin Franklin, one of the founding fathers of the USA, in the late eighteenth century.

Your faithful and affectionate Servant,

I am, my dear friend, Your's affectionately,

My best wishes attend you, being, with sincere esteem, Sir, Your most obedient and very humble servant,

Such phrases today would sound ridiculous in an email, even in a very formal letter. However, similar phrases exist in many languages of today. For example, a French person in a formal email might say *Would you accept, sir, the expression of my distinguished salutation* (10 words), or an Italian might say *In expectation of your courteous reply, it is my pleasure to send you my most cordial greetings* (17 words). Such phrases in English sound extremely pompous and would probably be rendered as *I look forward to hearing from you* (7 words) or simply *Best regards* (2 words).

In fact, most languages in their written form tend to be more formal than written English. This formality shows itself not just in the choice of words and expressions but also in the length of sentences and paragraphs. Below is an email to a professor from a Bangladeshi who wishes to become a research student. The parts in italics would be considered much too formal by most Anglos.

Dear Professor *Dr William* Gabbitas,

With due respect I would like to draw your attention that at present, I am working as an assistant professor in the Department of Engineering, Islamic University, Kushtia-7003, Bangladesh. I am *highly* interested in continuing my further studies in the field of reducing fuel emissions. I am therefore, very much interested to continue my higher studies for Ph.D. degree in your university under your supervision. I am sending *herewith* my bio-data *in favor of your kind consideration.*

I would be grateful if you would kindly send me information regarding admission procedures and financial support such as grants available from your government, university, or any other sources.

I would very much appreciate it if you would consider me for a position as your research student.

I am eagerly looking forward to your generous suggestion.

With warmest regards.

Sincerely yours

Hussain Choudhury

The above email might be appropriate for sending to academics who are accustomed to using such formal language themselves. However, a more appropriate version, for example, for sending to a professor in the USA, would be:

> Dear Professor Gabbitas
>
> I am an assistant professor in the department of Engineering, at the Islamic University in Bangladesh, where I am doing research into reducing fuel emissions. I would be very interested to continue my studies for a PhD under your supervision. From my CV (see attached) you will see that I have been working on very similar areas as you, and I feel I might be able to make a useful contribution to your team.
>
> I would be grateful if you would kindly send me information regarding admission procedures and any financial support that might be available.
>
> I look forward to hearing from you.
>
> Hussain Choudhury

In any case if it's your first contact with someone, it's generally best to use a formal style, particularly if you are writing to someone in a country whose culture you are not very familiar with. This is especially true of Eastern countries such as Korea and Japan, but even in Europe certain countries (e.g., Germany, Italy) tend to be much more formal than others.

5.9   Add a friendly phrase at the end of an email

There are various phrases that you can use at the end of an email, particularly if you think the rest of the email may be a little strong. These include the following:

Have a nice day.

Have a great weekend.

Keep up the good work.

5.10   Judge whether the email you have received is formal or informal and reply accordingly

Most people try to match the level of formality of the email that they have received. But this entails knowing how to recognize just how formal an email is. There are various clues.

FORMAL: LONG AND COMPLEX SENTENCES

If a phrase is long and / or complex, this is generally a sign of greater formality.

FORMAL	LESS FORMAL
We *have pleasure in confirming* the acceptance of your abstract for . . .	*This is to confirm* that your abstract has been accepted for . . .
Should you need any clarifications, please do not hesitate to contact us.	*If you* have any questions, please let us know.
You are requested to acknowledge this email.	*Please* acknowledge this email.
It is necessary that I have the report by Tuesday.	*Please* could I have the report by Tuesday.

It is important to be aware, however, that some short sentences (e.g., the first example sentence below) are not always the most informal and can also come across as rather cold. Writing in a telegraphic style can obscure the meaning from your reader, so always try to write complete and comprehensible sentences.

The examples below show how a simple concept, such as acknowledging receipt of a mail, can be expressed in many different ways from completely detached to quite warm.

I confirm receipt of your fax.

This is just to confirm that I received your fax.

Just to let you know that your fax got through.

Thanks for your fax.

FORMAL: MODAL VERBS

The four modal auxiliaries *may, can, could,* and *would* are often used to make a request sound more courteous and less direct. Compare the following pairs of sentences:

May I remind you that we are still awaiting your report on manuscript No. 1342/2 . . .
We are still awaiting your report on manuscript No. 1342/2 . . .

Can you kindly check with her that this is OK.
Check that this is OK.

Could you please keep me informed of any changes you plan to make to the presentation.
Keep me informed of any changes you plan to make to the presentation.

Would you like me to Skype you?
Do you want me to Skype you?

In a similar way, *won't be able to* is often preferred to *cannot*, and *would like* or *wish* to *want*. Both *cannot* and *want* tend to sound too abrupt.

I'm sorry but I *won't be able to* give you any feedback on your manuscript until next week.

We regret to inform you that we *will not be able to* offer your students any special rate for attending the congress.

The modal verb *may* is extremely useful whenever you want to give your mail a formal tone:

I would be grateful for any further information you *may* be able to give me about ...

You *may* also check the status of your manuscript by logging into your account at http://manuscript.zzxx.com/account.

To whom it *may* concern.

May I thank you for your help in this matter.

Note: The use of *shall* as a future auxiliary and *should* as a conditional auxiliary is outdated in English, and their use is a sure sign of formality. In the examples below, the first sentence in each pair is very formal, and the second sentence is normal English.

We *shall* give your request our prompt attention.
= We *will* deal with your request as soon as possible.

I *should be glad if you could* send the file again, this time as a pdf.
= *Please could you* send the file again, this time as a pdf.

FORMAL: NOUNS

The English language is essentially verb based. Many other languages are noun based. When there is a predominance of nouns rather than verbs, it gives an email a feeling of distance and formality:

Please inform me of the time of your *arrival*.
Please let me know when you *will be arriving*.

To the best of our *knowledge*.
As far as we *know*.

For more on this topic, see 5.4 in the companion volume *English for Writing Research Papers*.

FORMAL: MULTI-SYLLABLE WORDS

Generally, a clear indication of formality is given by the number of syllables in a word—the more there are, the more formal the email is likely to be. If you speak French, Italian, Portuguese, Romanian, or Spanish, a good tip is if the multi-syllable word in English looks similar to a word that you have in your own language, then it is probably formal in English. Compare the following pairs of verbs. The first verb is multi-syllable and formal, and the second is monosyllable or a phrasal verb:

> advise / let someone know, apologize / be sorry, assist / help, attempt / try, clarify / make clear, commence / start, consider / think about, contact / get in touch, enter / go in, evaluate / look into, examine / look at, inform / tell, perform / carry out, receive / get, reply / get back to, require / want, utilize / use

The same also applies to nouns, for example, *possibility* vs *chance*.

OMISSION OF SUBJECT AND OTHER PARTS OF SPEECH

A clear sign that an email is informal is when the subject of the verb and / or the auxiliary are missing. An email is even more informal when articles, possessive adjectives, etc. are also missed out in telegraphic style (last example).

INFORMAL	FORMAL
Been very busy recently.	*I have been* very busy recently.
Appreciate your early reply.	*I would appreciate* your early reply.
Hope to hear from you soon.	*I hope* to hear from you soon.
Speak to you soon.	*I will speak* to you soon.
Looking forward to your reply.	*I am looking* forward to your reply.
Will be in touch.	*I will* be in touch.
Just a quick update on . . .	*This is just* a quick update on . . .
Have forwarded Carlos *copy* of *ppt* to *personal* email too.	I have forwarded Carlos *a copy* of *the presentation* to *his personal* email too.

ABBREVIATIONS AND ACRONYMS

Some abbreviations are perfectly acceptable even in a formal email, such as *re* (regarding) and *C / A* (bank current account). Others, however, such as *ack* (acknowledge, acknowledgement), *tx* (thanks), and *rgds* (regards), should be used with caution—they give the impression that you could not find the time to write the words out in full.

SMILEYS

A smiley (see page 40) is a clear indication of informality. I strongly suggest that you use them only if your recipient has used them first. There are some people, particularly of older generations, who find smileys annoying. Also, avoid using them with anyone when you want to make a difficult request seem lighter. For example:

> Please could you send me the revision tomorrow :)

The above request for someone to revise a long document within a very short timeframe is not helped by having a smiley, which may actually make the recipient angry as he / she will certainly not be happy to do such a long task in such a short time.

5.11   An example of how a simple request can lead to a possible collaboration

Below is a string of emails between one of my students, Katia Orlandi, and the author of a paper, Olaf Christensen. As usual, I have changed their names and some details for reasons of privacy. Note how

- the string of emails becomes less and less formal
- they quickly build up a good relationship by showing interest in each other's work and countries
- they end up with a potential collaboration

Dear Dr. Christensen,

I'm a PhD Student at the Department of Engineering, at the University of Pisa in Italy.

I am doing research into energy-saving solutions for p2p overlay networks (e.g., Red BitTorrent).

I'm writing to you because I'm interested in your paper:

J. Breakwater and O. Christensen, "Red BitTorrents? The answer to everything".

I would appreciate it very much if you could send me a copy by email. By the way, I have found your previous papers really interesting; they have been a great stimulus to my research.

Thanks in advance.

Regards

Katia Orlandi

Hello Katia

Attached is our paper which we are going to present at the Fifth International Workshop on Red Communications next June.

I see you are from Pisa ... a small but beautiful city. I have been there (to see the Leaning Tower, of course).

Let me know if you have any questions about the BitTorrent work.

Olaf

Dear Dr. Christensen,

Thank you so much for your quick reply. I have already read half the paper - really useful.

Yes, Pisa is a great city, though I am actually from Palermo in Sicily. I see you work in Denmark; I was in Copenhagen this summer; it was really beautiful.

I am actually going to the Red Communications conference too! It would be great to meet up.

Ciao

Katia

Hi Katia

Out of curiosity I looked you up on your webpage at your department's website. You seem to have done a lot of research in the same area as our time. I was wondering whether you might be interested in working on a new project that my prof and I are setting up. In any case, let's arrange to meet at the Red C conference ... By the way, it's Olaf, I am not used to being addressed as Dr. Christensen :).

Part II
Writing and Responding to Reviews

Chapter 6
Requesting and Writing an Informal Review of a Colleague's Work

You will learn how to

- request a revision
- write informal comments on a colleague's manuscript
- be constructive

Sometimes we are given other people's work to comment on informally, for example, CVs, reports, posters, and presentations.

Writing a review for someone you know is tricky. You certainly don't want to offend them in any way, but at the same time if you find problems in their manuscript, it is clearly beneficial for them to know what these problems are and also how to remedy them. It is quite a responsibility because in effect you are acting as a referee, and the more issues you spot now, the more likely the paper will be published on first submission.

In this chapter, subsections 1, 9, and 10 refer to the person who is requesting an informal review. Subsections 2–8 refer to the person who is writing the review.

For useful phrases on this topic see Chapter 23.

A. Wallwork, *English for Academic Correspondence and Socializing*,
DOI 10.1007/978-1-4419-9401-1_6, © Springer Science+Business Media, LLC 2011

What the experts say

Tact is the art of making a point without making an enemy.

Isaac Newton, English physicist, mathematician, and astronomer

If the report is not what you were hoping for and seems needlessly critical, it is best to delay sending an email expressing your reaction. Instead, wait a few days, and then go back to it. Firstly, this allows your initial anger and demoralization to subside, and secondly when you re-read the report you may actually find something useful in it. Clearly, if you ask someone to do an informal review for you, it is not wise to then be critical of what they say. Thus your strategy is similar to the one you would adopt when you receive a referee's report from a journal: the referee is merely an obstacle to getting your paper accepted, so learn from him / her, and do whatever you can to say something positive about their suggestions, and then implement them into your manuscript. A few months' later you will not even be able to remember what changes you made and why you had to make them—all you will remember is the satisfaction of seeing your manuscript published.

Brian Martin, Professor of Social Sciences at the University of Wollongong, Australia,
author of Surviving Referees' Reports

Men tend to write emails that are approximately one and a half times longer than women, they also make stronger assertions, and disagree with others more than women. Women use diplomatic assertions, ask more questions, and make offers and suggestions. Men are much more prone to using profanity, insults and sarcasm than women.

Professor Susan Herring, School of Library and Information Science,
Indiana University, Bloomington

6.1   Give explicit instructions about how you want the recipient to review your work

When you ask someone to informally review your work, make sure first of all that you do so politely; see Chapter 23 to learn how.

Then be 100% explicit exactly what you expect the person to do; you cannot say *Please could you revise my manuscript.* You need to tell them what to focus on, bearing in mind that they may not have time to do a thorough job. Here is an example:

> Dear Carlos
>
> I hope all is well with you.
>
> I am currently working on a paper that I would like to submit to the journal's special issue for the conference. The paper is the extension of the work that I presented as a poster during the conference, which I think you saw. The draft is still at quite an early stage, but I would really appreciate your input.
>
> I know that you have a lot of expertise in this area and I am sure my paper would really benefit from your input. In any case, I have what I think are some really important new results, so I hope that you will find this paper of interest too. Obviously, I don't want to take up too much of your time, so perhaps you might just focus on the Discussion and Results. Also, if you could quickly browse through the Literature Cited to make sure I haven't missed any important papers (yours are all there by the way!).
>
> The deadline for submission is on Oct 10, so if you could get your revisions back to me by the end of this month (i.e., September) that would be great.
>
> I do appreciate the fact that you must be very busy, so please do not hesitate to let me know if you don't have the time.
>
> Thank you very much in advance.
>
> Maria

Note how Maria

- gives a brief overview of what kind of paper it is and what stage it is at
- outlines not only the benefit for herself but also a possible benefit for the recipient
- mentions the recipient's *expertise*

- gives the recipient precise details of the parts of the paper that most need the recipient's attention
- informs the recipient when she needs the manuscript return (she avoids using a formal and totally unhelpful expression such as *Please could you return it at your earliest convenience*)
- acknowledges that the recipient may be busy
- gives the recipient the option not to accept her request

The recipient thus has all the information he needs to decide whether to accept or decline the request. He does not need to ask for clarifications.

If you do not know the recipient very well, then you need to ensure that you are not making yourself a problem for the recipient. In such cases you can give them the option to decline your request by saying:

I appreciate that this must be a busy time of year for you, so please feel free to say "no."

I imagine that many people ask you for help in editing their draft manuscripts, so don't hesitate to let me know if you are overloaded with requests.

6.2 Carefully construct and organize your comments on your colleague's manuscript

When someone asks you to have a look at or edit their draft manuscript, they are sharing something with you that may have taken them many months to prepare and which they are probably very sensitive about. If you wish to maintain a positive relationship with the person who has asked you to review their work, then you might find the following structure useful:

1. Begin with a friendly comment. Try to create a bridge between you and the recipient in which you show that you want to be helpful and cooperative.

   Thanks for sending me your manuscript. It's looking really good, well done!

   I enjoyed reading your paper. It contains a lot of really useful data. I am impressed!

2. Show interest in the paper and find areas of the research / manuscript that you are in agreement with.

   Your aims seem well grounded and I think there is real innovation.

   I think you have highlighted your contribution clearly.

3. Identify those parts of the paper (or section of the paper) that you feel work really well and give a specific comment saying why you think they work well.

By saying something positive, you are putting the reader in the right frame of mind for accepting any criticisms that you may wish to make.

Your methods are really clear and I think readers would have no problem replicating them.

The abstract looks great. Very clear and concise, and not too much introductory stuff.

4. Tell the authors what you have done.

I have read the manuscript carefully and made several changes to the text, including a couple of additions. I hope that in doing so I have not altered the sense of what you wanted to say. In any case, please feel free to disregard .... Where possible, I have tried to ... Nevertheless, I think, the paper still needs some work before you send it to the journal.

5. When making criticisms be constructive (see 6.4). Rather than saying anything very negative, think about whether you could not transform your criticism into a query. For example, instead of saying *I don't understand why you have included the table on x—it seems completely redundant*, you could be more diplomatic and say *Could you clarify why you have included the table on x.*

6. Make any suggestions in a soft way.

Have you thought about ... ?

It might be a good idea to ...

When I am writing a paper, I find it useful to ...

Readers might appreciate it if you ...

The reviewers might be concerned about ...

7. Offer further help and tell them when you would be available.

If you need any more help, then don't hesitate to contact me. I am on vacation next week, but will be back the week after.

I would be happy to talk through the changes I suggested to the Discussion.

Please keep me up to date with the progress of this manuscript and let me know if you need any further help.

6.3   Use the first lines to say something positive

It is good practice to say something positive in the first few lines, but be careful how you phrase such comments. For example,

I have looked through your presentation and think it's quite good. Just a few comments:

can be interpreted as being a bit negative. The term *quite good* is a little dangerous in English because it can mean anything from "really good" to "sufficient but nothing great". This is partly due to the fact that words like *quite* very much depend on the intonation they are given when spoken. But of course in an email this intonation is completely lost.

Imagine how you would feel if you received the comments in the first column below. You would probably feel quite discouraged. The comments in the second column immediately put the recipient in the right frame of mind to receive any criticisms that you might have.

NOT VERY ENCOURAGING	ENCOURAGING
Your presentation is OK.	It's looking really good—I love the way you've used photos.
It looks fine.	Overall it looks excellent and the conclusions are very clear.
I looked at your presentation. Here is a list (non-exhaustive) of things you need to change:	I've now had a chance to go through the presentation and I thought you might like a few suggestions.
You need to improve the following points in your presentation:	It's pretty impressive, well done. Here are just a few comments which you are welcome to ignore.

6.4   Be constructive in your criticism

If you need to be critical of someone's work, your recipient is more likely to act on your comments if they are presented in a positive way.

Let's imagine that a co-author has written the first draft of the Methods section of a manuscript describing some research you have done together. Your respective professors set up the collaboration and in fact you don't know this co-author particularly well; he comes from another institute in another country. Most of your communication has been conducted via email and you have only met face-to-face twice.

In your opinion your co-author has committed three crucial mistakes. He has

1. missed out some important steps
2. not put the sources of some of the materials
3. misspelled the names of some of the materials

Here is a typical example of an email that fails to address these points in a constructive way:

Dear Paul

I have had a look at the Methods section and there are several problems with it. First you have missed out two crucial steps (i.e., blah and blah). Second, you haven't spelled some of the names of the materials correctly. Last but not least, you have failed to provide the sources of some of the materials.

I am reattaching the draft with various other suggested changes and additions.

Please could you make the other necessary changes and send me the draft back by the end of this week. It is now quite urgent.

Best regards

Maria

Maria has not thought about how Paul might feel when he reads her email. Paul is likely to be very angry and / or very upset. He may have spent months on writing the Methods. In addition, there may be very good reasons for the three apparent errors. Perhaps the two crucial steps were originally in the manuscript, but Paul had decided to change their position, and had thus cut them out but forgotten to paste them back in (maybe he was interrupted by a phone call when in the middle of the cut and paste). In his email to Maria, perhaps Paul had forgotten to tell her that he was locating the sources of some of the materials and would get back to her with the details. And finally, maybe Paul was waiting for Maria's revisions before doing a final spell check.

Maria's email will have a negative impact because

- it does not give the recipient the benefit of the doubt; it assumes that there is no other explanation for Paul's three errors other than that he is incompetent
- it is very direct; there is no introduction
- it over-emphasizes the problems by using words like *failed* and *last but not least*; it thus seems quite sarcastic
- its tone is not that of a co-author, but that of a severe angry professor

If you begin your email with an immediate criticism, your co-author will react negatively and this will set the tone for how he reacts to your other comments.

Instead find something positive to say. Here are some examples:

> Thanks for getting this section to me far ahead of the deadline; this will make my life much easier.

> I really like your succinct style of writing; I think it will help the referees, and the readers, to follow our methodology easily and quickly.

> Although I am not a native speaker myself, your English seems to be really good—so let's hope the reviewers are impressed!

Provided they are sincere, the above sentences help to get the recipient in a positive state so that he will then read your criticisms with a more open mind. You then have to deal with the three main mistakes in his draft. The first thing is to try and reduce the number of criticisms you make, and then begin with the most serious mistake. Thus, Maria's email could be rewritten as follows:

> I just wanted to point a couple of issues in your draft. Firstly, I may be wrong, but it seems to me that you have missed out two important steps in our methodology. These are . . .
> Secondly, the editor will expect us to provide the sources for all our materials, so I think we need to add these. I think I only noticed a couple of cases, so this shouldn't take you too long.
> By the way, would you mind doing a final spell check, but not just with Word as I don't think it will identify any spelling mistakes in the technical names (e.g., the names of the source materials).

In her revised version, it seems that she is only making one criticism (the two steps that are missing) and she does this by softening her comments with *I may be wrong, but it seems to me*. This gives Paul the option to prove her wrong. Regarding the sources of the materials, Maria takes joint responsibility for this by using the inclusive pronoun *us* and *our*, and she then minimizes the effort required by referring to the small number of sources involved and the short time required to sort out the problem. Finally, she presents the reference to the spelling mistakes almost as an afterthought (*by the way*) and as a friendly request (*would you mind*).

So, when Paul reads the above message, he will be appreciative of Maria's comments and will be more likely to both implement them and get back to Maria quickly.

6.5   Be diplomatic and make detailed comments rather than unspecific observations

When making your comments, it is generally appropriate not to sound overcritical and harsh but to adopt a more diplomatic, less direct approach. Compare these pairs of sentences and note how those in the second column adopt a softer approach.

DIRECT CRITICISM + TOO GENERIC	INDIRECT CRITICISM + MORE SPECIFIC
You should re-write parts of the presentation.	I think the introduction (i.e. Slides 2-3) may need some re-working.
Cut the redundant slides.	Could we manage without Slides 5 and 6? / It might be an idea to cut Slides 5 and 6
The Methodology is way too long.	What about making some cuts to the Methodology (e.g. the flow chart)?
You'll never have time to explain all those slides on the Results.	If we wanted to make any cuts anywhere, the Results might be a good place to start (e.g the first two tables). / I understand why you have gone into such detail in the Results, but ...

The examples above highlight various important points about softening the tone:

- choice of action words: *rework* is must less dramatic than *rewrite*

- use of modals of obligation (should, must): these are best avoided in active sentences as they tend to sound too authoritarian. If you are using such words simply to express an opinion, then begin your phrase with *I think*, or *it might be a good idea if*, etc.

- *may, might, perhaps, possibly*: these words are excellent ways to make suggestions without appearing to be a know-it-all

- phrasing criticisms in the form of questions: this allows for a certain amount of doubt, whether real or not, on the part of the commentator to be transmitted to the author. It also leaves the decision up to the recipient, thus leaving him / her feeling more in control.

- beginning sentences with *if*: the conditional can always be used as a more indirect means to criticize

- use of *we*: this makes you sound more involved in the process, as if you are sharing the responsibility with the author. This transmits a feeling of collaboration, rather than the idea of me vs you.

- use of words like *understand* and *appreciate*: again these help you sound more understanding, and show that you appreciate all the hard work the author has done

Also, note how the suggestions in the second column are much more specific than the vague comments in the first column.

6.6   Avoid being too direct when asking for clarification and making suggestions

When you are not sure about something that your colleague has written, it's a good idea to be careful how you ask questions and avoid being too direct otherwise you could sound more critical than you intend. You can make a question softer by

1. adding an extra little introductory phrase

2. making out that it's you that has a difficulty, but not necessarily that this difficulty is caused by some negligence on the recipient's part

3. phrasing the question in the passive, thus making it appear that the author was somehow not involved in the decision when in fact they were

DIRECT QUESTION	INDIRECT QUESTION
Why don't you have an "Outline" slide?	By the way, have you thought about having an "Outline" slide?
When are you going to mention the disadvantages of our approach?	Have you decided when you are going to mention the disadvantages of our approach?
Why did you include the table in the fourth slide?	It was probably my idea, but can you remind me why it was decided to include the table in the fourth slide?

Of course, if you have a lot of comments to make or if your comments are simple observations that will clearly help to improve the content of the presentation, then there is no need to always adopt a roundabout approach. For example:

The weight should be quoted to 3 decimal places, not 4.

An easier solution would be to swap the position of slides 5 and 7.

Don't forget to do a spell check at the end (I always forget!)

In the above cases you are not criticizing the recipient but merely making some helpful suggestions.

6.7   Conclude your report by saying something positive

Your concluding comments should always be positive, thus leaving the recipient thinking that they have not made a complete disaster of their work. Make sure you don't simply end with *Regards, Carlos* but include a phrase like one of the following:

Thanks for doing such a great job on this, and also thanks for offering to do the presentation (I am sure you will do it much better than I would have done).

Well, I think that's all—once again, a really excellent job, just a few things to tighten up here and there.

Hope you find these comments useful, and bear in mind that I've only focused on what changes I believe need making so I'm sorry if it comes across as being very critical.

6.8   Re-read everything before you hit the "send" button

Always re-read what you have written when you have been criticizing someone's work (or whenever you have something potentially awkward to say). Make sure you haven't said anything that could damage your relationship or offend in any way. Also, if you really have to be critical, consider leaving the email for a while and then coming back to it to see if you have been really fair or not.

6.9   Be diplomatic when sending reminders

If you are a PhD student or junior researcher and you make a request (e.g., to review your work), your recipient is generally under no obligation to fulfill the request. So if you hear nothing it is a good idea to send them a reminder (known as "chasing" in English). Ensure that you do so in a friendly tone with no sense of frustration or anger. Here are some examples:

> I was wondering if you had had time to look at my email dated 10 February (see below).

> I know that you are extremely busy, but could you possibly ...

> Sorry to bother you again, but I urgently need you to answer these questions.

> I know you must be very busy but if you could find the time to do this ...

When you chase someone with regard to a previous email that you have sent, always include the old email within your new email—this is why in the first example sentence above the sender has put *see below*. This indicates that the old mail is below his / her signature of the new email.

It may help to motivate your recipient to reply if you do one or more of the following:

- empathize with the fact that they are a busy person who probably has more important things to do than to reply to your request
- explain why this person is important for you and your work
- give them a brief explanation as to why you need a reply so urgently
- tell them how long it will take them to fulfill your request—people always tend to overestimate the time of a task that they don't want to do
- if time is running short, reduce your original request to what is absolutely essential for you (e.g., maybe originally you asked someone to read your whole manuscript, now you just ask them to read just one section)
- find a benefit for them of fulfilling your request
- give them a deadline for their response

Here is an example of an email from a student writing to a professor who she has never met for advice on her manuscript.

Dear Professor Li

I was wondering if you had had time to look at my email dated 10 February (see below).

I imagine that you must receive a lot of requests such as mine, but I really need your input as no one else has your expertise in this particular field. In reality, it would be enough if you could just read the last two pages of the Discussion (pages 12 and 13), just so that you could check that I have not reached any erroneous conclusions. I very much hope that my results might be of interest to you too as they diverge from what you reported in your paper *paper title*. I have a deadline for submission on the 20 April, so it would be perfect if you could get your comments to me by about 10 April.

I realize that this is a lot to ask, particularly as you have never even met me, but if you could spare 10-15 minutes of your time, I would be extremely grateful.

I look forward to hearing from you.

6.10 Be appreciative when thanking someone for doing an informal review of your work

When someone has done you the favor of reviewing your manuscript, it pays to be appreciative of their work. This is irrespectively of whether their comments were useful to you or not, and of whether you agree with what they say. You can begin an email of thanks by saying:

Thank you so much for your review, it was very kind of you to spare the time. The manuscript has certainly benefitted from your input—particularly the Discussion, where you have managed to really highlight the novelty of the research.

If they have made any specific criticisms you can say:

I understand what you meant by ... so I have adjusted that section accordingly.

Clearly, having read your comments, I need to rewrite the part about ...

I think you were right about the table, so I have ...

If you need any clarifications, you can say:

Thanks very much for all this. Just one thing—could you just clarify exactly what you mean by . . .

I may come back to you if I need further thoughts on some of the slides.

Also, bear in mind that if this person has made certain comments, they may be the exact same comments that the referees might make. Thus, it is worth taking your colleague's comments into serious consideration.

You can conclude your email by something like:

> Once again thanks for all your hard work—I found it really useful. I will keep you posted about the progress of the manuscript.

Chapter 7
Writing a Peer Review

You will learn how to

- focus on constructive feedback rather than negative criticism
- use a "sandwich" approach, in which your criticisms are sandwiched between positive comments
- choose a style and layout that is easy to follow and comment on for the authors

Peer review is an essential part of research. If you are chosen to do a peer review, it is because you are considered to have specialized knowledge of the subject. The fact that you were not involved in the research itself enables you to provide an objective and balanced critique of the authors' work. Thus, you are in a perfect position to really help, rather than discourage, the authors in their research, even if it means that you ultimately decide that a manuscript is not suitable for publication.

Please note that in this chapter and throughout this section, the terms *referee* and *reviewer*, and *report* and *review*, are used indifferently.

A. Wallwork, *English for Academic Correspondence and Socializing*,
DOI 10.1007/978-1-4419-9401-1_7, © Springer Science+Business Media, LLC 2011

Factoids

❖ An analysis of referees' reports by Magda Kouřilová from Comenius University in Bratislava found that less than 10% of her sample reviews used a sandwich technique (i.e., preceded and followed by compliments). Much more common was criticism alone, with no positive comments, even in those papers that were subsequently accepted for publication.

❖ In a paper entitled *How well does a journal's peer review process function? A survey of authors' opinions*, the researchers found that authors awaiting publication disagreed with their reviewers' comments about 25% of the time.

❖ Juan Miguel Campanario from the University of Alcalá, Madrid, Spain, published a thought-provoking paper asking the question *Have referees rejected some of the most-cited articles of all times?* And found that the answer was yes!

7.1   Be clear about your role as a reviewer

Your main aims as a reviewer are

1. to assess on behalf of the journal whether or not a paper is suitable for publication
2. help a fellow researcher who may be at the beginning of their career and who may not have access to all the data / equipment / experience / funds that you have

7.2   Read your journal's review guidelines

Most journals ask you to review a manuscript by following certain criteria. These criteria are normally contained within a form that you are asked to fill in, or may simply be in a downloadable document containing advice on how to write reviews. In some cases you may be asked to write an informal review for a colleague or a student. Below are some typical aspects that a review is likely to cover, followed by questions that you might like to ask yourself.

The paper should:

CONTRIBUTE TO THE SPECIFIC AREA OF KNOWLEDGE

Does the paper add sufficiently to the current literature? Does the review of the literature display patterns in earlier research that have not been noticed before? What original elements does it add and how? Does it have a clear message? Is the problem well defined and the purpose clearly stated?

HAVE A RELEVANT TITLE

Does the title attract the reader's attention and also reflect the actual content of the paper? Would an intelligent search be able to find this paper?

HAVE AN ABSTRACT THAT IS SHORT YET COMPREHENSIVE

Does the abstract give the reader a good idea of what to expect from the paper? Does the abstract clearly state the main objective (the research question), the conclusions, and how have they been reached, for example, theoretically, by case studies or through other measures?

MAKE GOOD USE OF KEY WORDS

Do the keywords describe the content? Will they enable potential readers to search for and find the paper?

REVIEW EXISTING LITERATURE AND GIVE APPROPRIATE REFERENCES

Have the authors avoided too many references referring to general knowledge or to papers published by the author's conationals or just in their own country? Are the references given in the literature cited section at the end of the paper relevant and up to date, have the important ones been included, and are there any important references missing? Are the references mentioned within the body of the paper?

FULLY DESCRIBE THE RESEARCH METHOD

Do the authors make it clear what was done and why certain methods were chosen and others not? Is the study designed well? Does the authors' data set seem appropriate to the questions that they pose? Have appropriate materials been selected? Is the sample of an adequate size? Are the methods adequately described? Can they be easily repeated?

HAVE A DISCUSSION AND CONCLUSIONS

Do their results answer their research question? Are the results well presented, discussed in light of previous evidence, and credible? Could they be strengthened? Are the conclusions justified from the evidence given? Are the conclusions adequately qualified? Are there any logical and obvious possible interpretations that the authors have not mentioned? Have any implications and applications been outlined?

BE CLEARLY ORGANIZED AND WRITTEN

Is the paper laid out clearly, with headings that enable the reader to understand the main points of the paper and to follow its structure? Is the order of the sections, paragraphs, and sentences logical—or should parts be shifted to another location in the paper? Is the style academic, but at the same time reader-oriented, that is, easy to read and assimilate? Is there any redundancy? Could the paper be shortened without losing any value?

HAVE FIGURES AND TABLES THAT ADD REAL VALUE

Do the figures and tables illustrate important points, or are they more confusing than clarifying? Are they explained in the text? Are the captions / legends appropriate?

You can find more possible questions at the end of Chapters 11–18 in the companion volume *English for Writing Research Papers*.

7.3   How to structure a referee's report: (1) acceptance subject to revisions

A referee's report which recommends possible acceptance subject to changes being made could be structured as follows.

1. SUMMARY OF PAPER

   This helps the authors to see whether you have understood the essence of their paper, and the editor to understand how relevant the paper is to his / her journal.

2. GENERAL COMMENTS ON THE QUALITY OF THE PAPER

   This is a good opportunity to say something positive and encouraging about the paper before beginning to make any criticisms (see 7.8). So, mention the strong points of the paper first, and then the weak points.

3. MAJOR REVISIONS REQUIRED

   Here you suggest what major changes you think the paper needs in order for it to be publishable in the journal. Again, try to present these changes in a constructive way and help the authors to see why such changes are necessary (see 7.12). Number each comment—this helps the authors when responding and the editors in judging the author's response.

4. MINOR REVISIONS REQUIRED

   These generally include typos, changes to numbering, changes to figure legends, suggestions for more appropriate vocabulary, etc. Number each comment.

5. FINAL COMMENTS

   Since your aim is to further knowledge in your field through new research, it helps if you offer some encouraging words of advice and to reiterate the positive elements that you have found in the manuscript. This is particularly important for researchers from less developed nations who may not have the equipment and experience that you have access to, but may nevertheless have discovered something that could benefit people living in their area of the world.

7.4   How to structure a referee's report: (2) complete rejection

If you are recommending that a paper be rejected either because it is outside the scope of the journal or because it would require too many revisions, then you would begin with Points 1 and 2 as in 7.3 above. Even if you are going to recommend rejection, you should still be able to find something positive to say. Points 3 and 4 are not necessary. So finish with Point 5 and if possible make suggestions on what would be required to make the paper more publishable. This will enable the authors to revise their paper and maybe submit it to another (possibly less prestigious) journal.

7.5   How to structure a referee's report: (3) acceptance as is

Even if you are recommending a paper for acceptance with no changes, you still need to provide authors and editors with a brief summary (Point 1 in 7.3). If you think the scientific quality is good, but that the English needs some improvement, then ask yourself how much the "poor" English really impacts on the reader's ability to understand. You can delay a paper's publication unnecessarily by making comments on the English. Of course, if the English is truly bad, then you must let the authors and editor know. See 7.14 for more on this important aspect.

7.6   Bear in mind the authors' expectations of you as a reviewer

I asked a group of 50 PhD students from around the world what they thought were the qualities of a good reviewer. Some of the adjectives they used to describe a good reviewer were as follows:

  competent
  consistent
  constructive
  highly knowledgeable
  neutral
  scrupulous
  sympathetic

Below are some of their comments. A good referee should

- understand the difficulties that PhD students have in writing their papers
- write their review in an organized way so that the corrections that need to be made (both in terms of data and the manuscript itself) can be easily followed
- be an expert in the field of reference of the paper and at the same time have no interest in promoting or censoring the papers he / she receives
- indicate how to improve the manuscript so as to make it more readable

- clearly explain the reasons why the paper could not be accepted, without being destructive
- understand what the authors have failed to do correctly and propose "best practices" to correct them based on his / her own experience
- search out errors in the text and clearly explain why they are errors
- have respect for different viewpoints and not be judgmental
- remember that the authors may have spent several years on the research and subsequent writing of the paper and so they should pay it close attention
- the more supportive they are in their comments, the more they will help the author(s)
- be quick to return their reports

7.7   Before you begin your report, put yourself in the author's shoes

It helps to remember the first time you received a referee's report. How did you feel when the referees made non-constructive negative comments? In my job as an editor of research papers, I get to see hundreds of referee reports. Here is one that a young PhD researcher received on her first paper. After reading this report, she was considering abandoning research forever.

> The claims made by the author are neither novel nor convincing. The study is of little or no interest to the community, and is probably inaccessible to anyone outside the author's presumably very small research group. Moreover, I believe there are no further experiments that would strengthen the paper.
> I found the manuscript painful to read, with no enthusiasm on the part of the authors, nor any regard to a potential application of their work, which would seem to confirm my suspicions that there are no possible applications for this line of research.
> The introduction of the work is poorly done with few references to related works. The writing itself is weak—multiple paragraphs are lumped into giant paragraphs without any thought for the poor reader. I struggled to find any connection between one sentence and the next. A literal translation using Google Translate would probably have produced a more meritworthy level of English.
> In short, this paper is not worthy of further consideration.

Fortunately, the other two reviewers were kinder, and after some modifications the paper was published in another journal.

7.8   Use the sandwich approach: begin and end on a positive note

Your report should always be constructive in its criticism. Your aim is to help, rather than destroy.

Always begin your report in a positive way. If you do this, the authors will be more prepared to accept the negative things that you have to say. And always end your report positively. Again, this will be appreciated by the authors who at the end of your report will thus not be too disillusioned. Very negative feedback is likely to produce very negative consequences. An author may feel very angry and resentful when their research is torn apart by the reviewer, and may end up actually learning nothing from the experience.

Below is a good example of a general summary of a manuscript. This summary precedes the detailed comments.

> The author should be commended for employing data on x in order to analyze y. Although these data present a rich source of information for studying y, they remain largely underutilized, so it is good to see them being used here.
> Unfortunately however, the paper, as it is, fails to make an important contribution to the literature, for two reasons. First, the analysis suffers from a number of methodological short-comings, which are summarized in the "main comments" section below. Second, most of the empirical results are quite obvious.
> Having said that, there is one result that seems non-obvious and interesting, namely that ...
> In fact, the paper could be improved significantly if the authors could answer the following questions ... If the answer is "yes" to these questions, then these aspects could be further explored. For example, it would be interesting to identify ...

In the first paragraph the reviewer shows her appreciation of one aspect of the paper and recognizes the novel value of what the authors have done. In the second paragraph, she outlines the reasons why she will subsequently recommend the paper be rejected subject to major revisions. In the last paragraph she gives the authors some possible avenues to help improve the quality and interest of the manuscript. She does so in a way which shows her obvious enthusiasm for the topic area. The result is that the authors have something positive to work on; they will not end the reviewer's report by thinking "maybe I should try to get a job in industry!"

To help the authors feel more positive about your comments, and thus more likely to implement your recommendations, try not to overuse such nouns as *failure*, *error*, *mistake*, *loss*, *problem*, *inaccuracy*, and *miscalculation*. And completely avoid words such as *disaster* and *catastrophe*. Resist the temptation to be sarcastic or funny at the author's expense; thus avoid adjectives such as *useless*, *hopeless*, *unbelievable*, *absurd*, and *debatable* and expressions such as *the poor reader*.

Make sure that any critical judgments you make are fully supported by detailed reference to the literature. Also, be realistic in the changes that you expect the authors to make. Journal editors always appreciate a positive and constructive approach. It reassures them that they made the right choice in choosing you as a referee.

7.9   Use a soft approach when criticizing

Given that your aim should be to help rather than destroy the author, try to adopt a soft approach. Here are some ways to write comments that are more likely to be accepted and appreciated by the authors.

By avoiding being too direct, the author is more likely to accept, and understand the need for, the negative feedback.

NO	YES
The whole data set seems to say: "OK, X does not change Y." Of course! what were you expecting from a one-year experiment? Why bother putting this in the paper at all?	The authors *might consider* removing this section from the paper as I am not convinced it leads to any worthwhile or conclusive results. Instead, *they could* focus on the interesting part of their work, which is ....

Make your comments sound subjective.

NO	YES
It is absolutely wrong to state that x = y.	*I feel that / As far as I can see, / In my opinion / I believe / Based on my knowledge of the topic I would* say that the assertion that x = y may be *open to discussion.*

If you state that something "must" be done, or that something is "not complete," try to think of how these problems could be remedied.

NO	YES
The presentation of results must be deeply modified.	I would suggest that the results be presented in a different way; for example, a table could be used rather than a figure. This would make the results stand out better and make it easier for the reader to understand the importance of them.
The description of methods is incomplete and does not permit a correct evaluation of the trials.	The description of the methods needs more details. For example, what criteria were used to select the three byproducts? Why was the field test conducted with KS only? Which parameters did the Authors evaluate in the field test and how?

Try to be helpful and give authors the benefit of the doubt.

NO	YES
The methodological part refers to rather old methods; how can they not be aware of the new procedures existing in the analytical literature?	The authors may not be aware that there are actually some new procedures existing in the analytical literature. They might try reading ....

There are some qualitative words in English that can be interpreted in more than one way (positively, but often negatively). So be careful of how you use words such as *OK* and *quite*.

If you say *The title is OK* it may be interpreted as "just sufficient but nothing special." It might be better to say *The title is fine / very appropriate*.

Similarly, *the results are quite interesting* is ambiguous. It could be they are surprisingly interesting, but more likely the interpretation will be that they really state nothing new.

The end result should be a report that the authors will find useful and which will encourage them to go forward. It should never make them feel angry (even if the paper is going to be rejected) or humiliated.

You will thus be potentially increasing knowledge in a particularly area by encouraging the authors to go back and try again.

7.10   Don't just use *should* to make recommendations

When you make recommendations, it is best not to be too strong or too direct, otherwise you may give the impression of being rather authoritarian. Using *must* and *have to* is generally not appropriate (e.g., *the authors must reduce the length of the manuscript*); it is better to use *should*. But to avoid repetition and tedium, you cannot use *should* every time you make a recommendation. Consider using the following alternatives:

The authors should explain X.

Please could you explain X.

I would recommend / suggest that the authors explain X.

It would be advisable to explain X.

It might help the reader if the authors explained X.

Also, in the cases above, you should make it clear why the authors need to explain X. If you don't provide the authors with a motivation, then they may not understand the necessity of explaining X. For example:

> Given that an understanding of X is crucial in order to appreciate the quality of the results, I suggest that ...

> I am not sure that readers will be able to follow the experimental procedure if they don't first have a clear understanding of X.

7.11   Use separate paragraphs to outline your comments

Try to make it as easy as possible for both the editor and the author to read your comments. If you write everything in one long paragraph, it will make it very hard for the authors to respond to what you have asked them to do.

Divide your comments into sections with headings—these are normally indicated by the journal.

Have separate paragraphs for each point you make. Give clear page and line references to show where your comments refer to in the paper.

If possible, number each comment.

7.12   Make sure your comments are explicit and explain how they could be implemented

Whether you are recommending acceptance or rejection, all the points you make should be clear to the authors.

The following unhelpful comment is quite typical of a referee's report. It makes a criticism, without suggesting any remedies:

> One of my main concerns is that the level of pollution in the sediments has not been clearly characterized: on the basis of metal contents in sediments (Table 1) it is hard to establish a level of pollution; consequently, the validation of the methodology is quite weak.

A more helpful report would be:

> I have three main concerns:
>
> (1) the aim of the work is not clear—I am not completely sure whether this is simply a validation of a widely-used bioassay or a field study. If it is indeed a validation, then I am not sure of its utility, given that many cases have already been reported in the literature (as cited by the authors themselves). If it is a field study, then it might be useful to add more parameters.

(2) the parameters that the authors measured are too similar to each other and there are too few of them (only four). I would recommend using at least six parameters.

(3) the sediments that the authors chose are not very revealing in terms of metal pollution. What about using sediments from .... ?

The revised version tells the authors what they can do to improve their work (see the last sentence in each of Points 1–3).

In the next example it is not 100% clear which part of the referee's sentence the author needs to address:

Can the authors explain why the artificial seawater for the control was replaced daily?

Is the problem with *artificial* seawater (rather than real seawater), with the *control* (rather than the sample), or with the replacement being on a *daily* basis (rather than hourly or weekly)? A clearer question would be:

Why didn't the authors treat the control in the same way as the other samples (which did not undergo daily replacement)?

In the following sentence the referee gives no reason for the "contrast" or why the sentence is not "clear"; therefore, the authors have little information on which to base the requested revision.

Lines 40–42: this sentence seems to be in contrast with the "Conclusion" section. Please clarify.
Line 51: ...sediments represent the major repository of integration and accumulation of...
This sentence is not clear.

The referee is forcing the authors to make an interpretation, which may or may not be correct. The above two comments could be made more explicit by saying:

In the Abstract (lines 40–42) the authors say that x and y were effective, but in the Conclusions it seems that only x is effective.
I am not sure how a repository can contain "integration." What exactly do the authors mean by "integration" in this context?

Always identify which part of a sentence you don't understand and why it is not clear for you.

Here are some more examples of unhelpful comments because they give no explanations.

The length of the paper could be reduced considerably.

The Discussion is rather poor.

The Conclusions do not add to the overall scientific knowledge in the field.

The format of the tables is inadequate.

The simulation analysis is not convincing.

In each of the above examples, the authors will want to know why the reviewer has made such comments and what they can do to remedy them. For example, how could they reduce the length—by cutting certain sections? by removing figures and tables? by reducing the literature cited? by reducing redundant words and phrases?

7.13   Use *you* to address the authors, and *I* (i.e., the first person) to make reference to yourself

Traditionally, referees address the authors as "the authors." Given that the referees' reports are above all for the authors, a much more direct and simpler way to refer to the authors is to say "you." This also avoids ambiguity if there are any third-party authors involved, for example, when the referee needs to talk about the authors of other papers in the literature.

A lot of trouble is taken to see that referees remain anonymous. However, this does not mean that if you are a referee you have to refer to yourself in a very indirect way. The first phrase below, to me at least, sounds very unnatural, and could easily be replaced with the second without any loss of anonymity:

> Specifically, this referee is concerned with the following issues ...

> Specifically, I am concerned with the following issues ...

The unnaturalness of not using the first person pronoun (I) is also revealed in the following example:

> However, *in the reviewer's opinion*, several critical weaknesses (enumerated below) affect the strength of the paper, which *it is believed* should not be accepted for publication.

It is believed presumably means *I believe.*

7.14   Don't make indiscriminate comments about the level of English

Here are some typical comments made about the level of English of the authors, the first by a non-native speaker of English, the second by a native speaker.

> A big problem with this work is the English form: there are so many language errors that it actually seriously compromises one's ability to understand what is being presented. The paper needs an extensive revision by a native English speaker.

> While I sympathize with the difficulties of writing in a foreign language, the poor quality of the English was asking too much of me. In the end I gave up. I also found their method of grandstanding their results to be quite obnoxious at times.

It is important to bear in mind that

- the authors' level of English may be quite low, so your report should be expressed in very simple English (words like *grandstanding* and *obnoxious* will not be familiar to most readers, and the tone is rather sarcastic)
- funds may be a problem for them, so anything you can do to avoid them spending extra money and to increase their chances of being published will be helpful
- they may be quite young, so you don't want to discourage them

If you are unsure about the level of English of the authors, it is advisable NOT just to say that the "the paper needs some revision".

The problem is that you may unnecessarily

- force the authors to spend money on a professional proofreader—it is possible that the editor of the journal too may not be a mother tongue English speaker and may not be very well qualified to judge the level of English
- delay the publication of the paper

In any case, do not be vague when criticizing the English.

1. If you are certain that there are lots of mistakes, you can say:

   This paper needs a thorough revision by a native English proofreader.

2. If there are only some typing / spelling mistakes:

   There are a few typos that need correcting (I suggest the authors turn on the spell check in Word)

3. If there are just a few grammatical mistakes:

   I noticed the following grammatical mistakes [*give a list*] but otherwise the English seems fine.

4. If you are certain there are some mistakes, but you are not sure how to identify them:

   I don't feel qualified to judge the English, as it is not my mother tongue; however, I do feel that in some parts the English is not up to standard and is sometimes rather ambiguous.

5. If you think the English is good, but you can't be certain, then the simplest solution is to say nothing and let the other referees decide. Alternatively, you can say:

   The English seems fine to me (but I am not a native speaker).

7.15   Be careful of your own level of English and spelling

If, as a reviewer, you make a comment about the author's English, then you need to be careful about your own too, as it might undermine your credibility. It is generally a good idea to use where possible only standard phrases (see Chapters 23). A sentence such as *The English must profoundly to be enhanced* may indicate to the authors that your level of English is actually even worse than theirs. Also be careful of misspellings and inappropriate language:

Figure 4 sounds wired to me—why is the resolution worst when does the flow rate increase?

The sentence above contains several mistakes: *sounds* should be *looks* (a figure is something you look at not listen to); *wired* should be *weird* (i.e., strange, but *weird* itself is a very colloquial word); and *worst* (superlative) should be *worse*; the last part of the sentence should read *when the flow rate increases* (*why* is the question word not *when*).

7.16   My plea to referees with regard to author's level of English

I would like to make my own plea to referees, particularly to non-native referees. I have seen many many papers that were initially rejected due to "poor English." These comments were made by referees <u>after</u> I and other colleagues had corrected the English of the paper in question. Clearly, there may have been a few errors that myself and my proofreaders missed or that were introduced by the authors as they made their final modifications. But the errors were rarely enough to justify rejection. Since I am an English teacher I have no difficulty in spotting whether the comments come from referees who are native or non-native speakers. Virtually all come from non-native referees.

If you are convinced that the errors are in sufficient quantity and sufficiently serious to impede an understanding of the paper, then of course it is legitimate to draw the editor's and the authors' attention to this fact.

However, please bear in mind the following:

- Having a paper proofread costs a lot of money. Funds for research are getting increasingly lower, and in some parts of the world are virtually non-existent. If you unnecessarily ask for a revision of the English, you are costing researchers time and money that would probably be better spent on research.
- If you find two or three banal errors such as *in literature* rather than *in the literature*, or *it was founded that* rather than *it was found that*, do not conclude that the rest of the paper contains many more examples of this type (it may do, and if so you should tell the authors; but it may not—so check).

- Spelling mistakes are also made by native speakers. Using Google Scholar, I looked for some typical mistakes; the results are reported in the table below. Note that (i) my findings are the result of a quick search and should not be considered as definitive results, and (ii) the last column contains occurrences of more than one type of misspelling for the same word. A good proportion of the spelling mistakes were committed by native speakers, and even appeared in the titles of their papers.

CORRECT SPELLING	TYPICAL INCORRECT SPELLING	OCCURRENCES OF CORRECT SPELLING	OCCURRENCES OF INCORRECT SPELLINGS	RATIO OF CORRECT TO INCORRECT SPELLING
occurrence	occurence	3,000,000	200,000	15:1
accommodation	accomodation	673,000	32,000	21:1
independent	independant	3,200,000	100,000	32:1
until	untill	5,200,000	57,000	91:1
separate	seperate	3,800,000	35,000	108:1

Typical spelling mistakes that are as common among native speakers as among non-native speakers.

Other frequently misspelled words by native speakers that I found on Google Scholar included *catagory* (instead of the correct spelling: category), *definately* (definitely), *equiptment* (equipment), *foriegn* (foreign), *fullfill* (fulfill), *goverment* (government), *maintainence* (maintenance), *neccessary* (necessary), *relevent* (relevant), and *transfered* (transferred). Native speakers also frequently confuse *they're*, *there*, and *their*; *its* and *it's*. So if, as I suspect, native speakers are rarely, if ever, criticized for there (sorry their) English, think twice before criticizing a non-native.

If you are a native speaker it may be tempting to criticize another researcher's English, but remember that unlike you they will have spent years learning English. In Italy, where I live and work, I have calculated that many academics spend around €10,000 to learn English, and an average of €150 per paper to have it corrected. These are costs that native speakers do not have to sustain and should not unnecessarily impose on their non-native colleagues.

Having said all this, if you think sloppy English and sloppy spelling may be indicative of a sloppy methodology and thus of sloppy data, then of course you should mention this in your report.

Chapter 8
Writing a Reply to the Reviewers' Reports

You will learn that

- your prime aim should be to have your paper published rather than to protect your pride
- the tone of your reply will have a big impact on whether your paper is accepted
- it generally makes sense to do what the reviewers suggest

I suspect, though I have no hard data to support this suspicion, that revised papers that might have been accepted for publication are sometimes rejected because of the negative and antagonistic stance taken by the authors when addressing the reviewers' comments. This chapter describes how to respond to the criticisms and opinions of the reviewers without being either rude or obsequious. The result will be to increase the chances of your manuscript being published.

In this chapter, 'referee' and 'reviewer' are used indifferently.

A. Wallwork, *English for Academic Correspondence and Socializing*,
DOI 10.1007/978-1-4419-9401-1_8, © Springer Science+Business Media, LLC 2011

What the experts say

I have trained hundreds of graduate students, and see a consistent pattern in the things they find difficult. Most notably, graduate students have usually been trained and selected for their technical skills, not their emotional intelligence, and often have to develop communication skills on their own. This means that when faced with sharp, anonymous feedback of the sort that can appear in referee comments, they're often at a loss as to how to respond. Developing the ability to maintain a self-aware, positive approach under these circumstances is at least as important for academic careers as it is in business.

Alex Lamb, Alex Lamb Training, trainer in empowerment for those in the worlds
of academia and business

One way to obviate the possible doubts and criticisms of referees is to be proactive and deal with them in the manuscript itself. It will help you considerably if you anticipate how the referees might react to your interpretations of your data. This is particularly true in the Discussion section. The secret is to present not only your own interpretation, but also to account for other possible interpretations. This means adding phrases such as 'Another possible explanation for this discrepancy might be … However, we feel that this is unlikely because …' By doing this you are defending yourself against possible negative comments that referees might make in their report on your manuscript. You will thus increase your chances of your paper being published without too many revisions.

Pierdomenico Perata, Professor of Plant Physiology, Scuola Superiore Sant'Anna, Pisa, Italy

In my work as an editor of scientific articles, I have read dozens of replies to referees reports. Sometimes I am amazed how rude the authors are to the referees—do they not realize that by being impolite they are dramatically reducing their chances of seeing their manuscript published? Clearly, as an author you should not simply accept everything the referees say. But when you give your reasons for such non acceptance it always pays to do so in a constructive way, without attempting to call into question the reputation, expertise or knowledge of the referee. My advice would be to wait at least 24 hours before hitting the "send" button—this enables you to vent your anger on one day, and then go back to remove all signs of that anger the next day.

Anna Southern, editor, English for Academics

Because email is instant it gives us the illusion that we are actually close to our recipient, as if we are actually having a face-to-face conversation. At the same time because we are not actually face to face we feel protected by the anonymity of email, and thus feel more free to make criticisms than we would be if were in front of the person. In an email exchange with a person we don't know very well, we tend to interpret ambiguous phrases in a negative light, making "sinister attributions" that might be unwarranted. Without the second-by-second feedback of a telephone or video exchange, in an email we may continue in a chain of increasingly rude emails.

Janice Nadler, Professor of Law, Northwestern University and Research Professor,
American Bar Foundation.

8.1   Structure your reply to the referees in a way that will keep referees and editors happy

If you want to increase the chances of having your paper accepted for publication, then you might like to try the following four-stage strategy.

First, try to find something about what the referee has said that you can agree with

> The referee is certainly right when he / she says that ...

> I thank the referee for pointing out that ...

> I agree with the referee's comments about ...

> We have implemented the referee's useful observations about ...

Such phrases do not undermine the referee's credibility or their feeling of importance. They will feel that their expertise has been taken into account.

Second, tell the referee that you have amended something that they mentioned.

> Referee 1 suggested providing more complete results. This was a very useful suggestion, so we have now applied the proposed method to a typical industrial application (see the new Section 5).

Third, now that the referee is happy, you can tell him / her why you didn't amend something else.

> Given that the paper is intended for a broad audience, we decided not to cut the first two paragraphs of the Introduction.

Fourth, if possible, finish with something else positive about the referee's comments.

> We would like to thank the referee once more for sparing the time to write so many detailed and useful comments.

8.2   Present your answers to the reviewers using the clearest possible layout

I have seen many different ways to structure the reply to the reviewers. The best ones are those that help both the referees and the editors to understand what changes have been made and where.

Deal with each referee's report individually. If the referee has numbered his / her comments and queries, then the simplest solution is to paste in your responses under each comment. For example:

REFEREE 1

> 1) *page 4, line 2: there is no clear connection between the two sentences.*
> The sentences have been clarified as follows: ...

2) *page 5, paragraph 3: this paragraph adds no value, I think it could be deleted*
Done.

3) *page 7, last line: What does "intervenes in the process" mean in this context?*
We have replaced "intervene in" with "affects the process." NB this line now appears at the top of page 8.

Note how the author has put all the referees' comments in italics, and his own replies in normal script. This avoids rather ugly and redundant solutions such as:

Referee: 1) page 4, line 2: there is no clear connection between the two sentences.
Author: The sentences have been clarified as follows: ...

Or even worse:

Answer to referee's comment No. 3) page 7, last line: What does "intervenes in the process" mean in this context?
WE HAVE REPLACED "INTERVENE IN" WITH "AFFECTS THE PROCESS."

The use of capital letters is particularly unattractive and is also more difficult to read than lower case script.

Sometimes referees do not indicate line or page numbers but simply write unreferenced comments in one long paragraph or in a series of paragraphs. If there is just one long paragraph, the best solution is to divide up the paragraph into paragraphs of three to four lines, and then paste your comments directly below each of the resulting sub-paragraphs.

The example below shows the referee's comment, again changed to italics by the author. This is followed by the author's response (in normal script), with pages and line references indicated where appropriate.

The experimental procedure is not sufficiently informative to allow replication. How was the overall procedure carried out? The author should explain the procedure in detail or cite a reference. Was this procedure applied to the whole sample or just to a part of it? In addition, the instruments for determining X and Y should be reported.
We agree with the referee's comment regarding replication. On page 6 we have inserted a reference to one of our previous papers that contains a detailed description of the total digestion procedure. We have specified that it is applied just to the elutriate. Regarding the two instruments, in the original manuscript we had in fact stated what they were, but in a different section. So we have now moved these statements to a more logical position in the Materials section (page 5, second paragraph).

A possible structure in both cases—with or without page and line numbering—is thus:

1. Optional: General comments on all the referees' reports but without comments on specific reports.
2. Comments on Referee 1, then comments on Referee 2, then comments on Referee 3. Where necessary, include old and new line and page numbering to help the referees and editors see where you have made the changes.
3. Final overall comments.

8.3   Be brief

Try not to write unnecessarily long explanations for things that you could say very quickly. For example, the following sentence:

> I greatly appreciate the fact that the referee highlighted the English mistakes. I really need this because I am not a native English speaker. In the new version of the paper I have fixed all the mistakes that the referee reported.

Could be rewritten more succinctly as:

> The English has been revised [by a professional mother tongue speaker].

8.4   Call yourselves *we* not *the authors*

Referring to yourselves as "the authors" is not only artificial but creates strange sentences such as:

> *The authors* were pleased that the paper was appreciated. With regard to the referees' concerns about the procedure, *they* have tried to explain it in more detail ...

If you call yourselves "the authors" then you are forced to use "they" as a personal pronoun to refer to yourselves. In addition to this sounding very strange (it sounds like you are writing the response to the referees on behalf of some other authors), it can also be ambiguous—who does *they* refer to in the extract above—the authors or the referees? A much easier, logical, and less artificial solution is to use *we*:

> *We* were pleased that the paper was appreciated. With regard to the referees' concerns about the procedure, *we* have tried to explain *our* procedure in more detail ...

8.5   Don't be embarrassed to say you don't understand the referee's comments

Sometimes the referee may make some comments that appear to make no sense. In such cases, you can write:

> Unfortunately, we were not able to understand this comment.

> We are not sure what the referee means here.

> It is not clear, in our opinion, what the referee is referring to.

8.6   Use the present and present perfect to outline the changes you have made

When you tell the editor what changes you have made to your manuscript, you will mainly use three tenses. Use the

- present perfect to describe the changes

  We have reduced the Abstract to 200 words.

  We have given names to each section.

- present simple to talk about how the manuscript looks now

  The Abstract is now only 200 words long.

  Sections are now referred to by name.

- simple past to talk about decisions

  We decided to keep the tables because ...

When you talk about things that you didn't change, you can use either the present perfect or the simple past.

  We have kept / kept Figure 1 because ...

The above are not rules but merely what I have observed from reading many replies to referees' reports.

8.7   Justify why and where you have not made changes

The editor will be interested just as much in the recommended changes that you did not make as much as those that you did make. If you decided not to make a change, then you need to justify your decision. Here are some examples—the referees' recommendations are in italics, and the authors' responses are in normal script.

  Remove Table 1 it contains no new information.
  We have kept Table 1 as we believe it does contain important information. In fact, in the second column we report the values of ... In addition, the third column shows ... We believe it is important for the reader to see these values in tabular form as they give a very clear visual comparison of the various approaches.

  The appendix can be deleted; it serves no purpose other than unnecessarily extending the length of the paper.
  Although we agree with the referee that the paper is rather long, we believe that the appendix is vital for those readers who ...

The authors have failed to provide details of the procedure for x.
These details are in fact provided in Ref. 2 (see page 6, line 17); for the sake of space we did not reproduce them in the current manuscript.

8.8   If you disagree with the reviewers, always be diplomatic

I suggest avoiding the use of the verb *disagree* and, if possible, minimize the use of adverbs such as *but, although, moreover, despite this, nevertheless,* and *in fact* where such adverbs are used to contradict what the referee has said. This should help your cause and will not draw attention to the fact that you are not in agreement.

REFEREE'S COMMENT	UNDIPLOMATIC RESPONSE	DIPLOMATIC RESPONSE
There is a lack of any innovative contribution.	We do not agree at all. Moreover, we have not found any examples of a similar contribution in the literature.	Having read the comment about lack of an innovative contribution, we rechecked the literature and could find no examples of anyone having used this method before. We believe that our work really is innovative for the following reasons:
Some of the results are misleading.	If Ref 1 had taken the time to read the whole paper, he / she would have seen that in Sect 4 we argue that the results were unexpected.	The referee certainly has a point in terms of x and y (which we have now corrected). Also, see Section 4, where we argue that the results were unexpected.
The results are incomplete.	Incomplete in what sense?	We understand what the referee is saying. We thought that we had covered all aspects, but on the basis of the referee's comment we have added a short case study to indicate the completeness of our results.
Cut Table 1—it repeats much of what is already in the text.	Although there is some repetition we disagree with the referee; in fact we think it is essential for reader comprehension.	We appreciate that Table 1 repeats some of what is already in the text, but in our experience this kind of table significantly helps readers to understand the concepts better.
The Conclusions are almost the same as the Abstract.	The referee may have a point; however, we have read many other papers published in the Journal, even by native speakers of English, which adopt exactly the same technique.	The referee is right and we have made several changes to ensure that the Conclusions are different from the Abstract, by • talking about possible applications • mentioning future work

I am not advocating simply accepting all the referee's comments, especially if they are clearly misguided. All I am saying is to do what you think is best, but to describe what you have done in the most diplomatic way possible so that the editor will be more inclined to accept what you have done.

The last example highlights the fact that if you have made a mistake you should admit it—don't try to justify the unjustifiable!

8.9   Don't find things to criticize in the referee's work or in the workings of the journal

When someone has spent several pages criticizing your work, it is often a natural reaction to find something to criticize in their work too. Below are three examples of how <u>not</u> to refer to the reviewers:

> EXAMPLE 1 I would also like to mention that Reviewer 3 seems rather superficial in his report, at least in the second part where he suggests that I should consider "other.... . books..., e.g. by Wilkins or Guyot," without any other reference data—I find such remarks extremely unhelpful.

> EXAMPLE 2 Reviewer 2 seems to be questioning my background and my level of expertise in the research area. I demand to know who has dared to assume the responsibility of making derogatory comments violating the integrity of a fellow academic. I pity your journal—why do you select people like this to humiliate other professionals? I will not hesitate to inform the community of your journal's practice.

One of the messages that I hope to get across in this book is that you should never forget what your main aim is. Your main aim in this case is to get your paper published.

In the second example, singling out Reviewer 2 for condemnation is not a good approach and will not improve your chances of publication. It is highly likely that after reading the above response, Reviewer 2 will NOT change his (or her) position—in fact the laws of human nature dictate that he is likely to be more convinced than ever of his original position. In addition, you cannot be sure that Reviewer 2 is not a personal friend of the editor.

> EXAMPLE 3 We would firstly like to thank Reviewers 1 and 3 for their contribution. Their suggestions were very useful during the revision process and have been incorporated into the revised manuscript. They helped us to understand the weak points of the paper and, as a direct consequence, we believe the quality of the revised paper has been improved significantly. However, we were frankly shocked by the comments of Reviewer 2, which we believe are biased and illogical. In fact, the review was insulting and indicated the reviewer had not read the paper and in any case was clearly biased against the work. He / She is entitled to disapprove of a paper but, in our opinion, most of the comments do not match the content of the paper or are unfounded. For example, the reviewer claims that only 7% of the paper is devoted to the topic outlined in the title of the paper, whereas we calculate it to be

68%. The positive and constructive comments from the other reviewers would seem to be in direct contradiction with Reviewer 2's unsubstantiated claims. Nevertheless, we acknowledge that the English and the reference section could be improved, so we have worked on that and the paper has undergone a thorough revision by a mother tongue professional, as recommended by Reviewer 2.

It is also part of human nature for authors to get annoyed by reviewers. Most authors would be annoyed by Reviewer 2's calculation of 7% (not 10% or an expression such as "most"), but there is nothing to be gained by imitating his style.

Below are two different ways of rewriting the third example in order to avoid compromising the chances of your paper being published.

REVISED VERSION 1 (RV1)	REVISED VERSION 2 (RV2)
First of all, we acknowledge, as the second reviewer correctly noted, that the English and the reference section needed improvement. We have now fixed the references and the paper has undergone a thorough revision by a mother tongue professional. However, we are a little perplexed by the reviewer's comments on the amount of the paper devoted to actual work descriptions. We have thought of ways of addressing this problem, but in any case we believe that in reality about 70% of the paper is dedicated to work descriptions—and this would seem to be confirmed by the positive and constructive comments from the other two reviewers.	We would firstly like to thank all the reviewers for their contribution. With regard to Reviewer 2's comment about the amount of space we have dedicated to the main topic, where possible we have tried to focus more on the topic. As also recommended by Reviewer 2, we have had the English reviewed by a mother tongue professional.

The strategy of RV1 is to

- start with something that you agree with about what the reviewer has said (this makes the reviewer and editor feel happy and makes them feel more positive about what you say afterwards)
- say what you want to say in a less critical manner which gives the reviewer some benefit of the doubt, but which still enables you to justify yourself
- modify any statements that you make that may be open to interpretation by saying *we believe / we hope / we think / in our opinion* or using conditionals (e.g., *would seem*)

The difference between RV1 and RV2 is that RV1 still risks irritating Reviewer 2 as it uses the word *perplexed* and then uses the support of Reviewers 1 and 3 to call into question what Reviewer 2 has said. This is also not helped by the reference to 70%.

In my opinion RV2 solves the problem by saying *where possible we have tried to focus more on the topic*. This is the perfect solution because it makes Reviewer 2 think that there was some truth in what he was saying (even if in reality there was no truth). At the same time it says that the authors have in some way implemented what Reviewer 2 suggested, though cleverly they don't mention how or where. This means that all parties are now happy. RV2 also has the advantage of being shorter.

The secret is not to call into question the reputation, professionalism, and expertise of any of the reviewers. Insulting the referee almost invariably leads to your paper being rejected.

If your reaction is to react heatedly or violently to the referee's reports, then it is best to write your response but then leave it for a few days. During those few days you will probably find that there is some truth in what the referee says, and that you may have overreacted because you were hoping to have your paper published straight away without any delays for revisions.

I strongly suggest that when you have written your reply, go through it very carefully and delete any sentences that might offend, even minimally, the referee. Such sentences add nothing to your quest of getting your paper published. All they do is to irritate the referee in question, and shed doubt on the editor's ability to choose a competent referee. They also preclude your chances of ever publishing in that journal again.

8.10 Be aware of what might happen if you ignore the referee's advice

Researchers are rarely satisfied with the reviews they receive. It can be a very disappointing (and unfortunately sometimes humiliating) experience to read a review that either rejects your manuscript completely or apparently requires too many changes for you to realistically make.

The secret is to try not to take the reviewer's comments personally, but to see them as sincere advice on how to improve your manuscript. Clearly, on some occasions referees totally misunderstand your paper. But often their misunderstanding is due to the fact that you have not expressed yourself clearly or because you have not really highlighted your results and their importance.

If you choose to ignore the referee's advice, particularly when it has been given to you in a constructive manner, then you risk receiving a second report from the referee, such as the following one:

> I very much appreciate the authors' efforts to meet the referees' requirements. However, I have re-read their new version several times to convince myself that may be I had reached the wrong conclusions in my previous assessment. Despite this I am now more convinced

than ever that the paper cannot be accepted. The manuscript is still confusing for the reader. The complexity of the topic does not justify the excessive length of the manuscript nor the excessive number of tables and figures.

In my previous report I suggested the authors should (i) try to be clear and concise in describing their aims and methods, (ii) present their most important relevant findings through an appropriate selection of significant data, and (iii) ensure that their Discussion and Conclusions reflected the data.

Unfortunately, the authors chose to ignore my suggestions, and consequently their manuscript is not substantially different now from its original version.

Consequently, I regret having to recommend that this manuscript should not be accepted for publication. This is a real shame as it contains much data of interest to the community, and also adopts a novel approach.

The above report indicates that the reviewer had no problem with the scientific content itself, but just in the way that the data were presented. He was concerned with a basic lack of readability and for that reason rejected the paper. It would not have been so difficult for the authors to have appeased the referee's concerns by making their paper easier to read.

Chapter 9
Communicating with the Editor

You will learn

- the importance of the cover letter in affecting the outcome of your paper
- to avoid saying anything negative about the editor and the journal

As you will see from what the experts say on the next page, it is vital not to underestimate the importance of establishing and maintaining a positive relationship with your editor. This chapter teaches you how to do that and thus improve your chances of having your research published.

A. Wallwork, *English for Academic Correspondence and Socializing*,
DOI 10.1007/978-1-4419-9401-1_9, © Springer Science+Business Media, LLC 2011

What the experts say

I have been editor and guest editor of many scientific journals. As an editor I always try to establish a good relation with all the researchers / authors who wish to publish their work. It very much eases the publishing process if the authors adopt a constructive approach, both in their responses to reviewers and in the cover letter to the editor. Clearly, the most important thing for an editor to do is to judge the scientific merit of a paper. However, editors are human, and as such they are affected, consciously or subconsciously, by any negative or aggressive stance taken by the author.

Luciano Lenzini, Professor, Department of Information Engineering, University of Pisa, Italy

The cover letter is the first step to getting your article published. A poorly written letter containing grammatical and / or spelling mistakes will not make a good first impression and may affect how the editor subsequently reads your paper. Also, remember that you are not necessarily doing the journal a favor by sending them your manuscript. You need to convince the editor of the importance of your work. Use as few a words as possible: editors receive maybe a hundred emails a day and don't normally appreciate lengthy explanations. If you always try to see things from the editor's point of view and make life simple for them, then that will certainly help your chances.

Mark Worden, editor, Speak Up

Over my long career as an author a lesson that I have learned, which I would like to pass on to first time authors, is always to be diplomatic with your editor. Editors have a tough job, and it pays to be appreciative of what they do. Essentially, your main aim is to get your work published as quickly as possible. Anything you can do to smooth this process will help you in this objective. Be diplomatic at all times, even if you are in strong disagreement. Always do everything you can to appreciate, and if possible accommodate, their point of view.

Keith Harding, ELT author and trainer

9.1   Focus only on what you need to achieve

As with other types of email, when you write to an editor you need to

- decide what your primary objective is
- only write things that will achieve that objective

I often set the following exercise for my PhD students.

Imagine that you submitted your paper for publication in a journal several months ago. The editor has never replied even though you have written him / her two emails.

1. Think of a subject line.
2. Explain the situation and find out whether your paper has been accepted or not.
3. Use appropriate salutations at the beginning and end.

Below is the kind of email that about 90% of my students write. NB: this email contains mistakes in the English (see page 318 for a corrected version).

Subject line: Paper submission

Dear Sir

My name is Pinco Pallino and I submitted my paper to you several months ago and I am still waiting for your judge.

This is the third email I write to know if my paper was admitted or not. Please answer me in any case.

Best regards

The problem with the above email is that instead of increasing your chances of having your paper published you have decreased them. This is because you have

- used a completely generic subject line—an editor's primary work is dealing with paper submissions, so this kind of subject line is very unhelpful
- not taken the trouble to find out the name of the editor
- criticized (explicitly and implicitly) the editor—what kind of person doesn't answer three emails?
- showed the editor that your English is poor; therefore he / she might conclude that if the English in your email is poor, then there is a good chance that it will be poor in the paper too

A much better version would be

> Subject line: Paper submission Manuscript 1453
>
> Dear Helena Smith
>
> I was wondering if you had received my email sent 14 September (see below) regarding the submission of my manuscript (1453).
>
> Please find attached a copy of the paper for your convenience.
>
> Best regards

The above is much better because it thinks about the editor's point of view. You provide

- a meaningful subject line
- the name of the editor
- all the info the editor needs + you save him / her time by attaching another copy of the paper and by incorporating your original email at the end of the current one

In addition, there is absolutely no sense of criticism. You are aware that the editor may have had more important things to do than reply to your email. After all, he / she is doing you a favor if he / she publishes your paper. You are not doing him / her a favor by sending your paper (unless you are already a Nobel prize winner!).

9.2   Ensure your cover letter is clear and accurate

Writing a good cover letter is crucial in increasing the chances of your paper being published. It will be the first example of your writing skills that the Editor sees. If it is clear and accurate, then the Editor may also make the assumption that your manuscript is equally clear and that your data are accurate. If however it is poorly structured and contains mistakes in the English, this might condition the Editor's expectations with regard to your manuscript. Below is an example of a good cover letter.

> Dear Professor Seinfeld
>
> I would like to submit for publication in the *Journal of Future Education* the attached paper entitled *A Proposal for Radical Educational Reform* by Adrian Wallwork and Anna Southern.
>
> Our aim was to test the efficiency of short vs long degree courses. Our study of 15,000 male and female graduates aged between 35 and 55 found that they would have performed far

better in their careers from a financial point of view if they had undertaken a one-year course at university rather than the traditional three- to four-year course.

Our key finding is that people on shorter courses will earn up to 15% more during their lifetime. The implications of this are not only for the graduates themselves but also for governments as i) governments could save considerable amounts of money and ii) universities would be free to accept more students.

We believe that our findings will be of great interest to readers of your journal, particularly due to their counterintuitive nature and the fact they go against the general trend that claims that university courses should be increased in length.

This research has not been published before and is not being considered for publication elsewhere.

I look forward to hearing from you.

The structure and content of the above letter and many of the recommendations below are based on advice given on the *British Medical Journal's* website (http://resources.bmj.com/bmj/pdfs/wager.pdf):

- Find out the name of the current editor, rather than simply writing *Dear Sir / Madam*. This shows that you have made an effort, which reflects the fact that you are serious about getting your paper published in their journal
- Ensure that the editor's name is spelt correctly (e.g., *Seinfeld* rather than *Sienfled*). No one likes to see their name misspelled
- Ensure that the journal's name is spelt correctly and is the correct one (be careful of using old cover letters, you may forget to delete old information)
- Provide a brief summary of the aim and outcome of the research (paragraph 2 in the above example)
- Outline the key findings and the implications (paragraph 3)
- State why readers of the journal will be interested in your findings and how it fits in with recent articles in the journal (paragraph 4).
- Reassure the editor that his / her journal has an exclusive on your manuscript (paragraph 5)

If you have had your paper revised by a professional proofreader, send him / her your cover letter to check as well

If you are writing to a non-specialized journal such as *Nature* or *Scientific American*, then you need to convince the editor that your paper is topical, that it will interest a non-scientific audience, and that an interdisciplinary journal is a more suitable form of publication for your research than a single-discipline or archival journal.

In both cases—specialized and non-specialized—make sure you read the instructions for the author on their websites, which often give instructions not only regarding the manuscript but also about the cover letter.

9.3   If you've only made a few changes, describe them in the letter to the editor

If the reviewer has only asked for minor changes, and if you can describe these changes in around 20 lines or less, then you can incorporate these changes directly into the letter to the editor.

> Dear Professor Seinfeld
>
> Please find attached the revised manuscript (No. FE 245.998 Ver 2) by *names of authors*. Following the reviewers' comments, we have made the following changes: ...
>
> There was only one change (suggested by Ref. 2) that was not made, which was to delete Figure 2. We decided to retain Figure 2 for the following two reasons: ...
>
> I hope you will find the revised manuscript suitable for publication in *name of journal*.
>
> Best regards

If your replies to the reviewers take up more than one page, then they should be written in a separate document. In this case you can write:

> Please find attached the revised manuscript (No. FE 245.998 Ver 2) by *names of authors*. Also attached are our responses to the reviewers, including all the changes that have been made.

9.4   Be diplomatic in any emails to check the progress of your manuscript

Your manuscript is very important to you and you will obviously want it to be published as soon as possible with the minimal amount of trouble. However, your manuscript is far more important to you than it is to an editor who may be handling 50 or 60 manuscripts at a time. If you have submitted a manuscript and you have not heard from the editor for three months, then it is certainly a good idea to check what is happening. The email below shows how <u>not</u> to do this.

Dear Professor Carling,

On January 14 of this year I submitted a manuscript (ID 09-00236) entitled *name of paper* for possible publication in *name of journal*. On March 14 I was informed that the paper had been accepted with MINOR REVISIONS. On April 3, I resubmitted my manuscript (ID 09-00236.R1), revised according to the Editor's and Referees' comments.

So far, more than THREE months after submitting the revised manuscript, I haven't received any news about the final decision.

Given that:

1. nowadays most journals have reduced their publication times
2. the paper was accepted on the basis of only minor revisions
3. I submitted the revised manuscript strictly following the suggestions of the Referees

it seems reasonable to wonder what the reasons are for this unexpected and unusual delay.

I look forward to hearing from you.

Basically, the email above (which is absolutely genuine apart from the names and ID numbers) could have been rewritten as *Dear Editor, You are an incompetent imbecile. You have had my paper for more than three months—do you want to publish it or not?*

You have absolutely no idea for the reasons in the delay in the final decision regarding your manuscript. Perhaps the editor has

- been replaced with a new editor
- had serious family problems
- had problems with his PC and has lost your email and / or manuscript
- still not received a reply from one of the reviewers despite chasing this reviewer three times

The email above would be particularly irritating for the editor because

- it does not attempt to see things at all from her point of view
- the use of capitals is extremely impolite
- the use of the numbered bullets and the content of these bullets is completely unnecessary
- it contains many unnecessary details (e.g., the chronology of events)
- it has an aggressive and sarcastic tone

Your aim should simply be to get your paper published not to express negative comments on the way the journal carries out its activities.

Also, remember that writing in another language often acts as a filter and you may not be able to judge either the level of aggression in what you have written or the kind of reaction you might receive. A much better approach, which does not compromise the establishment of good relationships, is the following:

I wonder if you could help me with a problem.

On April 3 of this year, I resubmitted my manuscript (ID 09-00236.R1), revised according to the Editor's and Referees' comments.

I am just writing to check whether there is any news about the final decision. As you can see from the attached emails below, I have in fact raised this problem twice before.

Anything you could do to speed the process up would be very much appreciated.

Thank you very much in advance.

The revised email above contains the same information as the original "aggressive" email, but presents this information in a friendly, professional, and non-aggressive way that will not make the editor feel either angry or guilty. Attaching the previous correspondence (*as you can see from the attached emails below*) enables you to give the editor clear evidence of what you are saying yet at the same time do so in a totally neutral way.

Part III
Telephone and Teleconference Calls

Chapter 10
Preparing for and Setting Up a Phone Call

You will learn how to

- plan in order to make the call more effective
- react when you don't understand your interlocutor
- conclude the call

A memorandum written in 1876 by the US company Western Union stated that *This telephone has too many shortcomings to be seriously considered as a means of communication. The device is inherently of no use to us.* This chapter is designed to help you overcome any of the shortcomings you may experience while using the telephone.

For useful phrases on conducting telephone calls see Chapter 24.

A. Wallwork, *English for Academic Correspondence and Socializing*,
DOI 10.1007/978-1-4419-9401-1_10, © Springer Science+Business Media, LLC 2011

What the experts say

Whatever your field, you will create a strong impression when you communicate by phone; this can be either good or bad, and may well last. It is thus critical to prepare for any important telephone calls in advance, so that your listener will grasp the reason for your call immediately and will be motivated not just to listen, but to act on any request you may make. Telephone communication is not as straightforward as it may seem, and the fact that we cannot see facial reactions and that misunderstandings may more easily arise and be more difficult to resolve must always be born in mind.

Patrick Forsyth, Touchstone Training & Consultancy

If you have something important to say to someone with whom you have never previously had contact, then use the phone rather than email. Through an initial phone call people become real to each other. This sets up a positive relationship which can then be continued via email. On the other hand, a rushed email may contain errors and create the wrong first impression. People pay more attention to a phone call than they do to email. Future communication will be more successful, if you start the relationship in a positive manner.

Susan B. Barnes, Associate Director, Lab for Social Computing, Rochester Institute of Technology

10.1   Decide whether another form of communication might be more suitable

It is generally a good idea to speak to someone directly on the phone rather than send an email if you want (i) to establish a good relationship and (ii) to solve any misunderstandings that have already arisen via email.

However, bear in mind that phone calls are possibly the most difficult form of communication in English for non-native speakers. So first of all consider whether your phone call is really necessary, and whether it wouldn't be simpler for you, or at least for your counterpart, simply to send an email or fax.

10.2   Prepare and practice

The level of success of your phone call can be enhanced considerably if you have a very clear idea of what you want to say before you actually make the call. Write down some notes about what you want to say, and then make sure you know how to say everything in English.

You could also find out something about the person who you want to talk to. Is this person a man or a woman, old or young? What level of formality will you have to use? What is their level of English? Are they a native speaker? Have any of your colleagues spoken to this person? What can you learn from their experience: for example, does this person have a reputation for speaking very fast? If so, you need to learn appropriate phrases for encouraging them to slow down.

Think about what the other person might ask you, and prepare answers to such questions. If you do so, you are more likely to be able to understand the question when it is asked.

If you have an important call to make, you may find it useful if you simulate the call with a colleague, and ask the colleague to ask you pertinent questions.

10.3   Consider using an email as a preliminary information exchange before the call

The more both parties are prepared for a telephone call, the more likely the call will be successful. If you have a call that will require a complex discussion, it is not a bad idea to send each other a list of points that you wish to discuss. This will enable you to

- think about what you need to say and how to say it
- think about what useful phrases in English you may need
- tick the items from the list as you discuss them, and make notes next to each item

You could suggest such an email exchange by writing:

> Before we make our call I thought it might be useful to send you this list of items that I would like to discuss. If you have any additions I would be glad to receive them. Then it would be great if you could give me a few hours to look through them. Thank you.

10.4   Be prepared for what the interlocutor might say

It is important not only to practise what you want to say, but to prepare for what you might hear, for example, the typical phrases that a switchboard operator might say.

> Could you tell me what it is in connection with?

> Has he spoken to you before?

> I'll just check for you. Could you hold for a moment?

To learn more about the phrases you might hear on the telephone, see Chapter 24.

10.5   Think about the time and the place of the call

Some people find that the quality of their English is also affected by the time of day, the level of stress they are under, and their location. Try to analyze at what point of the day your English seems to work best. Choose a place to make your call where you will have minimal external interference.

You may find it easier to speak in English when your colleagues are not listening to you, so you will feel less inhibited.

10.6   Beware of ringing people on their mobile phone

You are unlikely to have the person's full attention if you call them on their mobile: you may well be disturbing them in the middle of something else. It is generally a good idea to ask:

> Is this a good time or are you in the middle of something?

> Am I interrupting something?

If they then say *Well, actually I am with someone at the moment. But go ahead, what can I do for you?* it is probably best to call back later:

> Sorry, I have obviously got you at an inconvenient time. What time do you think I could call you back?

10.7   Give your name and the name of the person you want to talk to

Announce to the switchboard operator who you are slowly and clearly. Spell out your name clearly, for example:

> This is Riccardo Rizzi, that's R-I-Z-Z-I, calling from the Italian National Research Council, in Pisa, Italy; can I speak to Andrea Caroli please.

It's always a good idea to give both the first name and surname of the person you want to speak to. First, your listener will have a greater chance of understanding who it is you want and second if you had asked for Ms Caroli or Mrs Caroli, you would have totally confused the operator because Andrea (in Italy at least) is a man's name, not a woman's name.

For spelling out names see 11.4.

10.8   Help the person that you want to speak to

The person you wish to speak to may not be expecting your call. When they receive your call, they will probably be in the middle of something else and need a few seconds to reorient themselves. To help them

- say your first and second names (the switchboard operator may not have given your correct name to your interlocutor)
- explain the context—that is, the relevant communication you've had with this person, for example, *you may remember that I sent you a document two weeks ago, well I am calling because ...*
- explain why you are calling

If you are talking to someone with a low level of English, frequently summarize what you say. Ask questions to make sure your listener has understood. Don't merely say "OK?," "Have you got that?" because even if they say "yes" it doesn't mean that they have necessarily understood.

If they don't understand what you are saying and you are speaking reasonably slowly, it may simply be that they don't understand a particular word or phrase. Try and rephrase what you've said, instead of repeating what you've said before.

10.9   Speak slowly and clearly

You may be nervous about making the call, and when we are nervous we tend to speak fast, particularly at the beginning of a conversation. However, given the fact that

- we give our interlocutor important info (our name and institute, and why we are calling) at the beginning of a call
- our interlocutor is probably still thinking about what he / she was doing before you interrupted them

it is best to speak slowly and clearly, with pauses between each piece of information. Also, you can offer to repeat things:

> Would you like me to repeat my name again?

10.10   Don't be afraid to interrupt and make frequent summaries of what you think you have understood

If you are talking to a native English speaker, it may help you to remember that communication is two way. The responsibility for the fact that you do not understand something lies with your native-speaking interlocutor too. Your interlocutor will also want you to understand what he / she says. So keep checking that you have understood what is being said, and make summaries of your understanding so that your interlocutor can check whether you have correctly interpreted what he / she has said. See Chapter 14 to learn these skills.

10.11   Compensate for lack of body language

Unless you are using Skype (or equivalent), the other person will not be able to see the reaction on your face, or whether you are nodding in agreement or not. You can compensate for this by using one of the following expressions: *I see*, *yes*, *OK*, *right* or noises such as *a-huh* and *mmm*. Using such expressions also shows your interlocutor that you are still on the phone and are absorbing the information being given to you. This is extremely important when making phone calls with the Japanese, who expect to hear a constant flow of listening signals.

10.12   Avoid being too direct

When on the phone, you lose a substantial part of your communicative power because the other person cannot see the expression on your face, nor can they read your body language. This is even more true of email (where vocal clues are also lost), but even on the phone it is worth trying to make an extra effort to be polite and diplomatic. If you use very direct language, you may be in danger of sounding rather rude.

The second column in the table below shows some "softer" versions of the phrases in the first column.

POSSIBLY TOO DIRECT	SOFTER
Why didn't you send us the report earlier?	I was wondering why I hadn't received the report earlier.
You were supposed to be sending me a report.	Sorry but I was expecting to receive a report.
I need the revisions by tomorrow.	I was wondering if you could send me the revisions by tomorrow.
	Would it be possible by the end of the morning?
	Do you think you could send me the revisions by lunchtime today?
I'm calling you about . . .	The reason I'm calling you is . . .

What you will notice from the "softer" versions is that they require more words and more complex grammar (e.g., use of conditionals, and the past continuous and past perfect). Even if your English is low level, you could simply learn the phrases as if they were idioms rather than as grammatical constructions.

10.13   Take notes during the call and summarize the important points at the end of the call

If you take notes during the call, it will help you to paraphrase what the other person has said so that you can check your understanding. Obviously, notes will also help you to remember what was said and this will be useful if you decide to send your interlocutor an email summarizing the call (see 10.15).

At the end of the call, in order to check that you have not missed anything, make a mini summary of what has been said. This gives your interlocutor an opportunity to clarify any points. You can say:

> Can I just check that I have got everything? So we have decided to resubmit the manuscript to another journal. You want me to check the bibliography, and you are going to rewrite the last part of the Discussion. We have set ourselves a deadline for the end of this month. Does that all sound right?

10.14   If you really can't understand, learn a way to close the call

There will be occasions when you simply cannot understand. Rather than panicking and putting the phone down with no explanation you can say:

- *I am afraid the line is really bad. I will try calling back later.* You can then prepare yourself better for the next time you call, or alternatively ask a colleague to make the phone call for you

- *I think it might be better just to send an email. I will do this as soon as possible.* You can summarize what you think you have understood in the email, and then ask for clarifications

10.15   Follow up with an email

You and your interlocutor may remember little more than 10% of what was said during your call. Even if you think the phone call has gone well and that you have understood everything, it is always good practice to send your interlocutor an email summarizing the main points. This allows the interlocutor to check his / her understanding of the call as well. In addition, you can ask any questions or clarify points that you forgot to make during the call itself.

Chapter 11
Leaving a Telephone Message

You will learn how to

- spell out names and addresses
- give numbers
- ensure that your message is understood

Leaving and receiving telephone messages generally entails taking note of vital numbers and information. This is not too difficult provided that you are aware of a few tricks for ensuring that you and your interlocutor understand everything that needs to be passed on to the third party.

A. Wallwork, *English for Academic Correspondence and Socializing*, 137
DOI 10.1007/978-1-4419-9401-1_11, © Springer Science+Business Media, LLC 2011

Factoids

❖ There is considerable variation in the way people in various parts of the world say telephone numbers: some read telephone numbers in single or in double figures, others in groups of three numbers, for example, 224, by saying "two hundred and twenty four".

❖ People answer the phone in many different ways. In Britain, many people answer by saying their number. In Italy they say *pronto* meaning "ready". In the Philippines they use the English word "hello" due to the influence of US soldiers, and it is used in combination with the local language *hello, sino po sila?*, which means "hello, who is this please?" In Japan they use the same phrases, *moshi moshi*, to answer the phone, when they can't hear the person very well, and to confirm that the other person is still on the line.

❖ Telephone directories are not standard throughout the world. In Iceland and some parts of Brazil, people are listed by the first name rather than their surname. In Italy, they are organized by surname but only within the village or municipality where the person lives. In China, where listing names alphabetically is clearly a problem, many people simply ring directory inquiries.

11.1 Learn the structure and typical phrases of a telephone message

The following example is designed to show you the language used in a typical telephone conversation, where one party leaves a message.

Department of Engineering. Good afternoon can I help you?
Yes, this is Professor Baumann from the University of Munich. Could I speak to Professor Yang please?
Sorry I didn't catch your name, could you speak up a bit please the line's bad.
Yes, it's Professor Baumann.
And where did you say you are ringing from?
The University of Munich.
OK, I'll try and connect you. ... Sorry, the line's busy. Do you want to leave a message?
Could you tell her that Heinrich Baumann called, and that the meeting's been postponed till next Tuesday.
That's Tuesday the seventh right?
Right. But if she needs to speak to me she can get me on 0049 that's the code for Germany, then 89 656 2343. Extension fifteen.
That's one five right?
That's it.
Can I read that back to you to make sure I've got everything?
Sure.
Professor Baumann, that's B-A-U-M-A-N from the ...
No, two Ns, M-A-double N.
OK, from the University of Munich. The meeting's been postponed till Tuesday the seventh, and she can reach you on 0049 89 656 2334
Sorry that should be four three, not three four.
OK 2343, extension 15, one five.
That's it. Thanks very much. Bye.
Goodbye.

For more phrases, see Chapter 24.

11.2 Speak clearly and slowly

If you need to leave a message, speak very slowly and clearly. Repeat each bit of information at least twice, particularly any numbers. Even the most proficient of English speakers often take down the wrong numbers. If you need to mention days of the week, especially Tuesday and Thursday, which are very easily confused, then always say the day with the date: "Thursday the 16th," so that there's a greater chance of being understood.

11.3 Make the call as interactive as possible

If you want to ensure that your interlocutor carries out your requests, it helps if you encourage them to be active rather than passive. You can ask your interlocutor to

- confirm what you have said
- to read back an email or website address to you
- to repeat the spelling of any name

These techniques force the interlocutor to pay more attention. Conversely, if you are the receiver of the message then you can follow exactly the same techniques. You can say:

> Can I just confirm what you have said. So, the meeting has been moved to ...
> I'll just read back your website address. www dot u-n-i-p-i slash ....
> So it's Anna Southern, that's S-O-U ...

11.4   Spell names out clearly using the International Alphabet or equivalent

When spelling a word, make sure you differentiate clearly between easily confused letters such as B and P, and D and T, and N and M. There is an International Alphabet (see first column below - Alpha, Bravo etc), but few people are familiar with it. So you might find it easier to use the names of countries (second column - Argentina, Brazil etc), which you may also find easier to pronounce.

Note: Where the name of the country is not commonly known or could easily be spelt very differently in another language, I have suggested another word.

Always repeat the spelling and always do so slowly.

A	Alpha	Argentina
B	Bravo	Brazil
C	Charlie	Congo
D	Delta	Denmark
E	Echo	Ecuador
F	Foxtrot	France
G	Golf	Germany
H	Hotel	Holland (hotel)
I	India	India
J	Juliet	Japan
K	Kilo	Kenya
L	Lima	Lebanon (lemon)
M	Mike	Mexico
N	November	Norway
O	Oscar	Oman (orange)
P	Papa	Panama
Q	Quebec	Qatar (quick)
R	Romeo	Russia
S	Sierra	Spain
T	Tango	Turkey
U	Uniform	Uganda

V	Victor	Venezuela
W	Whisky	Wales (Washington)
X	X-ray	
Y	Yankee	Yemen (yellow)
Z	Zulu	Zambia

When you spell out a name, you can say:

> My name is Schmidt. That's S as in Spain, C as in Congo, etc.

Alternatively:

> My name is Schmidt. That's Spain, Congo, etc.

Be especially careful when spelling out vowels, whose sounds tend to be very different from country to country.

Note how the following letters have the same final sound. In the second column there are common words with the same sound.

b, c, d, e, g, p, v, z	be, see, we
j, k	way, say
i, y	I, my, why
q, u, w	you, two

The letters below have the same initial sound, which is the same as the vowel sound (in italics) in the example words.

a, h	pl*ay*, s*ay*, w*ay*
f, l, m, n, x	b*e*d, g*e*t, w*e*ll
o	g*o*, n*o*, sh*ow*

11.5   Practice spelling out addresses

Being able to spell out your email address without confusing your listener is a key skill when participating in a telephone call. This is because if communication between you and your interlocutor is difficult or impossible due to language difficulties, the easiest solution is to continue the communication via email. To be able to continue via email, at least one of you needs to give their email address. In reality you increase your chances of continuing the communication if you both give your addresses. Here is an example dialogue of someone giving their email address:

> My address is anna_southern at virgilio dot it. That's anna A-N-N-A underscore ...
> Sorry, what is after ANNA?
> Underscore.
> Underscore?
> The little line between two words.
> OK.
> So, underscore then Southern. That's S as in Spain, O, U, T as in Turkey, H, E, R, N.
> Is that N as in Norway?
> Yes, that's right. Then at virgilio dot it. That's V, I, R, G, I, L, I, O dot I, T.
> OK. I'll just repeat that. anna that's with two Ns right?

Yes, A double N A.
Then underscore S, O, U, T, H, E, R, N. So annasouthern, that's all one word, right?
Yes, that's right-
Then at virgilio, that's V, I ...

If your address is rather complicated (e.g., with an underscore, slashes, or very long), it is not a bad idea to have a personal email address that is short and which is simple to say, which you can use for emergencies!

Here is an example dialogue of someone giving their website address:

So it's www englishconferences forward slash R1256 dot pdf.
Sorry does englishconferences have a dot between the two words?
No it's all one word.
Then forward slash. The letter R. Then the numbers 1, 2, 5, 6 as digits not as words. Then dot pdf. Have you got that?
I'll just read it back to you. So, that's forward slash ...

Below is an example of how to dictate the following traditional postal address over the phone: Adrian Wallwork, Via Murolavoro 17, 56127 Pisa, Italy

Adrian Wallwork. That's a-d-r-i-a-n new word w-a-l-l-w-o-r-k. New line. Via Murolavoro. That's v-i-a new word m-u-r-o-l-a-v-o-r-o, number 17, that's one-seven. New line, 56127 Pisa. New line, Italy.

11.6   When spelling out telephone numbers, read each digit individually

Every language seems to have its own system of reading out telephone numbers, and conventions differ even within the same country. The simplest system is to read each digit individually. Thus to say 113 4345, you would begin by saying *one one three* rather than *one hundred thirteen*.

When reading out landline numbers, it is generally best to separate the country code from the rest of the number. Below is an example of how to spell out 0044 161 980 416 71.

zero zero four four—that's the code for England—one six one; nine eight zero; four one six; seven one

Note that some people say *oh* rather than *zero*.

Whether you are dictating or noting down an address or phone number, make sure you repeat them at least twice. Even people who speak the same language often make mistakes with numbers.

11.7   Consider sending a fax, rather than an email, confirming what has been said

If you think that your message may not have been understood, then ask for their fax number, and then fax the information to them. A fax is better than an email in this case, as reading out and understanding an email address is often considerably more difficult than dictating a number.

Chapter 12
Conference Calls

You will learn how to

- coordinate and participate in a call
- set up and follow a protocol
- introduce yourself
- interrupt if you cannot follow

Conference calls, in which participants can only hear each other but not see each other, are tricky even when all participants are native speakers of the same language. Most of the problems are connected with a lack of familiarity with the technology. When native and non-native speakers are involved, then there are also additional problems of communication. This chapter is designed to help you go into a conference call feeling relaxed in the knowledge that you know how to participate. I will also show that it is both normal and perfectly acceptable to interrupt when you don't understand something.

A. Wallwork, *English for Academic Correspondence and Socializing*,   145
DOI 10.1007/978-1-4419-9401-1_12, © Springer Science+Business Media, LLC 2011

Factoids: 200 years of telephony

1876   First words spoken on a telephone

1877   First phone sold

1880   London's first phone directory (255 names)

1889   First coin pay phone

1901   First transatlantic wireless message

1922   First fax

1933   First speaking clock

1949   First answering machine (initially called the Electronic Secretary)

1960   First fully automated mobile phone system for vehicles

1983   First cordless phone sold

1984   One of the first videoconferencing systems sold

1989   First satellite telephone service

1999   First full Internet service on mobile phones

2000   Turkish inventor markets a phone with a built-in lie detector

2003   First Skype call made (originally called Sky peer-to-peer, then Skyper, and finally Skype)

2006   In only three years of operations, 100 million people are already using Skype (the telephone took 36 years to reach just 10 million users)

2007   First iPhone sold

2076   Fault-free telepathy replaces need for telephones of any kind

12.1   Prepare for the call

Conference calls are a difficult form of communication for non-native speakers. However, if you prepare well, and learn some useful phrases to help you out of difficulty, then these calls need not be such a terrifying experience!

The dialogs in the rest of this chapter come from a typical conference call. The speakers are James (a native English speaker), Sarah and Steve (two other native speakers), Luigi (an Italian), and Sergey (a Russian). James has organized the call and is acting as chairperson.

12.2   Announce yourself when you join the call

As people join the call there is generally a beep sound. As you join, introduce yourself:

Sarah   Hi, this is Sarah. Who's on the call?
James   Hi Sarah, this is James. We are just waiting for Luigi, Sergey, and Steve.

12.3   Check that everyone can hear

If you are the chairperson, it is a good idea to check that no one is having any technical difficulties.

James   Is everyone picking up all right?
Luigi   This is Luigi. I can hear you fine.
Sarah   This is Sarah. I can't hear what you're saying—there's a high-pitched noise
        going on.
James   Is that any better?
Sarah   That's fine now.
James   Are you on speaker phone Sergey, because everything is echoing.
Sergey Yes, I am. I'll try turning it off. Is that any better?

12.4   Establish rules for the call

It is essential to set some rules at the beginning of the call. Unlike a face-to-face discussion with multiple participants, in a conference call people cannot use body language to indicate that they wish to interrupt. This means that rules need to be made with regard to turn taking and also to avoid several people speaking at the same time.

In the next dialog James begins the meeting by laying down the protocol.

> OK everyone is here now. First could I ask you all to introduce yourselves? Just your name
> and university will be enough. *everyone introduces themselves* We have a couple of people
> on the call who are not native speakers. If this call is to be successful, we need the native
> speakers to speak as clearly as possible. If anyone isn't sure about something, please feel
> free to request for the information to be repeated or clarified. Also, can I just remind you all
> to say your name when you speak. At least the first few times. And if you ask a question,
> try and direct it to someone in particular.

If the chairperson makes no reference to the difficulties of the non-native speakers,
then it is a good idea for you to mention it immediately. Here is what Luigi could
say:

> I don't know about Sergey, but I would really appreciate it if you could all speak very slowly
> and clearly.

12.5   Allow time for "tuning in"

Understanding someone on the telephone can be hard, particularly if it is the first
time that you have heard that person's voice. So it is useful to dedicate a minute or
two to small talk, so that everyone can get used to the sound of each other's voices.
Banal questions can be used:

> So Sergey, what's the weather like in Moscow?

> Luigi, how did the conference go?

> Here it is pouring with rain, what's it like with you?

> Sergey, what time is it with you?

> Sarah, how was your holiday?

> Steve, how are things going in Boston?

12.6   Remind participants about the agenda

Conference calls are often arranged at quite short notice. It is always a good idea to
announce the goal of the meeting and the agenda. So James could say some of the
following:

> The goal of this call is to discuss ...

> Well, I think you know the agenda. First Luigi is going to tell us about how much funding
> we can expect. Then Steve is going to talk about where we are with the draft of the proposal.
> And finally Sergey will update us on ...

12.7   Check that everyone has all the documents required

Conference calls often involve looking at documents, so it is worth checking that everyone received them and has them to hand.

> Did you all get the files I sent you last night?

> Do you all have a copy of the agenda?

> Have you all got the presentation open at slide 1?

> Do you all have the document in front of you?

If you are not sure what is being referred to, you can say:

> Sorry what presentation are you talking about?

> Sorry, but I am not sure I received the document.

12.8   Get the meeting started

If you are the chairperson, ensure that you make a clear verbal signal to show that you wish the meeting to start. And clearly say who you wish to begin talking.

> OK, let's begin.

> Right. If you are all ready I'll begin.

> OK. Luigi do you want to start?

If you are called on to start, and you think that someone else should start, then you can say:

> No you go first James.

> No, I think Sergey should probably start.

12.9   Be prepared for what to do and what to say if you "arrive" late

Below is an example of what procedure could be followed if someone joins the call when the main discussion has already begun.

Steve   Hi, Steve here. Sorry I am late.
James   Hi Steve, could you wait a second. Then I'll recap everything for you. *finishes conversation with the others* OK, Steve, just to summarize what we have discussed so far. *makes a summary* I think that's everything, do any of you have anything to add?

Steve   Thanks. Sorry about being late, but for some reason I couldn't get a connection.
         Just before we continue, could the others just introduce themselves so that
         I can recognize their voices.

12.10   Ensure you are clear when you are taking participants through a presentation or document

If you are in a teleconference rather than a video conference, it can be quite difficult for people to follow your explanations of presentations and documents. Thus, you need to clearly state what slide you are on and what part of the slide you are talking about, or what page / section / line of a document you are referring to.

So, I am going to move on to the next slide now, which is slide 12.

So, we are on slide 12 now. I'd like you to focus on the figure at the top left. The one that says "functionality."

Can we just go back to the top of page 20?

OK, so is everyone on page 40? The middle of the page where it says "How to set up version 2."

12.11   Don't be embarrassed to admit that you are not following

Given the fact that there are multiple participants, it is easy to get "lost." This may or may not have anything to do with the fact the call is being held in English. In any case, it is always a good idea to interrupt.

Sorry, I am not sure who is talking. Can I suggest that everyone announces who they are before they speak?

This is Luigi again. I'm sorry but it's hard to understand two people talking at once.

Sorry, but the line isn't great at my end, could you all speak more slowly?

Sorry, what slide are we up to?

Sorry, what page are we on now?

Sorry, I am not sure which figure you are talking about.

12.12   Announce that the call is reaching an end

Typical things that people say to signal that the conference call is over include the following:

I think we've covered everything, so let's finish here.

Right, I think that about finishes it.

This is a good point to end the meeting.

Luigi mentioned that he needs to stop at 11.45, so I think we should conclude here.

OK, I've said all I want to say, so unless any of you have anything to add, I think we can stop here.

Has anyone else got anything they want to add?

It is a good policy to tell people what you are going to do next, and what you expect them to do next.

I have taken a few notes, and I will email everyone with a summary of what we have decided. If I miss anything out, then please let me know.

I'll get the minutes of this sent out to you. Sergey, if you could send in the draft proposal for funds that would be great.

Final remarks:

Thanks everyone for making this call, particularly you Sergey, it must be in the middle of the night for you!

Thanks for your time everyone.

Bye everyone.

See you next week.

12.13   A note on videoconferences

Most of this chapter is also valid for videoconferences. The main difference is obviously that you can see the other participants, so there is no need to introduce yourself every time you speak. Also, if the video quality is good you can make eye contact (if the quality is poor it may seem that your remote interlocutor is avoiding eye contact with you) and you can see the reactions of the other participants.

So the only extra phrases you might need are

Can everyone see OK?

How is the sound quality for you guys?

Can you see the slides OK? Do you want me to make them bigger?

Part IV
Dealing with Native English Speakers

Chapter 13
How to Improve Your Understanding of Native English Speakers

You will learn that

- many native speakers have difficulty understanding each other. For example, someone from Dallas, Texas, might find someone from Newcastle in England totally incomprehensible, and vice versa—simply because they both have strong accents, though they may also use a different vocabulary

- key words in English tend to be enunciated more clearly, with greater stress and louder volume. Focus on these key words rather than trying to understand each individual word. You should thus be able to understand the logical flow

- much of what people say in spontaneous speech is redundant, so there is no need to try to understand each individual word

Only a quarter of conversations carried out in English in the world are between native English speakers, so it might seem that understanding the English of native speakers is not particularly important. However, many interesting research opportunities can be found in countries where English is the first language, and many interesting scientific presentations are given by native or near native speakers. Consequently, being able to understand native speakers is still important. This chapter is designed to show you why you may have difficulty in understanding native English speakers. Knowing why you can't understand may then help you to improve your listening skills.

What the experts say

The day native English speakers learn to speak English slowly and clearly, the world will breathe a huge sigh of relief.

Adrian Wallwork, founder, English for Academics

If you fail to communicate successfully with a native speaker, do not immediately assume it is because of your English ability. Many native speakers are unaware that their spoken English is difficult to understand. This means that they often speak too fast, use inappropriate language (e.g., colloquial structures and expressions), and may also have a strong regional accent that you have probably never been exposed to before. The secret is not to be afraid or embarrassed, but to inform the native English speaker that you are unable to understand.

Dr Sue Fraser, lecturer in English, Seisen Jogakuin College, Japan

Although many millions of textbooks for learning English are sold every year, very few focus on teaching students what to say when they can't understand spoken English. But knowing how to interrupt someone and the phrases that you can use to ask for clarification, is probably the most important thing to learn when studying a foreign language—particularly English.

Annette Kelly, EFL teacher, Italy

13.1   Accept that you will not, and do not need to, understand everything

When we are learning a foreign language, we tend to think that it is important to understand everything that we hear. But when you are listening to someone talking in your own language, you probably don't listen at 100% and nor do you probably need / wish to.

Thus, an essential rule for improving your understanding of native English speakers is not to expect to understand everything they say. My wife and I are both from Manchester in England. When we watch DVDs of US television series, we watch with subtitles—if we don't have subtitles, we sometimes miss about 30% of what is said. However, even if we don't turn on the subtitles and thus miss 30%, we still understand enough to follow the story.

And this is not only for US movies. We recently watched the British classic *Billy Elliot*, which is set in the far north of England, where the accent is quite strong. We watched it on videotape—so no subtitles. We only understood about 70–80% of what was said. However, this did not stop us from following the plot and loving the film!

Understanding enough to follow the plot should be your objective too. By "plot," I mean a conversation in a bar, a formal presentation, a telephone call.

In non-strictly technical / scientific encounters, conversations are often more a means of being together, a socio-cultural event in which relations are established, rather than an opportunity for exchanging information. Most of the time, what is said may be completely irrelevant. Quite often talking is merely an end in itself. When we go out for dinner with friends, the main object is not to glean useful information but simply to bond with the people we are with and to enjoy their company.

13.2   Be aware that not understanding a native speaker may have little to do with vocabulary

Below is an extract a transcript of a recording of someone talking about cultural differences. When I played it to my students, most found it extremely difficult to understand. They said that one of the main causes of this lack of understanding was vocabulary (the other main cause was the speed of the voice).

> I think the British culture is to a degree puritanical which contains aspects of sort of you know carefulness with money and not demonstrating lavishly one's feelings in terms of you know gift giving and things like that and I think you know that that's contrasted with you

know possibly with the Italian attitude to family, it being incredibly important and that you know what you have you share with your family and you show your sort of, your love for your family by gift giving. What I mean is that . . .

As you can see there are very few words (e.g., lavishly = abundantly, generously) that are not of common usage. In reality, the words that my students thought they did not know were actually common words they knew very well but just pronounced in what for them was an alien way.

The key to better understanding is not to focus on each individual word but just on the general meaning. In fact as you see many words add no value at all—he says *you know* five times and *sort of* twice in the space of 90 words, thus representing around 15% of his speech.

Another problem is the total lack of structure in what the speaker is saying. Thus your reason for not understanding a native speaker may have little to do with vocabulary. It will probably be due to their accent. As highlighted in the transcript above, it may also be due to a high level of redundancy in what the speaker says combined with a low level of organization. These issues are dealt with in more detail in 13.3.

13.3   Understand why you don't understand

When you read a text, the punctuation (commas, full stops, capital letters, etc.) helps you to move within a sentence and from one sentence to the next. Brackets, for example, show you that something is an example or of secondary importance. Punctuation also helps you to skim through the text without having to read or understand every single word. You don't really need to read every single word as you can recognize certain patterns and you can often predict what the next phrase is going to say.

A similar process takes place when you listen to someone speaking your native language. You don't need to concentrate on every word they say. Unfortunately, although we can usually quite easily transfer our reading skills from our own language into another, we cannot transfer our listening skills—particularly in the case of the English language. English often sounds like one long flow of sounds and it is difficult to hear the separations between one word and the next.

However, spoken English does follow some regular patterns, and if you can recognize these patterns, it may help you to understand more of what you hear and enable you to understand the general meaning rather than trying to focus on individual words and then getting lost!

In the spoken language, we often begin phrases and project our intonation in a particular way, but then we may abandon what we are saying—even in the middle of a word. Thus, unlike the written language, which generally has some logical sequence, the spoken language often seems to follow no logical track and is therefore more difficult to understand. However, by recognizing the intonation we can get a clearer idea of the "direction" in which the speech is going.

The following is an extract from a conversation between an Indian and an Australian, who both now live in England, talking about how impolite they find the English and how this contrasts with the impression they had before they arrived in England.

> Indian: I was astounded as to how often impolite people were in England, whereas I was always taught that English people were incredibly polite and courteous.

> Australian: *Yeah, I, you see* this is what happened to me. I thought, *I thought* because I'm brash or because I'm more confident and *you know* outspoken because that's the way generally Australians are, I thought that I would be the rude person *you know* but I was offended a lot more than I expected to be by people's behavior. I thought *you know* because people *would*, wouldn't say things.

> Indian: It's almost *as if*, as if the messages that are sent back to your country and my country are completely different to the reality of *actually* what's going on at the time.

What you can notice is that they don't speak in a logical flow, particularly the Australian. They have not prepared what they are going to say, so they just talk as ideas come into their head. There is a lot of redundancy (highlighted in italics) due to repetitions of words and fillers (*you know*). So they use a lot of words but don't actually say very much in terms of real content.

I think it is extremely important not to focus on every single word and not to think that every word a person says will be important. For example, you might think that the words *brash, confident*, and *outspoken* are all key words, but they essentially mean the same thing. Basically, the Australian is saying that he thought the English people might find him a little offensive, but in reality he was the one who was offended.

It is also important to remember what the function of a social exchange is. It is not essentially to exchange useful information, but instead, to create a relationship. At the end of this conversation the Indian and Australian will feel closer to each other because they have shared a common experience or common perception—this is what they will remember; they will not remember necessarily the exact words that each other used to describe this perception. Note also that sharing similar cultural perceptions will generally have a more positive result in terms of the relationship between the speakers, than talking about differences in culture (see 13.7 and 17.4)

13.4   Learn how to recognize key words

When spoken at high speed, English words seem to merge together to create one long noise. For example, the simple question "do you want to go and get something to eat?" when spoken fast becomes "wannagetsomingteat?"

The problem for you and other non-native speakers is that you have probably learned to say the first version in which each word is clearly separated from its neighboring words, and you will therefore be unable to clearly recognize the native version.

So if spoken English is similar to the noise of an express train, how can you possibly understand a native speaker? The key is not to try and differentiate between the sounds and words, but to focus only on those parts of the phrase that are said the loudest and with the most emphasis. When native speakers say *do you want to go and get something to eat*, they don't give each word the same stress and the same volume.

English is what is known as a stress-timed language, which means it has a kind of in-built rhythm that native speakers follow. This may be one of the explanations for the success of rock music and rap sung in English.

The words that are given the most stress are generally those that have the most importance in the phrase: *do you <u>want</u> to go and <u>get</u> something to <u>eat.</u>*

If someone said to you *want get eat* with an intonation that suggested they were asking you a question, you would not have too much difficulty in understanding their meaning. So what you need to try and train yourself to do is just to focus on those words with the most stress. By "stress" I mean a combination of three factors: clarity, volume, and length. Thus, the key words in a phrase tend to be articulated more clearly, at a higher volume, and at a slower speed.

This means that the words that add little value to the phrase are said much less clearly, at a lower volume, and considerably faster. However, given that these words tend not to give key information, you can just ignore them and still have a good chance of understanding the overall meaning of the phrase. Basically, the time it takes to say *eat* will be approximately the same as it take to say *to go and*.

In theory this might sound very logical and even obvious. Of course, in practice it is much harder. However, with some self-training, a more relaxed approach, and more realistic expectations about what you are likely to understand, this method is certainly less stressful than anxiously trying to understand each individual word in a phrase. If you focus on individual words and sounds, you will soon get lost and lose track of the conversation. If, instead, you focus on every fifth or sixth word, i.e., the words that create the rhythm, then you will be more able to keep up with the conversation.

Here is an example from a conversation between an Anglo-Italian, an American, and an Indian talking about the role of the family in their respective countries. The words in the larger font were stressed by the speakers—by 'stress' I mean that the speaker's voice was louder and he / she spent a longer time to say the words. The words in the smaller font were said much more quickly.

Note that if you only understood the words in the larger font, you would still have a general idea of what was said during the conversation. On the other hand, if you tried to concentrate on understanding all the words, you would soon get lost and would be unable to continue participating in the conversation.

> Anglo-Italian: I think in Italy, I mean the family has to take priority, it always has done, I mean that's the kind of core of society and then it kind of unwinds from that, it spirals out from that and I think on the whole they've managed to keep it together through very basic traditions like, for example, the whole sort of ritual of eating together. It's important that at least once a week the whole extended family coming together to fight and scream and laugh and joke or whatever.

> American: I wonder if that has something to do with the size. It's interesting to me for instance that because most countries in Europe are much smaller than the North American experience, where family units are closer together. So for instance in North America it's not unusual to have a son or a daughter two thousand miles away in you know New York city, while the family is in Los Angeles, and moving around for economic reasons is just considered normal.

> Indian: I think that that happens in India as well but it often depends on where, where you come from, a vast majority of the country is quite poor and the main emphasis is just on existing and surviving and what you say about the family being important is certainly absolutely crucial and key.

Some of the stress words you might still not understand (e.g., *unwinds, spiral, scream*) but if you only heard the words—*Italy, family, priority, core of society, eating, extended family*—you would still have an idea of what the Italian was talking about.

13.5   Listen rather than focusing on what you are going to say next

We speak at between 120 and 150 words per minute, but as listeners our brains can process between 400 and 800 words per minute. This means that we get distracted easily and start thinking about other things. If you really want to improve your listening and thus to understand better what other people are saying to you in English, then you need to focus exclusively on what this person is saying. If you start thinking about your next question (or other things), you will quickly get distracted. Try to think at the same speed as your interlocutor rather than being constantly ahead of them.

13.6   Improve your listening habits

American author Robert McCloskey once remarked: *I know that you believe that you understood what you think I said, but I am not sure you realize that what you heard is not what I meant.* People hear what they want to hear.

You can improve your chances of hearing what your interlocutor wants you to hear if you

- focus not just on the first part of what someone says but also on the last part (our tendency is to listen attentively at the beginning and then half listen toward the end)
- participate in a conversation with an open mind, that is, you need to put aside any prejudices you have about, for instance, politics, ethics, and religion - if you listen without prejudice you will hear more of what is actually said rather than what you think is being said
- decide that the topic being discussed is potentially interesting, rather than immediately deciding that it is of no interest to you and thinking about other things
- pay attention, rather than pretending to pay attention
- try not to get distracted by how your interlocutor speaks or any other mannerisms they may have
- focus not just on the facts that you are given, but how these facts are given, and what interpretation your interlocutor is giving them

13.7   Don't immediately blame cultural differences for misunderstandings

Most misunderstandings boil down to communication—think about the most recent misunderstandings in your life and how they arose. It's clearly not only a case of the words we use, but how we use them and how we say them. If this is true within our own language, when communicating across cultures the problem becomes far more critical. However, because we know we are of different cultures, we tend to blame misunderstandings on differences in culture, ignoring the fact that we may simply have misinterpreted or mistranslated what they have said to us and vice versa.

Thus, again it is important to listen very carefully to what our interlocutors say, and to constantly make summaries and ask for clarifications (see Chapter 14).

Chapter 14
What to Do if You Don't Understand
What Someone Says

You will learn how to

- interrupt your interlocutor and ask for clarification without losing face
- identify for the interlocutor exactly what part of their sentence you did not understand
- find a way to help your native-English-speaking interlocutor be sensitive to the fact communication is a two-way process, in which both parties are responsible for helping each other understand. It is thus perfectly acceptable, and indeed often essential, to interrupt your interlocutor, and you shouldn't be afraid or embarrassed to do so

Often when you don't understand what someone says or writes, it has no other consequences than embarrassment and frustration. However, on some occasions, for example, in interviews and technical meetings, it may be crucial to understand all the key points. In such cases it is imperative that you ensure that you are able to follow at the least the main points of what is being said.

This chapter will show you ways to improve your understanding of native speakers and to transform a potentially frustrating exchange into a positive collaboration. The strategies I outline are those that native speakers use with each other all day and every day in the native-English-speaking world. They are not strategies that I have specifically designed for non-native speakers. This means that a native speaker will be very familiar with them, and therefore you do not need to be afraid to use them.

For useful phrases on this topic see Chapter 25.

A. Wallwork, *English for Academic Correspondence and Socializing*,
DOI 10.1007/978-1-4419-9401-1_14, © Springer Science+Business Media, LLC 2011

Factoids

❖ Nearly one-third of the citizens of the USA feel that it is not too important or not important at all to speak a second language. The number of children and students studying languages in the UK has dropped considerably, and less money is being invested in language research. Apparently, this lack of language skills has led to a lack of interpreters and is making it harder for international anti-terrorism squads, for example, to work together.

❖ Misunderstandings are as common with people who share the same language as they are in exchanges between people who are talking in a second language. A study in the UK revealed that as many as 6 out of 10 conversations in the workplace lead to a significant degree of misunderstanding.

❖ According to communications expert Tony Buzan, 85% of native English speakers in Britain rate their listening ability (in English) as average or less.

❖ Native speakers often listen at only 25% of their potential. The other 75% is made up of ignoring, or forgetting, distorting, or misunderstanding what the other person has said. Concentration rises above 25% if the interlocutor thinks what he / she is hearing is important or interesting. But in any case it never reaches 100%.

❖ Research conducted by Gass and Varonis highlighted that some native speakers are reluctant to enter into conversations with non-native speakers when they are feeling tired, as the effort required is much greater than when talking to another native speaker.

14.1 Be reassured that even native English speakers sometimes do not understand each other

Many of my students say they have a feeling of inferiority and inadequacy when they are talking to native speakers. They feel nervous. They feel stupid. They feel that they cannot participate on an equal level.

Native speakers do not always understand each other. As Oscar Wilde noted, "We have really everything in common with America nowadays, except, of course, the language." And another Irish playwright George Bernard Shaw once said, "England and America are two countries separated by a common language."

I am English and frequently in my life I have had experiences when I fail to understand another native English speaker. I once spent 20 minutes in a taxi in Glasgow (Scotland) in which the taxi driver chatted away to me in a strong Glaswegian accent, and I understood absolutely nothing. When I am in London, I am often unable to understand a single word in the first 30 seconds of what a native Londoner says to me because they speak so fast.

I once told a colleague from Texas, Tim Mitchell, that I had just come back from a seaside holiday in Corsica and had stepped on a sea urchin while swimming. Tim's face filled with shock and horror. He was clearly very concerned and asked me if I had had blood tests done at the local hospital. I couldn't understand his extreme reaction until I realized that he thought I had stepped on a syringe. The words *sea urchin* and *syringe* sound quite similar. Neither of us felt inadequate or stupid, we both just laughed about it.

In the English language world we accept that often we do not understand each other.

The solution for you as a non-native speaker is to change perspective. Think about situations within your own country. Presumably there are people in your country who speak with a very different accent from yours, and may even use a slightly different vocabulary or dialect. If you do not understand what they say, I imagine that you do not feel any sense of inferiority—at the most you might feel a little embarrassed. In any case, you probably collaborate with each other to understand what you are saying.

So when you have to speak to native speakers, try to imagine that English is simply a rather obscure dialect of your own language! Your objective and that of your interlocutor's is to understand each other. You should both be on an equal level.

14.2   Raise awareness in your interlocutor of your difficulty in understanding

A key factor in your ability to understand native speakers is letting them know that you are not a native speaker and thus your command of the language is not the same as theirs. The problem with a lot of people whose first language is English is that they often don't learn languages themselves. They thus have no idea of the difficulties that you might experience in trying to understand them. Also they are not aware that you might, for instance, have a good command of spoken English and written English but that your listening skills are much lower.

If you don't encourage the native speaker to speak clearly, then you will significantly reduce your understanding of what they say. This is certainly not a benefit for you, and is probably not good for them either.

Instead you need to make it immediately clear to the native speaker that you need him or her to speak slowly and clearly, make frequent mini summaries, and be prepared for many interruptions for clarification on your part. You could say something like this:

> It would be great if you could speak really slowly and clearly, as my English listening skills are not very good. Thank you. And also please do not be offended if I frequently ask you for clarifications.

But the problem does not end there. Even if the native speaker acknowledges your difficulties, they are likely to forget these difficulties within two or three minutes, as they then become absorbed by what they are saying. This means that you frequently have to remind them to speak more slowly.

> I am sorry, but please could you speak more slowly.

14.3   Identify the part of the phrase that you did not understand

Avoid saying "repeat please" if you don't understand what someone has said. Instead it is much more beneficial for both you and your interlocutor if you precisely identify what part of the phrase you didn't understand. Let's imagine that the part in italics in the sentences in the first column in the table on the next page is the part said by your interlocutor that you did not understand. Your questions for clarification are shown in the second column.

YOUR INTERLOCUTOR SAYS THIS:	TO CLARIFY, YOU SAY THIS:
I thought the presentation was *amazing*.	You thought the presentation was *what* sorry? Sorry, *what* did you think the presentation was?
I made *a terrible mess* with my presentation.	You made *a what* sorry? Sorry, *what* did you do with your presentation?
We have all just come back from *the trip to the mosque*.	You have all come back from *where* sorry? *Where* did you go, sorry?
I have just had an interesting conversation with Professor Suzuki.	With Professor *who* sorry. *Sorry*, who did you speak to?

In the examples above, I have given two possible clarification questions. For example:

> I *thought the presentation was* amazing.
> Type 1) You *thought the presentation was* what sorry?
> Type 2) Sorry, *what* did you think the presentation was?

Type 1 is easy to use because you simply repeat the words immediately preceding the word that you didn't understand (in the example the repeated words are shown in italics).

Type 2 is more complex because it entails using an auxiliary verb (*did* in the example). It also means that you have to remember to put the words in a question form.

So it is simpler to use Type 1, which you can further reduce to *the presentation was what?*

Both Types 1 and 2 have the advantage that your interlocutor will only repeat the word that you didn't understand (*amazing* in this case). This means that you now have a far greater chance of actually hearing the word, as it will now be isolated from its surrounding words. If you don't understand the meaning you can simply say *Sorry what does that mean?* Or simply repeat the word with a rising intonation to indicate that you don't understand: *amazing, sorry?*

Obviously, you can only use this strategy of repeating words if you hear the words in the first place. And this is another reason why it is very important to listen carefully.

The examples given in the table on the next page are useful when you are focusing not just on an individual word but on a whole sequence of words. If you don't identify the precise part of the sentence, your interlocutor will just repeat everything probably exactly as before, but perhaps a bit louder. By identifying the part you did not understand, there is a chance that the interlocutor will use different words and say that particular part more slowly. The second column also shows alternative forms of clarification.

WORD / S MISUNDERSTOOD	CLARIFICATION QUESTION
It chucked it down yesterday so I couldn't summon up the courage to venture out.	Sorry, I didn't understand the *first part* of what you said. Sorry *what* did it do yesterday?
It chucked it down yesterday so I couldn't *summon up the courage* to venture out.	Sorry, I missed the part in the *middle*. Sorry *what* couldn't you do?
It chucked it down yesterday so I couldn't summon up the courage to *venture out*.	Sorry, I didn't catch the *last part*. Sorry, I didn't understand *the bit after "courage"*. Sorry, I didn't understand *what* you didn't have the courage to do.
Note: The sentence means: It was raining very hard yesterday and I didn't feel like going outside.	The courage to do *what*, sorry?

14.4   Identify the key word that you did not understand

Here is an extract from a conversation. It highlights the strategies that a non-native-English-speaking woman uses to identify what the native-speaking man has said.

1. Man	Could you tell her that the meeting has been put off until next Thursday.
2. Woman	The meeting has been what sorry?
3. Man	It's been put off until next Thursday.
4. Woman	Sorry, "put off?"
5. Man	Postponed. It has been postponed till next Thursday.
6. Woman	So it's been delayed, but not canceled?
7. Man	Yes, that's right.

The key problem in the above dialog was that the woman did not know the term *put off*. The first time the man says *put off* (line 1), the woman probably hears the following sound: *zbinputofftil*, that is, one long sound where several words have been merged together. Basically, she has no idea what the man said between *meeting* and *next Thursday*. So her tactic is to say all the words she heard until the point where she stopped understanding (line 2). The man then simply repeats the second part of his initial sentence (line 3), but this time probably with more emphasis on *put off*. Because the man puts more emphasis on *put off*, the woman is now able to identify the part of the sentence that she had failed to identify before.

Note how in line 4 the woman begins her sentence with *sorry*. If she had simply said "Put off?" the man might have just answered "Yes, put off" as he would think she was just asking for confirmation. Instead the word *sorry* tells the man that the woman is not familiar with the term *put off*. *Sorry* is very frequently used by native speakers when asking for clarification.

The man now uses a synonym for *put off* (postponed). The woman's final strategy (line 6) is to check, using her own words, that she has understood correctly the meaning of *postponed*. And finally in line 7, the man confirms that she has understood.

The woman never says *Repeat please*. If you say *repeat please*, your interlocutor will just repeat the whole phrase again and you will probably not understand any more than you did the first time. Basically the woman asks a series of increasingly specific questions to identify the exact part of the man's phrase that she did not understand.

The above dialog and strategies used are typical of the strategies used by native speakers too. If you use them with a native speaker, he or she will not think you are doing anything strange.

14.5 Avoid confusion between similar sounding words

Some words sound very similar to each other and are frequently confused even by native speakers. Below are some examples of how to clarify certain pairs of words.

WORDS	POSSIBLE MISUNDERSTANDING	CLARIFICATION
Tuesday vs Thursday	We have scheduled the meeting for Tuesday.	That's Tuesday the sixth right?
13 vs 30	We need thirty copies.	That's thirty, three zero, right?
can vs can't	I can come to the meeting	So you are saying that you <u>are</u> able to come to the meeting?
	I can't come to the presentation	So you mean that you <u>not</u> able to attend the presentation? So you mean that you <u>cannot</u> attend?

In the first example, the secret is to combine the day of the week with its related date. This means that your interlocutor has two opportunities to verify that you have understood correctly. If you have misunderstood, your interlocutor can then say *No, Thursday the eighth*.

The confusion in the second example happens with numbers from 13 to 19 and 30, 40, 50, etc. Using the correct stress can help: thir<u>teen</u> vs <u>thir</u>ty. However, particularly on the telephone, this subtle difference in pronunciation may not be heard. So the secret is to say the number as a word (e.g., *one hundred and fourteen*) and then to divide it up into digits (*that's one one four*). If you have misunderstood, your interlocutor can then say *No, thirteen, one three.*

In the third example, the problem is increased if *can* is followed by a verb that begins with the letter T. Thus, understanding the difference between *I can tell you* and *I can't tell you* is very difficult. There are also significant differences between the way native speakers pronounce the word *can't*—for example, in my pronunciation *can't* rhymes with *aren't*, but for others the vowel sound of "a" is the same as in *and*. The solution is to replace *can* and *can't* with the verb *to be able to*. You also need to stress the *are* in the affirmative version, and the *not* in the negative version, as illustrated in the table. If you have misunderstood, your interlocutor can then say *No, I am able to come* or *no, I am not able to come* (alternatively *I cannot attend*).

14.6   Turn your misunderstanding into something positive

One way to understand more of what your interlocutor says is to make frequent short summaries of what your interlocutor tells you. Your interlocutor will appreciate the interest you are showing. You can use phrases such as the following to begin your summary:

Can I just clarify what I think you are saying? You mean that ...

I just want to check that I am following you correctly. So you are saying that ...

Your listener will not interpret such clarifications as a lack of English comprehension skills on your part, but that like a native speaker you simply want an accurate understanding of what has been said.

Using this tactic means that you could turn a potentially embarrassing situation into something positive.

Chapter 15
How to Improve Your Pronunciation

You will learn that

- your listening skills will improve dramatically if you improve your pronunciation
- even though English pronunciation seems quite random, there are a few basic rules

I teach in Italy and I have done the following experiment with around 1,000 PhD students. I say *Sofia Loren*, the name of perhaps Italy's most famous actress. I pronounce the name as an English person would, with the stress like this _Sofia Loren_. I repeat the name several times. Over the five years that I have been doing this experiment, only two of the Italian students have ever understood what I was saying. The reason? I pronounce the name in a different way from how Italians pronounce it: *Sofia Loren*. I achieved the same results by saying *Marilyn Monroe*, one of America's most famous actresses. Again, I say it as a British or American would say it: _Marilyn Monroe_. Italians pronounce *Marilyn* using different vowels sounds and *Monroe* with the stress on the first syllable—thus they do not understand me when I say it.

The point I was making to my students is that if you pronounce a very familiar word with even a minimal difference in pronunciation there is a chance that you will not be understood. Although grammar mistakes will rarely cause breakdowns in communication, problems with pronunciation sometimes do. It is thus imperative that you improve your pronunciation if you wish to understand and be understood by a native English speaker.

A. Wallwork, *English for Academic Correspondence and Socializing*,
DOI 10.1007/978-1-4419-9401-1_15, © Springer Science+Business Media, LLC 2011

Factoids

❖ In some research by Dr Sue Fraser, some Japanese high school students were asked to rate their difficulty of listening to and understanding the English of certain native speakers, of a Taiwanese speaker, and of their fellow Japanese. Fraser found that 95% of the students found the Japanese speaker "easy to understand," 52% the Taiwanese, 38% the American, 31% the Scottish person, 18% the English person, and 12% the person from Zimbabwe (where English is the official language).

❖ W.W. Skeat, a professor at Cambridge University, once declared, "I hold firmly to the belief ... that no-one can tell how to pronounce an English word unless he has at some time or other heard it."

❖ British and American pronunciation differ considerably, particularly with regard to vowels sounds, for example: route = *root* (GB), *raut* (US). British people tend to pronounce the second *t* in *twenty*, unlike many North Americans who say *twenny*. The stress within a word may also be different: *detail, frustrated* (GB), *detail, frustrated* (US).

❖ The vast majority of English surnames have the stress on the first syllable, for example, Babbage, Berners-Lee, Darwin, Dawkins, Faraday, Hawking, Newton, Turing. British towns also have the stress on the first syllable, for example, Birmingham, Cambridge, London, Manchester, Newcastle, Oxford.

15.1   Avoid the typical pronunciation mistakes of people who speak your language

The first factoid on the previous page highlights that

- if you are a non-native speaker, you will find the English spoken by people of your own native language easiest to understand and to imitate
- speakers of languages within the same language group (e.g., Japanese and Chinese; Italian and Spanish) generally understand each other's English relatively easily
- there are big differences in levels of understanding of the varieties of English spoken by native speakers

There are two very important implications:

- just because your colleagues in your own country can understand your English, it certainly does not mean that people from other countries will understand you. For example, if you are from Japan, an Italian may have difficulty understanding your English and likewise you may not understand his / her English
- if you are a native English speaker there is a chance that non-native speakers will have difficulty understanding you, and may be even native speakers

15.2   Learn to listen to the correct pronunciation

When learning languages we often meet a word for the first time when we are reading (rather than listening). As we are reading we assign a pronunciation to any new words we meet without actually knowing whether that pronunciation is the correct pronunciation or not.

For example, many students in Europe go to study English in London, and one popular district of London is called Shepherd's Bush. Anyone who has never heard *shepherd* being pronounced by a native speaker might assume that the *ph* is pronounced *f* (as in **ph**ilosophy), and so they think the pronunciation is *sheferd*. In reality it is pronounced *shep herd* because it means someone who *herds* (looks after) *sheep*. These students then look at the map of London, imagine the pronunciation of *shepherd* (without thinking that they might be completely wrong), go to England, and say *sheferd's bush*. They are lucky because the Londoners manage to understand them as the word *sheferd* is associated with *bush*, so the two words together make it easy to decipher.

Typically, because these students think they have confirmation of their own pronunciation from the fact that they appeared to have been understood by the native

Londoners, they come back to their native country and tell their English teacher that they went to *sheferd's bush*, that is, still using the incorrect pronunciation. This reason is that they never listened to hear how the word is really pronounced even though they will have heard it being pronounced many times correctly (e.g., whenever they use the underground system). This is because the pronunciation they have in their head overrides (dominates) their ability to hear the correct pronunciation.

The rest of this chapter gives some very general guidelines on word stress (e.g., *manager* rather than *manager*), but there are many exceptions to the guidelines. I have not made an analysis of all the different sounds of English as this would require an entire book!

It is a good idea to write a list of words that you think you may need at a conference. Then you can convert your list into a pdf file and use Adobe "read aloud" (see page 313 for a link to a pdf explaining how to use this feature). You will then hear the correct stress and vowel sound for each word.

For more on pronunciation, see 3.1–3.8 in the companion volume *English for Presentations at International Conferences*.

15.3   Word stress: two syllables

A good simple guideline is that if you have a doubt about the pronunciation of a two-syllable word that is not a verb, then put the stress on the first syllable. In fact, the vast majority of British surnames and place names have the stress on the first syllable. Examples: *Thatcher, Newton, London, Bristol*.

This is not the case of many US names as these have been more influenced by American Indian, Spanish, and the languages of the settlers: *Los Angeles, New York*.

TWO-SYLLABLE WORDS	SOME EXAMPLES	SOME EXCEPTIONS
nouns: first syllable	China, country, effort, colleague, method, minute, person, program, statement	amount, canal, cartoon, cassette, effect, event, exam, guitar, hotel, Japan, police, success, technique
verbs: second syllable	allow, accept, depend, forget, support	happen, listen, wonder, manage, mention
adjectives: first syllable	common, English, famous, heavy, perfect, pretty, private, previous, recent, various	afraid, aware, Chinese, complete, concise, correct, polite, precise
conjunctions, prepositions, adverbs: second syllable	ago, before, perhaps, toward, until	after, also, likewise, seldom

Some words change stress depending on whether they are nouns (on first syllable) or verbs (on second syllable).

Examples: contact, exploit, increase, insert, object, present, progress, record, report, research, upset.

Apart from those words, if a word can be both a verb and a noun I don't think there is any way of knowing where the stress will be. In the table below all the words are both verbs and nouns.

FIRST SYLLABLE		SECOND SYLLABLE	
answer	invoice	address	reply
access	measure	command	report
archive	promise	concern	request
comment	profit	control	respect
contact	question	correct	result
discount	schedule	debate	return
issue	survey	effect	support

Unfortunately, some words are stressed differently by different people, for example, *research*—some people say *research* and other *research*, irrespectively of whether it is a noun or verb.

15.4   Word stress: compound nouns

A word that is made up of two words has the stress on the first syllable (e.g., *software*). Here are some examples:

> boyfriend, everyone, feedback, headline, highlight, income, input, interface, interview, layout, newspaper, outcome, overview, podcast, sidetrack, supermarket, switchboard, workshop

Exceptions: afternoon, understand

15.5   Word stress: three syllables

Most three-syllable words (nouns, verbs, and adjectives) that don't have a suffix (e.g., *un-*, *pre-*) have the stress on the first or second syllable. Only a few have the stress on the third syllable (e.g., expertise, introduce, Japanese, personnel).

FIRST SYLLABLE		SECOND SYLLABLE	
absolute	hierarchy	acceptance	embarrass
agency	industry	accompany	example
alias	influence	advantage	explicit
apparent	interested	assistant	financial
architect	interesting	component	ideal
article	modify	configure	important
atmosphere	monitor	consultant	objective
attitude	paragraph	convenient	percentage
bicycle	personal	determine	performance
company	prejudice	develop	strategic
conference	premises	dishonest	sufficient
confident	principle		
consequence	quality		
deficit	satellite		
difficult	sufficient		
excellent	triangle		

15.6 Word stress: multi-syllables

Words ending with *-able*, *-ary*, *-ise*, *-ize*, *-yse*, *-ure* have the stress on the first syllable:

suitable, secretary, category, realize, analyze, organize, recognize, architecture, literature

Words ending with *-ate*, *-ical*, *-ity*, *-ment*, *-ology* have the stress on the third to last syllable

graduate, immediate, separate, logical, reality, feasibility, management, development, government, environment, psychology

Some exceptions (stress on second syllable): equipment, fulfillment

Words ending with *-ial*, *-ic*, *-cian*, *-sion*, *-tion* have the stress on the penultimate syllable:

appearance, artificial, specific, expensive, politician, occasion, specialisation

Most words ending in *-ee* have the stress on *-ee*.

attendee, employee, interviewee, referee

An exception (stress on second syllable): committee

The majority of other multi-syllable words have the stress on the second sylla-ble (e.g., identify, particular, parameter, enthusiasm), but some on the third (e.g., fundamental, correspondence).

A number of commonly used multi-syllable words are usually pronounced with-out certain syllables (i.e., the ones in italics below are not pronounced in normal speech):

> average, bus*i*ness, categ*o*ry, Cath*o*lic, comf*o*rtable, diff*e*rence, *eve*ning, gen*e*ral, int*e*rested, int*e*resting, lab*o*ratory, lit*e*rature, med*i*cine, pref*e*rable, ref*e*rence, temp*e*rature, veg*e*table, Wedn*e*sday

15.7   Acronyms

Acronyms are pronounced in three ways:

1. with each individual letter pronounced separately and with equal stress on each letter, for example, DVD, EU, UN, WWW
2. like a normal word, for example, NATO, UNESCO, URL
3. like a normal word but with vowel sounds added, for example, FTSE (pronounced *footsie*)

15.8   Sentence stress

Generally you should stress the word that carries the key information or that helps to distinguish one thing from something else. This means that normally we stress adjectives rather than their nouns:

> *I am a* software *developer.*

You would only stress the noun if it is the noun that helps to differentiate between two things.

> *I am a software* developer *not a software salesperson.*

Stress verbs rather than pronouns:

> *I want to* show *you.*

Only stress the pronoun when you want to differentiate one group of things or people from another.

> *I want to show* you *not* them.

Stress the main verb rather than an affirmative auxiliary, unless you want to give special emphasis.

This has happened *several times.*

I can assure that this has *happened several times.*

Stress the negative auxiliary rather than main verb (first example below), unless you are distinguishing between two verbs (second example).

This hasn't *happened before.*

I haven't spoken *to him but I have* seen *him.*

Chapter 16
Exploiting Audiovisual Resources

You will learn that

- watching movies is more frustrating and less productive than watching most other types of TV programs
- how much you will understand will depend on the type of TV series you watch
- there are endless resources on the web to help you improve your listening skills

Many people rely on English lessons to improve their English without considering the fact that you can learn a considerable amount outside the classroom. Given that a major difficulty for most people is understanding native English speakers, it makes sense to take every opportunity you can to listen to English—in the car, on your PC, and on TV. This chapter gives advice on what to watch and how often.

A. Wallwork, *English for Academic Correspondence and Socializing*, 179
DOI 10.1007/978-1-4419-9401-1_16, © Springer Science+Business Media, LLC 2011

Factoids

❖ The inhabitants of countries which broadcast movies and other TV programs directly in English (e.g., Scandinavian countries, Holland, Portugal) tend to speak and understand English much better than those countries where movies are dubbed (France, Germany, Italy).

❖ In the 1930s and 40s Germany, Italy and Spain dubbed British and US movies (i.e. replaced the English audio with that of their own language) to defend their national language and as a form of censorship to protect their regimes. It was also a problem of illiteracy as many people at that time would not have been able to read the subtitles. In Poland they initially used the same actor to dub every single part—male and female—of imported movies. The first countries to introduce subtitles were Denmark and France, in 1929.

❖ Dutch teenagers have a very wide vocabulary of everyday English because they tend to watch TV series—they thus hear the same expressions being said repeatedly over many episodes.

❖ The mayor of New York from 1933 to 1945 spoke English, Italian, and Yiddish fluently. If you watch his televised speeches with the volume off, you can still tell what language he was speaking in by noting his body language, particularly the way he used his hands and arms.

16.1   The news

Listening to the international news on TV or on the radio is good practice because you are probably already aware of some of the stories and you will thus be able to follow them much better. Watching news that is all local to one country is much more difficult.

16.2   TED.com

This is a great website and in my opinion is probably the best way to improve your listening (apart, of course, from interacting directly with native speakers). The site is packed with fascinating talks (i.e., presentations) given by experts in various fields from around the world. You will learn not only English, but also interesting facts. You can

- choose the topic you are interested in by using their internal search engine— the main topics are technology, entertainment, design, business, science, culture, arts, and global issues
- choose the speaker
- choose the most watched talks, the most recent talks, the most talked about talks
- choose the length of the talk depending on the time you have available for watching—they vary from a minimum of around 2 minutes up to a maximum of around 20 minutes
- read a transcript of the talk either in English or in your own language—you can do this before you watch to get a clear idea of the topic, and also while you are watching. The transcript is interactive in the sense that you can click on words within the transcript and be automatically taken to that same point in the video
- use the subtitles—there are English subtitles for all the talks, and for the very popular talks there are often subtitles in many other languages
- download the talk and play it on other media
- read comments made by people who have watched the talk and contribute to a discussion on the topic

Note that the existence or not of subtitles and translations into various languages depends on how recently the talk was posted (if it is within the last few months, it may not have either of these features) and how popular the talk is.

If you are really serious about improving your listening, then another option is to copy and paste the transcript and invent your own listening exercises by deleting random words and then while listening you can try to fill in the gaps. It helps if you delete the words a few days before, and then you listen, otherwise you might remember what you deleted.

16.3   TV series

The main advantages of TV series are that they

- can often be addictive, so you are really motivated to watch the next episode
- are shorter than movies (from 20 to 50 minutes maximum)—this makes finding time to watch them much easier
- show characters who keep reappearing so that you get tuned in to the voices; also these characters tend to have particular phrases that they say repeatedly
- go on for years, so you have a constant source of entertainment

16.4   Movies

Movies are much harder to understand because

- the plot is totally new
- the voices are all new
- the film tends to last at least 90 minutes, which requires intense concentration

Nevertheless, watching movies is fun. So

- choose films you have already seen in your native language, so then you do not have to worry about following the plot
- check out on YouTube to hear what the actors sound like, and try to find extracts from the film to judge whether you are likely to enjoy it and understand it
- consider watching it over several days

The easiest movies to understand are

- science fiction—full of technical words that you may be familiar with, and there is little humor (humor tends to be quite difficult to understand)
- documentaries—the narrator tends to speak clearly and from a script, so even though you can't see the lips moving you will still be able to understand
- historical

The most difficult are ones that contain non-standard English, ones with lots of slang, and ones with a lot of humor and thus full of word plays, for instance:

- ones containing dialects
- wacky comedies

- thrillers
- crime stories

You might also consider watching old movies. Ones that precede the 1970s tend to be a little easier to understand as the actors tended to enunciate the words more clearly. Also, the plot is slower and easier to follow.

16.5   Reality shows

If you want to hear "real" English, then watch a reality show. The problem is that reality shows contain a lot of slang which is (i) difficult to understand and (ii) unlikely to be very useful for you in the world of academia!

16.6   YouTube

There are hundreds of thousands of short videos that you can watch on YouTube. The vast majority have no subtitles. However, many are simply fun. Let me just make one example. There are extracts from the shows of magicians and illusionists. These are great videos to watch because they are short and highly entertaining. You are also motivated to rewatch them to try and understand how the trick works. By watching them several times, you will also be hearing again and again what the magician says, and therefore hopefully improving your understanding.

16.7   Subtitles

There are no rules for the use of subtitles. The main problem is that if you use subtitles you will probably read the subtitles rather than listen. However, try to watch some parts of the video with subtitles and some without, or watch a part with subtitles and then rewatch the same part without subtitles.

If you do opt for subtitles, I suggest that you use English subtitles—select "English for the hard of hearing."

If there is a part that you simply don't understand, then switch on the subtitles from your language. It is also fun to watch films in your own language with English subtitles!

16.8   Songs

If you have any favorite English-speaking bands or singers, then try listening to their songs while reading the lyrics. They may contain a lot of slang but the ear-training that you will get will be very useful.

16.9   Audio books and podcasts

You can buy audio books and download podcasts on a huge variety of topics. If you put them on your iPod, you can then listen to them while you are traveling. The BBC provides a lot of downloadable materials (bbc.com).

16.10   Give yourself a clear objective

Be realistic about what you want to achieve. Just as you can't lose 10 kg in weight in one weekend, you can't learn English in two days.

Here are some ideas.

(1) Once a day watch the news or a podcast in English or one presentation on Ted

(2) Every week watch two episodes of a 20-minute TV series or one episode of a 50-minute episode

But be patient. The first 10–20 times you watch you will only understand 10%. Then you will gradually manage to reach about 50%, and then hopefully even more.

Only watch things that you would have watched anyway in your own language. You are only going to learn if you are motivated and enjoy yourself.

Part V
Socializing

Chapter 17
Preparing for Social Events

You will learn that

- you can prepare for a social event in the same way that you can prepare for a work meeting
- if you want to meet a specific person, it is best to organize this in advance
- much of the success of a social meeting is decided before it even takes place

You may find social events much more difficult to manage than work-related events. When you are talking about your research, you will generally have more command over the vocabulary that you need in order to conduct a discussion. However, even in a social situation, you can shift the conversation to topics where you have greater command of English or a wider general knowledge. The first part of this chapter teaches you how to prepare for typical conversations. In the second part (17.9 and following) you will also learn how to arrange meetings with key people in advance of the conference.

A. Wallwork, *English for Academic Correspondence and Socializing*,
DOI 10.1007/978-1-4419-9401-1_17, © Springer Science+Business Media, LLC 2011

Factoids

❖ Surveys have shown that 87% of people fear having to suffer boring conversations at social events.

❖ Topics that are acceptable for conversations between people who have just met vary considerably from culture to culture. Whereas in some Asian cultures it might be perfectly acceptable to ask someone how much they earn, in Western cultures this might be considered very impolite and embarrassing.

❖ Social psychologist Sidney Jourard from the University of Florida investigated how often people touch each other while having meals together in restaurants. In a restaurant in San Juan (Puerto Rico) people touched each other up to 180 times in the space of one hour, in Paris 110 times, in Gainesville (USA) twice, and in London never!

❖ People with more active social lives are both healthier and live longer. This is even more true, the more diverse your social relationships are.

17.1   Exploit conferences for publishing your research and for networking

Apart from being an excuse for spending a few days in an exotic location, there are many additional benefits of attending a conference. If you give a presentation or have a poster session, then you can "publicize" your results and give your readers a chance to learn something about you and your work. You will thus gain valuable visibility, and hopefully credibility too. This should give you a good opportunity to then set up new contacts and collaborations.

Those who go to conferences frequently recommend not attending too many events or going to too many presentations. The idea is not just to learn everything you can about your research topic, but to use every moment you can to network (i.e., to meet new people in the hope of setting up new collaborations). Other professors I spoke to recommended going to more marginal workshops rather than the big-name presentations. You are likely to learn more at the workshops (you can read the big name's paper by yourself at home) and will have more opportunity to participate and meet other people.

How you come across as a person both during your presentation and afterwards at the social events is often just as important as the content of the presentation itself. My own studies with PhD students have revealed that after only 10 days most people remember more about what they thought about the presenter and how he / she made them feel, than they can about what the presenter actually presented.

But even if you only attend a conference without giving any presentations, you will still have many opportunities to

- find out what the hot topics are, and what other researchers are working on, and keep up to date regarding technical progress. This is important if you are a member of an international technical working group or if you wish to set up cooperations
- get feedback on your published work
- get new ideas while listening and talking to other people
- network and meet up with old friends, colleagues, and people who until now you may have only contacted via email or telephone

You can do all these things successfully if you feel confident about talking to people in English. It will help you considerably if you have the right English phrases available. This section is designed to help you achieve those goals.

17.2   Identify typical conversation topics and prepare related vocabulary lists

You will massively increase your chances of understanding a conversation in a social context, if you prepare vocabulary lists connected with the kind of topics that might come up in conversation. It is true that an infinite number of topics could be discussed at a social dinner, but what is also certain is that some topics come up very frequently. These topics include

- the location and how the conference has been organized
- the social events (including tourist excursions) connected with the conference
- the weather
- the food
- other people's presentations
- latest technologies (cell phones and applications, PCs, etc.)

If you learn as much vocabulary as possible connected with the above points, you will feel

- more confident about talking, that is, offering your opinions and responding to others
- more relaxed when listening

The result will be that you will be able to participate in the conversation actively, and thus have a more positive and rewarding experience.

Other topics which are typically covered at social events include family, work, education, sport, film, music, and the political and economic situation of one or more countries. Again, if you learn the words (meaning and pronunciation) associated with these topics, you will be able to participate much more effectively.

17.3   Learn what topics of conversation are not acceptable for particular nationalities

There are some topics of conversation that are universally acceptable, such as those used for breaking the ice (e.g., the ones listed at the beginning of 17.2). As an example, money is a topic that some British people might consider inappropriate for discussion with strangers at a social event—this means that they might find it embarrassing to be asked questions about how much they earn, how much their house is worth, and how much they spend on their children's education.

What is appropriate varies from nation to nation. I spoke to a Japanese researcher who told me,

> In Japan we are hesitant to talk about personal matters. For instance, many British people I have met like to talk about their families and show photographs, but the Japanese don't do that, at least not in depth. We would say "I have a husband. I have a son and I have two daughters." Japanese men like talking about hobbies, golf, for example. We talk about food. Women even like to talk about what blood type they are.

Sometimes you may think that your interlocutor is asking too many questions, which may be also too personal. Most Anglos would not consider questions such as Where do you study? What kind of research do you do? What did you major in? What seminars are you planning to go to? Did you take your vacation yet? to be too personal. Such questions are merely a friendly exploration in a search to find things that you may have in common.

Some questions would be considered inappropriate by most Anglos, for example:

How old are you?
What is your salary?
What is your religion?
Are you married?
How old is your husband / wife?
Do you plan to get married?
Do you plan to have children?
How much do you weigh?
Have you put on weight?
How much did you pay for your car / house (etc.)?

17.4   Think of other safe topics that involve cultural similarities rather than just differences

The social events organized at international conferences provide a perfect opportunity for discussing similarities and differences in culture. If you focus on the similarities, it will generally create a better atmosphere, rather than trying to claim that your country does things better than another country.

This does not necessarily involve having heavy ethical or political discussions but can be centered on more straightforward, but nevertheless interesting, topics such as

- legal age to do certain things (e.g., drive a car, vote)
- dialects and different languages within the same national borders
- the role of the family (e.g., treatment of the elderly, ages people leave home)
- things people do for fun (e.g., bungee jumping, karaoke)
- tipping habits (e.g., hotels, restaurants, taxi drivers)

- holiday destinations
- jobs and how often people change them, how far people commute to work
- national sports
- natural resources
- shop and office opening and closing times
- punctuality and its relative importance

If you prepare vocabulary lists for the above topics and learn the pronunciation of the words, then you will have more confidence to initiate and / or participate in a conversation.

17.5   If you live near the conference location, be prepared to answer questions on your town

If you live in the region where the conference is being held, then you have the perfect opportunity to share your knowledge and practice your English! Here are some typical questions and answers:

Are there any good restaurants where I can try / sample the local food?
Yes, there is a good one near the town hall, and another one just round the corner from here on Academia Street.

What local sites would you recommend that I go and see?
Well the standard places where all tourists go are .... But I suggest that you visit the museum of ... and if you like food you could go to the market on Academia Street.

Do you have any suggestions as to where I might buy a ...
You could try the department store which is on the main road that leads to the mosque.

Note the construction with suggest and recommend: to suggest / recommend that someone do something

If someone is critical of the local services or about the organization of the conference, and if you don't want to enter into a long defense, you can simply say:

Yes, I know what you mean.

Or if you want to be more defensive you can say:

Well, to be honest, I just think you have been unlucky.

17.6   Prepare anecdotes that you can recount over dinner

You will probably be able to participate more effectively in a conversation if you initiate the topic area yourself. You could prepare short anecdotes on one or more of the following:

- travel stories (e.g., missing planes, terrible hotels)
- misadventures in the lab
- the worst presentation you ever did
- the best / worst conference you ever attended

These are good topics because they are neutral and everyone in your group is likely to have something to contribute. If you initiate the conversation, it will help to boost your confidence.

An alternative to stories / anecdotes are factoids (i.e., interesting statistics), for example, factoids about your country, about your research area, or about anything you find interesting. I find a good way of collecting interesting facts or quotations is to note them down from any book you are reading. For instance, I have just finished reading Andy Hunt's excellent book *Pragmatic Thinking and Learning*. These are just a few of things that I wrote down:

> The majority of all scientific information is less than fifteen years old.

> You'll be at the peak of intelligence at the very end of the project and at your most ignorant at the beginning.

> We have "bugs" in the way we think—fundamental errors in how we process information, make decisions, and evaluate situations.

> Did you ever sit down and deliberately decide to be liberal, conservative, libertarian, or anarchist? A workaholic or a slacker?

> Because it was fun, the presentation was much more effective. Normally, no one pays any attention to the standard talk.

> Multitasking can cost you 20 to 40 percent of your productivity.

You can introduce a factoid by saying:

> I read in the newspaper this morning that ...

> I was surfing the web the other day and I found an interesting statistic that says ...

> Did you know that ...?

> I read some research that says you can tell the difference ...

> I have heard that apparently most people would prefer ...

Or you can just slip the factoid or the quote / idea into the middle of an ongoing conversation. Basically, you just need to be curious about the world. So keep a note book of interesting things that you read. And make a list of interesting experiences that you have had. Then you can use such facts and stories on social occasions.

It is also helpful to learn something about psychology and communication skills. Socializing is all about relating to people and communicating well with the other attendees. Learning good communication skills and social skills entails knowing how the human brain receives information, and how we perceive each other.

17.7   Practice being at the center of attention in low-risk situations

Do you like standing up in front of other people or do you feel nervous and self-conscious? If you are the kind of person who usually does not talk much at dinners, parties, and even in everyday banal social situations (e.g., in front of the coffee machine, on the telephone), then try and make an effort to talk more and find yourself at the center of attention.

Don't just listen to people, learn to have the courage to interrupt them and comment on what they have said. For instance you can relate what they have said to your own experience. You could say:

I know exactly what you mean. In fact ...

Actually I had a very similar experience to what you have just described.

I was once in exactly the same situation.

I completely agree with what you are saying. In fact, ...

I am not sure I totally agree with you. In my country, for instance, ...

Tell people things that have happened to you or that you have read or heard about. You can do this in low-risk situations (i.e., where your conversation skills and level of English are not going to be judged), for example, when you are with a group of friends.

You could practise doing two-minute presentations with a group of colleagues. You could do this either in your own language or in English. Possible topics:

- what you enjoy doing most in life
- your favorite movie or book and why you like it so much
- the worst journey of your life

- the best holiday
- your dreams for the future
- your ideal house

Another solution is to offer to do teaching work at your department or institute. Teaching experience is excellent training for presentations as you have to learn to explain things clearly and engage your students.

If you practice being at the center of attention, you will gain more confidence.

17.8   Anticipate answers to questions that people might ask you after your presentation

If you are going to a conference to give a presentation, there is always a good chance that someone will come up to you after the presentation and ask you questions or set up a meeting for later.

If you want to create a good impression and avoid possible embarrassment, it is good idea to prepare answers to as many possible questions you can think of. You should do that in advance of the conference so that you can create suitable answers in English.

For more on this aspect, see Chapter 16 *Questions and Answers* in the companion volume *English for Presentations at International Conferences.*

17.9   Decide in advance which key people you want to meet

People do not go to conferences just to watch presentations. One of the primary reasons is networking, that is, finding people with whom you can set up collaborations or who can give you useful feedback on your work. Networking is much simpler if you have a clear idea in advance of who you would like to meet (hereafter "your key person"). A simple way to do this is to

- look at the conference program and find the names of key persons
- find information about them from their personal pages on their institute's website
- find a photograph of them so you will be able to identify them in a room from a distance

Then you need to prepare questions in English that you wish to ask them.

You should also predict how they might answer your questions. This will increase your chances of understanding their answers and will also enable you to think of follow-up questions.

17.10   Email your key person in advance of the conference

You will massively increase your chances of having a conversation with your key person if you email them before the conference to say that you would be interested in meeting them. Here is an example:

Subject: XYZ Conference: meeting to discuss ABC

Dear Professor Jones

I see from the program for the XYZ Conference that you will be giving a presentation on ABC. I am a researcher at The Institute and I am working in a very similar field. There seems to be a lot of overlap between our work and I think you might find my data useful for ... I was wondering if you might be able to spare 10 minutes of your time to answer a few questions.

There is a social dinner on the second night - perhaps we could meet 15 minutes before it begins, or of course any other time that might suit you.

I look forward to hearing from you.

The structure is as follows:

1. say how you know about the key person (i.e., they are attending the same conference as you)
2. briefly describe what you do
3. show how what you do relates to what they do
4. indicate how long the meeting might last (keep it as short as possible)
5. suggest a possible meeting place and time, but show flexibility

Of course, there is no guarantee they will even open your email, but if they do you will have created an opportunity for a meeting. Such an email requires minimal effort. It also helps to avoid the embarrassment of having to walk up to a complete stranger and introducing yourself in English.

17.11   Think of how the meeting could be beneficial not only to you but also to your key person

Although we sometimes do things purely for altruistic reasons, we are generally more motivated to help people if it seems that there might also be some benefit for us. It is thus a good idea to think of how a collaboration with you could benefit your key person—what knowledge do you have that would be useful for them, what part of their research could you do on their behalf, what contacts do you have that might be useful for them too?

17.12   Find out as much as you can about your key person, but be discreet

If you think that the meeting you have arranged could help you significantly in your career, then you need to do everything you can to ensure a successful outcome. Find out everything you can about the person—read their papers, find them on LinkedIn or Facebook, locate their personal website, or find about their academic achievements on their department's website. Find out what is important for them and what they are interested in aside from their research work. Look for things that you might have in common.

> I read in one of your papers that ...

> I was looking at your profile on your university's website and saw that ...

> Diego mentioned that you are doing some research into ...

Most people will be flattered that you have taken the time to read their papers or looked at their work profile. However, although most people will not mind if you have investigated a little about their professional life, they may find it creepy (i.e., weird and disturbing) if you have been looking at their holiday photos on Facebook and know all about their hobbies. So be extremely careful how you refer to the things that you have learned about the person.

You can make your meeting much more beneficial if you determine to find any person that you meet interesting. This will make you more animated and thus appear more interesting to your interlocutor. You will also be less distracted as you will be focusing totally on the other person.

During the conversation restate and / or summarize the key points to check that you have understood. This is also a way to keep your mind alert and at the same time proves your appreciation of your interlocutor's remarks.

17.13   Encourage your key person to come to your presentation or poster session

The more people who come to your presentation, the more people are likely to come up to you directly (or contact you via email) to discuss your work. To increase your chances of people coming, particularly your key person, you can do some self-publicity. To everyone you meet at the social events, at the bar, at the coffee machine, or wherever, you can say:

> I am doing a presentation on X tomorrow at 10.00 in Conference Room number 2. It would be great if you could come.
>
> If you are interested in X, then you might like to come to my presentation tomorrow. It's at 11.00 in Room 13.
>
> I don't know you would be interested, but this afternoon I am presenting my work on X. It's at three o'clock in the main conference hall.

Then you give the person your card, with a previously handwritten reminder on the back of the card stating the topic of the presentation, the time, and the location.

Chapter 18
Introducing Yourself and Conducting One-to-One Meetings

You will learn how to

- introduce yourself face to face in a variety of situations
- walk up to a complete stranger and ask to arrange a meeting
- set up and conduct informal meetings with key people
- ensure the best possible outcome of the meeting
- follow up on the meeting

Research shows that three factors determine a successful career: performance 10%, image and personal style 30%, and exposure and visibility 60%. The more visible you are as a researcher, the more likely you are to find more interesting and remunerative research positions. If you use a conference as an opportunity to introduce yourself to as many people as possible, you will help to widen your opportunities for new collaborations. However, merely introducing yourself is not sufficient. You also need to create a good first impression on your interlocutors and engage with them in small talk. Peter Honey, chartered psychologist and creator of Honey & Mumford Learning Styles Questionnaire, says,

> So far as other people are concerned, you are your behavior. Although there are other things which go towards making you the person you are—your thoughts, feelings, attitudes, motives, beliefs and so on—your behavior is apparent to everyone.

This chapter focuses on typical ways that Anglos introduce themselves and set up meetings. I am not suggesting that this is the best way to conduct such activities, but simply that this would be the norm if you were visiting countries where English is spoken as the first language.

In this chapter all the points apart from 18.7 refer to the person who wishes to set up the meeting.

A. Wallwork, *English for Academic Correspondence and Socializing*, 199
DOI 10.1007/978-1-4419-9401-1_18, © Springer Science+Business Media, LLC 2011

Factoids

❖ Why do people in some cultures shake hands when they meet or introduce themselves? One piece of popular folklore claims that when one caveman went to visit another caveman in his house, he put down his club (i.e., of a branch or stump of a tree used as a weapon) outside the house he was visiting. He reassured his "host" that he did not have any violent intentions by offering his hand—this proved that he was not holding his club. A similar story surrounds the origin of clubs (i.e., meeting places of associations)—everyone put down their club before entering the room!

❖ The word *protocol* refers a set of rules governing how communication should take place (e.g., behavior at a conference). Originally, in ancient Greece, it referred to a piece of paper that was glued onto a manuscript in order to identify the author. Similarly, the term *etiquette* (i.e., acceptable rules for social behavior) had its origins in the French custom of giving a little ticket to those who attended public ceremonies. This ticket gave attendees instructions on how to behave during the ceremony.

❖ The first visiting cards (i.e., a card that you left with the person whose house you had called on) appeared in France during the reign of Louis XIV. Business cards were first introduced to Britain in the eighteenth century and shortly after to the USA. In Japan, business cards are presented with both hands. Brazilians also exchange business cards on private occasions. The size of a standard business card varies from country to country with some of the biggest being in Scandinavian countries, Australia, and New Zealand.

❖ The English word *Goodbye* was originally four words: *God be with you*. These four words were said so fast that they merged into one word.

18.1   Learn how to introduce yourself for both formal and informal occasions

Most Anglos today introduce themselves in a very simple way by saying:

Hi, I'm James.

Hi, I'm James Smith.

Hello I'm James Smith.

Good morning I am Professor Smith.

Anglos say their first name (*James*) followed, in more formal situations, by their family name (*Smith*).

If someone asks *What is your name?* you would normally reply with both first and family names.

Anglos often give their own name rather than directly asking the interlocutor for his / her name. This may take place several minutes into the conversation, particularly if the conversation appears to be worth continuing. A typical introduction is as follows:

By the way, my name is Joe Bloggs.

Sorry, I have not introduced myself—I'm Joe Bloggs from NASA.

I don't think we have been introduced have we? I'm ...

At this point you would be expected to reply with your name.

Pleased to meet you. I'm Stomu Yamashata.

If you didn't hear the name of the person you have just been introduced to, you can say:

Sorry, I didn't catch your name.

Sorry, I didn't get your name clearly. Can you spell it for me?

Sorry, how do your pronounce your name?

Don't be reluctant to ask for a repetition of the name, otherwise you will spend the rest of the conversation looking at their name tag! Also, we all like it when people remember and use our name; we feel important and consequently we are more responsive to people who remember it.

If you are too embarrassed to ask someone to remind you of their name, then you could offer them your card and hopefully they will then give you their card. Giving someone your card also means that you immediately have something to talk about:

Oh, I see you are from Tokyo, I was there last year.

So you work for the Department of Linguistics, do you know Professor Kamatchi?

So you work in Italy, but I think you are from China, is that right?

18.2   Use people's titles where appropriate

In English there is only one form of *you*. If you wish to show someone respect, then you can use their title, for example, Dr or Professor. However, many Anglos consider titles as being quite formal, and they might simply say:

Please call me John.

This means that from that moment on the communication can take place in a more friendly atmosphere. In other words, if you are a PhD student and you are talking to Professor Smith, you should continue to address him as Professor Smith until he suggests otherwise.

In English there are a very limited number of titles; in the academic world there are only Dr and Professor. Your country may have many other titles, for example, lawyer and engineer. Such titles are impossible to translate into English. This means that if you are for example an engineer, you should not address another engineer as Engineer Smith, but simply as Dr Smith or Professor Smith. However, in emails (see 2.2) you might wish to address an engineer whose native language is not English using the word engineer in their language, for example, Herr Diplom Ingenieur Weber (for a German).

If you wish to give someone a title and that person is not an academic, then for men you can use *Mr* (pronounced *mister*) and for women *Ms* (pronounced *muz*, like the *cause* in *because*). *Mr* and *Ms* do not indicate whether the person is married or not. The terms *Mrs* (pronounced "misses") and *Miss* are not so commonly used nowadays as they indicate that the woman is married and unmarried, respectively— such information is not considered necessary for the interlocutor (see 2.3).

18.3   Prepare strategies for introducing yourself to a presenter after his / her presentation

After someone's presentation, you might like to ask them questions at the bar or at the social dinner. First you will probably need to attract their attention and introduce yourself.

> Excuse me, do you have a minute? Would you mind answering a few questions?

> Excuse me, do you think I could ask you a couple of questions about your presentation? Thanks. My name is ... and I work at ... I am doing some research on ... What I'd like to ask you is: ...

Other questions you might like to ask are as follows:

> Could you give me some more details about ...?

> Where can I get more information about ... ?

> Can I just ask you about something you said in your presentation?

> I'm not sure I understood your point about ... Could you clarify it for me?

> Have you uploaded your presentation? If so, where can I find it?

Many presenters are very tired immediately after doing their presentation and just want to get away and have a drink or something to eat. Also, if you are in a line with other people, the presenter will probably want to deal with each person in the line as quickly as possible.

So, when you finally get to talk to the presenter say:

> I don't want to take up your time now. But would it be possible for us to meet later this evening? I am in the same field of research as you, and I have a project that I think you might be interested in.

18.4   Learn how to introduce yourself to a group of people

To avoid having to introduce yourself into a group, you could try to arrive early at any social events. This means when you see your key person entering the room, you can go up to them immediately before they get immersed in a conversation.

If your key person is already chatting to another person or a group of people, then you need to observe their body language and how they are facing each other. If they are in a closed circle, quite close to each other and looking directly into each other's faces, it is probably best to choose another moment. However, if they are not too close, and there is space between them, then you can join them. In such cases you can say:

> Do you mind if I join you?

> I don't really know anyone else here. Do you mind if I join you?

> Is it OK if I listen in? [*to listen in* means to listen without actively participating]

> Sorry, I was listening from distance and what you are saying sounds really interesting.

Then you can wait for a lull (pause) in the conversation and introduce yourself:

> Hi, I'm Adrian from the University of Pisa.

At this point your have their attention. You can continue by asking a question to check that you have correctly identified your key person.

> Are you Professor Jonson? Because I have been really wanting to meet you.

If there is no key person in the group, but in any case the conversation seems interesting. You can say:

> What you were saying about x is really interesting because I have been doing some similar research and ...

> So where do you two work?

Thus, you can either immediately start talking about what you do or ask the other people a question. Asking a question is the most polite strategy as it shows that you are interested in them. It also gives you a chance to tune into their voice.

At some point, someone in the group will probably ask you what you do. Rather than stating your position in academia (e.g., *I am a PhD student. I am a lecturer. I am an assistant professor.*), it is generally best to say something more descriptive and specific:

> I am investigating new ways to produce fuel efficient cars.

> I am doing some research into the sensations people have when beggars ask them for money.

If you are more descriptive, people are more likely to make comments or ask questions. If you just say *I am a PhD student*, then the conversation may then be directed to someone else.

In any case, make sure you do not spend too much time talking about yourself. Find out what the other members of the group are interested in and focus on that.

If you no longer wish to keep talking to the group, you can say:

> Well, it's been really interesting talking to you. I'll see you around.

> I've really enjoyed talking to you. Enjoy the rest of the conference.

The use of the present perfect (*it has been, I have enjoyed*) immediately alerts the rest of the group that you are about to leave.

18.5   Exploit opportunities for introductions at the coffee machine

If your key person is alone by the coffee machine, this is a great opportunity as you will hopefully get their undivided attention.

First you need to attract the key person's attention. Here are some phrases you could use:

> Excuse me. I heard you speak in the round table / I saw your presentation this morning.

> Hi, do you have a couple of minutes for some questions?

> Excuse me, could I just have a word with you? I am from ...

> I am X from the University of Y, do you think I could ask you a couple of questions?

Second, it is generally a good idea to say something positive about the person and / or their work:

> I really enjoyed your presentation this morning—it was certainly the most useful of today's sessions.

> I thought what you said at the round table discussion was really useful.

Third, suggest you move to somewhere where you can sit.

> Thank you, shall we go and sit in the bar?

> Shall we go and sit over there where it is a bit quieter?

If you see that they are in a hurry, then it is best to arrange to meet later. Show that you understand that the person is busy and that you don't want to take up much of their time. In fact, tell them the exact amount of time involved, this is more likely to get them to accept.

> Would after lunch suit you?

> Shall we meet at the bar?

> When do you think you might be free? When would suit you?

> Would tonight after the last session be any good for you?

> Could you manage 8.45 tomorrow? That would give us about 10 minutes before the morning session starts.

> I promise I won't take any more than 10 minutes of your time.

If they agree to your proposal, then you can say:

> That would be great / perfect.

> That's very kind of you.

18.6   Be prepared for what to say if your proposal for a meeting is not accepted

If they don't agree to your proposal, then you can say:

Oh, I understand, don't worry it's not a problem.

That's fine. No problem. Enjoy the rest of the conference.

OK I have really enjoyed speaking to you in any case.

In any case, maybe I could email you the questions? Would that be alright?

18.7   Be ready for someone wanting to set up a meeting with you

If you are happy to meet with the person, you can agree by saying:

Yes, that's fine, but would you mind meeting tomorrow as I am bit busy now?

Yes, fine, but I do only have about 10 minutes available.

If you want to find out more, you can ask:

What exactly is it that you need to know?

Could you tell me what information you need?

But if for some reason you cannot or do not want to meet with the person, you can make an excuse:

I'm sorry but I really don't have time at the moment.

Sorry, but I'm really very busy.

I'm sorry but I just need to have a look at my notes and I'll catch up with you later—I'll see you around.

18.8   Prepare well for any informal one-to-one meetings

Your meeting will be far more beneficial if both parties prepare for it. It is a good idea to let the person know in advance exactly what information you need. For this reason, setting up meetings for the following day is a good tactic as it gives the other person time to think about the answers. In such cases you can say:

Would you mind giving me your email address, so that I can email you my questions?

I have prepared a list of three questions that I would like to ask you—they are here on this sheet. If perhaps you could take a look at them before we meet, that would be great.

Having questions prepared indicates that you are a serious person who is not going waste the person's time.

18.9   Be positive throughout informal one-to-one meetings

The outcome of an informal meeting often depends on how well it begins. If your key person is late for the meeting, reassure them that it is not a problem:

> Don't worry, I am very grateful you could come.

> No problem, it doesn't matter.

> Can I get you a coffee?

If you are late:

> I am so sorry I am late—I got held up paying my bill—have you been waiting long?

First, acknowledge that you are grateful that the person has found the time to meet with you.

> First of all, it is very kind of you to come.

> Thank you so much for coming. I really appreciate it.

> Did you have time to have a look at the questions I sent you?

Ensure that you only make positive comments about the conference, its location, and its organization. People respond much better to positive-thinking people and are more likely to listen to them and consequently to consider future collaborations. So avoid negative comments such as:

> Last year's edition of this conference was much better don't you think?

> I have been so bored by some of the presentations.

> I have been surprised by the total lack of any decent social events.

Instead, find something positive to say:

> I really enjoyed the first presentation yesterday.

> The trip to the museum was very interesting I thought.

> I am enjoying trying out all the local food.

There is always a chance that the person provides you with no useful information at all. Nevertheless, it is always best to show interest and take a few notes.

Give your key person time to express themselves, but be sure you respect the timeframe that you arranged, and then conclude by saying:

> OK, I don't want to keep you any longer.

> Well, I don't want to take up any more of your time.

Well I think we've covered all the questions ... but would it be OK if I email you if I need any further clarifications?

Well, it was really kind of you to spare your time / of you to come

What you said has been really interesting and useful, thank you.

I am sure there are other people you will be wanting to meet.

18.10   A verbal exchange is like a game of ping pong: always give your interlocutor an opportunity to speak

It is fundamental never to dominate any verbal exchange, particularly if your interlocutor is someone who could potentially help you.

An exchange should be like a game of table tennis (ping pong). You speak for a few seconds, then you send the "ball" to the other person by finding a way to let him / her speak, then he / she speaks and passes the ball back to you.

Compare the following two dialogs, in which a researcher, Carlos, is interested in collaborating with an expert in neurolinguistics, Professor Jaganathan. Carlos hopes the professor might offer him a position in her laboratory.

DIALOG 1

Carlos: Good morning Professor Jaganathan. I saw your presentation this morning and in my opinion it was very good. My name is Carlos Nascimento and I work at the Brazilian National Research Council. My field of interest is neurolinguistics applied to second language learning. Last year we began some experiments on blah blah blah blah ... [*talks continuously for another three minutes*]. I believe our fields of interest have much in common. I was wondering if you might be available to discuss a possible collaboration together. Would you be free for dinner tonight, or tomorrow evening? It would be very useful for me if we could meet. And also ...

Jaganathan: Um, sorry I am rather busy at the moment, could you send me an email?

Professor Jaganathan's reaction may be to think that an evening with Carlos would be hard work. She would have to listen to the constant flow of Carlos's incessant talking. The impression might be that Carlos is only interested in himself and that for him Professor Jaganathan is just a means to his end. Also, his comment about Professor Jaganathan's presentation being "very good" sounds like he is the expert rather than her.

Carlos's perspective may be very different. He may think that by talking in this manner he will be creating a good impression because it shows that he is confident.

Another possible reason for him talking so much is that he is nervous. When we are nervous we often talk a lot more and at a faster speed than we would normally do. This usually does not create a good impression on our listener.

DIALOG 2

Carlos: Good morning Professor Jaganathan, my name is Carlos Nascimento. (1) Do you have a minute?

Jaganathan: Er, yes. But I have to be at a meeting in ten minutes.

Carlos: (2) Well, I promise I won't take more than two minutes of your time. (3) I thought your presentation was really very interesting. (4) I am just curious to know how you set the last experiments up. It must have been quite challenging.

Jaganathan: You are right it was. In fact, we had to . . . and then we had to . . . and finally we . . .

Carlos: That's really interesting. Well, my group in Rio did a very similar experiment, and I think our results and our project in general might be (5) very useful for you in terms of speeding up the test times.

Jaganathan: Really?

Carlos: So I was wondering if you might be free for a few minutes at the (6) social dinner tonight, or tomorrow evening? (7)

Jaganathan: Sure, that sounds great. Let's make it tonight.

The second dialog is much more successful because Carlos

1. gives the professor an opportunity to say that she cannot speak now; this is also a sign of respect
2. tells her how much of her time he requires (i.e., *two minutes*)—this will reassure her that she will not miss her meeting
3. compliments her on her presentation in a way that makes him sound genuinely appreciative
4. asks her a question about her work and makes a supposition about the difficulties involved (*challenging*)—this gives her an opportunity to talk and also puts her at the center of attention rather than just him
5. gives a reason why she should be interested in talking with him.

6. does not ask her to have dinner alone with him but in the context of a social event—this means that she doesn't feel any embarrassment or pressure

7. makes an arrangement without mentioning anything about a "collaboration" —Carlos will then delay mentioning a collaboration until he has given the professor enough valid reasons to be interested in such a collaboration

The result is that Professor Jaganathan is happy to meet with Carlos.

To be able to communicate in the way I have suggested in Dialog 2, you really need to practice beforehand. You need to think carefully about what you are going to say. But just as importantly you must think about how you can avoid dominating the exchange by finding ways to encourage your interlocutor to speak. Given the importance of such exchanges, I strongly recommend that you simulate the exchange with a colleague. Try it first in your own language, and then in English.

The same principles are also true when you say goodbye—either at the end of a conversation, or at the end of the conference itself. Again you play ping pong, as highlighted in the dialog below in which Carlos says goodbye to Professor Jaganathan on the last day of the conference.

DIALOG 3

Carlos: Professor Jaganathan, I just wanted to say how much I enjoyed meeting you the other night. The food was great wasn't it?

Jaganathan: Yes, it was really delicious and the location was great too.

Carlos: So, when I get back to Rio I will discuss what we said with my professor and then he will contact you. Is that still OK with you?

Jaganathan: Yes, of course.

Carlos: And finally can I just thank you again both for your presentation and particularly for finding the time to speak with me—I really appreciate it. Have a great trip back to Bombay.

Jaganathan: Thank you.

Of course, the professor doesn't participate as much as Carlos in the exchange, but at least she feels she is being considered.

Again, if you simply improvise such exchanges, rather than preparing for them in advance, you may give a rather negative impression on your interlocutor.

Carlos also takes the opportunity to summarize what has been decided (*I will discuss . . .*). Making such summaries of important meetings is vital for both sides to ensure that there are no misunderstandings.

18.11   Ensure that you follow up on your meeting

One of the most important aspects of networking is to follow up on a face-to-face meeting. Many of the potential benefits of the meeting will be lost if you don't take advantage of them by sending an email, such as the one below.

Dear Professor Kisunaite,

I am the student in Social Psychology from *name of institute / country*.

Thank you very much for sparing the time to meet with me last week. Your comments were particularly useful.

As I mentioned at our meeting, if by any chance a position arises in your laboratory I would be very grateful if you would consider me - my CV is attached.

I am also attaching a paper which I am currently writing that I think you will find of interest.

Once again, thank you for all your help and I do hope we will meet again in the near future.

Best regards

This email acts as a reminder to the professor of

- who you are
- what you discussed
- what decisions were reached and / or what offer was made

Chapter 19
How to Have Successful Social Conversations

You will learn how to

- show interest in your interlocutor
- make small talk and have informal discussions
- improve your listening skills by taking a more active part in conversations and by perceiving listening as a productive rather than passive activity
- find excuses for ending a conversation

To have a successful conversation and consequently to improve your chances at being involved in new research collaborations, you need to learn a series of social skills. These include being able to break the ice, carry forward a conversation, listen carefully, create an interpersonal bond, take turns in talking, collaborate with your interlocutor to fill silences by referring back to something that was said earlier, react sensitively to what is being said, contribute and make the right comments / noises when someone is telling a story, embark on safe topics, and exit when required. When speaking in another language, we tend to forget the social skills that we have in our own language. However, these skills are imperative for successful business and social encounters.

For useful phrases to use in the context of socializing see Chapter 26.

A. Wallwork, *English for Academic Correspondence and Socializing*,
DOI 10.1007/978-1-4419-9401-1_19, © Springer Science+Business Media, LLC 2011

What the experts say

The art of conversation is the art of hearing as well as of being heard.

William Hazlitt (1778–1830), English writer and grammarian

It is an impertinent and unreasonable fault in conversation for one man to take up all the discourse.

Richard Steele (1672–1729), Irish writer and politician

Never speak of yourself to others; make them talk about themselves instead: therein lies the whole art of pleasing. Everyone knows it and everyone forgets it.

Edmond de Goncourt (1822–1896) and Jules de Goncourt (1830–1870), French writers

Encounters with people of so many different kinds and on so many different psychological levels have been for me incomparably more important than fragmentary conversations with celebrities. The finest and most significant conversations of my life were anonymous.

Carl Jung (1875–1961) Swiss psychiatrist, founder of analytical psychology

Apart from theology and sex there is really nothing to talk about.

Harold J Laski (1893–1950), English political scientist

Beware of the conversationalist who adds "in other words." He is merely starting afresh.

Robert Morley (1908–1992), English actor

19.1   Analyze what makes a successful conversation

Different people from different cultures have different ways of conversing. Even men and women of the same nationality converse in a different way. Various researchers in the USA and UK have shown that in many countries in the West, women tend to disclose more about themselves than men, and men tend to focus more on their accomplishments and sport. Women often use more words and give more details than men, with the consequence that men "tune out." In a work environment women tend to take things more literally, and men tend be more lacking in sensitivity. Finally, men tend to interrupt more in a discussion or conversation than women.

The dialog below is an example of what in many countries would be considered as an unsuccessful conversation. It is between a woman (W) and a man (M), but it is not intended to show any differences in the way the two sexes converse. They have never met before and they are waiting for a presentation to begin at a conference.

W   Sorry, is this seat taken?
M   No.
W   There are a lot of people here for this session, aren't there?
M   Yes, there seem to be.
W   Do you know the presenter? I think she is from Harvard.
M   Yes.
W   Hi, my name's Eriko Suzuki, I work for a Japanese pharmaceutical company. And you?
M   I'm in medical research.
W   What kind of medical research if I can ask?
M   Smoking-related diseases.
W   Really? That's interesting because we are developing some medicine to help smokers stop smoking.
M   Oh.
W   I work in the research department there and we are looking for collaborations. *pause* So is this your first time in Istanbul?
M   No, I have been here many times.
W   Many times?
M   Yes.
W   Oh, I have just seen a colleague of mine over there. Bye.

The dialog is obviously exaggerated, but it does highlight a common problem in conversations—ones that are completely one-sided. The woman is trying to be friendly, but the man rejects all her attempts at getting the conversation going. It may simply be that the man is shy and / or is worried about not speaking good English. But the impression he gives to the woman is that he simply does not wish to communicate. This leads to a breakdown in the communication and the result is that the man misses a possible opportunity to collaborate with the pharmaceutical company where the woman works.

Below is a different version of the same dialog. Note how the two speakers

- immediately start a friendly conversation
- share experiences
- show interest in what the other person is saying
- repeat back the same question that they have been asked
- repeat back what their interlocutor has just said to encourage him / her to continue
- avoid dominating the conversation and take equal responsibility for its success
- interrupt a lull (i.e. a silent pause) in the conversation by referring back to what the other said earlier

The context of the dialog is the same, but the dynamics are very different.

W   Sorry, is this seat taken?
M   No sorry I just put my bag here that's all. I'll just move it so you can sit down.
W   Thanks. There are a lot of people here for this session, aren't there?
M   Yes, I think we are all here to hear the professor from Harvard, she's supposed to be really good.
W   Yeah, I have read a lot of her papers. Really excellent. Have you come far to be here?
M   Well not too far, from Cairo actually. And you?
W   From Cairo wow! I've come from Tokyo I work for a pharmaceutical company. I'm Eriko, by the way.
M   Ahmed. Pleased to meet you. So you work for a pharmaceutical company?
W   Yes, I am in the research department. We are developing an anti-smoking drug.
M   Well that's a coincidence. At my lab we are working on smoking-related diseases.
W   Well I must introduce you to my boss, he will be interested.
M   Great idea, maybe you could introduce him to me after this morning's sessions.
W   Yeah, definitely. [*silence for a few seconds*] So you were saying you are from Cairo, do you mean you were born there?

The keys to a successful conversation are as follows:

- take equal responsibility for keeping the conversation going
- introduce new topics naturally—don't jump from one topic to another
- link what you say to what other person has just said
- show interest

The rest of this chapter is dedicated to outlining strategies for a successful conversation.

19.2   Try to judge how formal or informal you should be

A frequent cause of misunderstanding and embarrassment is when two people expect a different level of formality from each other.

Let's imagine a meeting between a male Spanish researcher and a male researcher from India, both with identical roles within their respective universities.

The Spanish researcher is probably accustomed to conducting social exchanges on an informal and friendly level. He would be surprised if his interlocutor referred to him as "Sir" during such a conversation. In such cases, he might feel that his interlocutor is putting him on a superior level, which he does not feel comfortable with.

By contrast, the Indian may perceive the Spanish researcher as trying too hard to be friendly and this may make him feel uneasy. The Indian is used to showing people respect and in return being shown respect.

There is no easy solution to this very common situation when different cultures meet with differing ideas about the norms of communication. Both the Spanish and the Indian researchers are conducting a conversation following their own norms. The secret is probably just to be aware that we don't all socialize in the same way, and to try and adopt some neutral middle ground where we are neither too friendly nor too formal, and where both parties feel comfortable.

19.3   Be aware of what is and what is not interesting for your interlocutor

I was telling my wife, Anna, about a new PhD student of mine, Sofia, from Estonia. The conversation went something like this:

Me: I've got this new student from Estonia.
Anna: Uh huh [*has an expressionless face*].
Me: She speaks Estonian, and her father's from Russia, so she speaks fluent Russian too. Apparently the two languages, Russian and Estonian, have nothing in common. Estonian is Uralic language, so it's actually got more in common with Finnish. She speaks Turkish too, and some other languages, and her English is great.
Anna: Uh [*starts looking out of the window*].
Me: She said that the population is only one and a quarter million, and that Tallinn, the capital, is a Unesco world heritage site. It's meant to be incredibly beautiful.
Anna: Oh [*takes out her Blackberry*].
Me: She was really enthusiastic, I thought we could go there some time for a short holiday.
Anna: A holiday? [*stops playing with her Blackberry*] Great idea. When? A Unesco site did you say?
Me: Yes.
Anna: Wasn't Estonia once part of the USSR?
Me: That's right.
Anna: So does she speak Russian?

My wife had only been half listening to me until the point where I suggested we could go to Tallinn. What I was telling her was really only of interest to me (I love languages). But once the holiday (Anna loves traveling) was mentioned, she became interested not only in Estonia but also in Sofia, and asked me if Sofia spoke Russian—she had no recollection that 20 seconds before I had told her that Sofia's father was Russian and that she spoke fluent Russian.

If I had begun the conversation saying *I think we should plan a short holiday to Tallinn*, then Anna would have paid much more attention to the other things I mentioned.

This is important because if you want to be a successful networker and be able to set up new collaborations, then it helps if you can talk about things that will be of interest to your interlocutor. Imagine the topic of conversation is holidays. A lot of people may not be particularly interested to hear what hotel you stayed in, what museums you visited, how much the metro cost, and so on—unless of course they are planning to go there themselves. They are more interested in holiday disasters: planes rerouted or cancelled, luggage lost, food poisoning.

By listening and analyzing the conversations going on around you, you should be able to get a clearer idea of what topics people find interesting, and more specifically, what aspects of those topics generate interest.

19.4   Begin by making small talk

Small talk means the initial exchanges people have on non-risk topics such as the weather, the hotel where you are staying, and how you traveled to your meeting place. Cultures differ considerably in the way they attempt to establish a relationship using small talk. In much of Europe and North America, initial conversations often focus on the person's job, and in Japan on the organization they work for. Arabs, on the other hand, may initially attempt to find out about each other's family identity.

Such exchanges enable you and your interlocutor to

- get used to each other's accents and style of speaking. You are not giving each other essential information, so it does not matter at this point if you do not understand everything you say to each other
- find your voice in English
- make a connection with each other
- learn a little personal information that you might be able to refer to in future conversations
- make some positive comments about each other. This positive feeling will then be useful if any negative comments need to be made later on (e.g., in a technical discussion)

Typical questions that people ask while making small talk are as follows:

It's a bit cloudy, isn't it?

Do you think it's going to rain later on?

Did you have to travel far to get here?

Which hotel are you staying in?

What do you think of the conference so far?

Have you been here before?

Did you go on the excursion yesterday?

To move the conversation forward, you can introduce yourself and exchange cards. This gives you an easy way to begin talking about your research areas.

By the way, my name's *your name*. Here is my card.

Oh, I see you are from the university of *name of town*.

So, how long have you been a researcher at *name of institute*?

How long have you been working for *name of institute*?

Are you here with anyone else from your institute?

What exactly do you do at *name of institute*?

If you quickly exhaust work-related questions, you can ask more personal questions such as

So, where are you from? Whereabouts exactly?

So, what's it like living in *name of town / country*?

Are you giving a presentation? What on?

Are you coming to the social dinner tonight?

19.5   Show interest

Everyone likes it when people show genuine interest in them—it gives them a feeling of importance and recognition. You can show interest in other people by asking questions and by showing that you are 100% focused on listening to the answers. If you find a topic that seems to interest them more than other topics, then try to ask more questions about this particular topic. In any case, focus on questions that you think that your interlocutor will take pleasure in answering.

If you are not naturally curious about other people, a good way to think of questions is to use *how*, *where*, *why*, *when*, *what*. For example:

> *How* did you get to the conference? By plane? By train?

> *Where* are you staying?

> *Why* did you decide to come to this conference?

> *When* are you doing your presentation?

> *What* are you planning to visit while you are here?

When you listen to the answers, try to show some reaction or at least that you are listening to what your interlocutor is saying. The most typical word native speakers use is *really* which is said in the form of a question and is designed to encourage the speaker to continue. Another typical comment is *right*. For example, let's imagine that the dialog below takes place in Budapest (Hungary).

> So where are you from?
> From Stockholm in Sweden.
> Oh right, so how did you get here?
> By train.
> Really?
> Yes, I don't like traveling by plane.
> Right.
> And you, where are you from?
> Well, I'm from Budapest actually.
> Oh really?
> Yes, I was born here.

Other expressions you might use are

> I see.

> That's interesting.

> Wow.

> Fantastic.

It might feel very unnatural for you to use any of these phrases, but remember you should not say them in an exaggerated way with a lot of emphasis. Just say them in a neutral way and quite quietly. They are basically verbal noises that demonstrate to your interlocutors that you are interested in what they are saying.

19.6   Ask open questions

Some questions could simply be answered *yes* or *no*. For instance:

> Did you have a good time at the museum?

> How was the presentation?

The above questions are called closed questions, because potentially the person could simply answer *yes* or *no* and thus "close" the conversation. Typically, they make use of auxiliary verbs (*did, can, are, have*, etc.). If you find that your interlocutor is just giving you *yes no* answers, it will soon become an effort for you to continue the conversation. So you could rephrase the questions as follows:

So, what did you see at the museum? Where is the museum exactly? Which exhibits did you see?

What did you learn from the presentation? Why did you choose to go to that particular presentation?

The above are what is known as open questions, and again they make use of question words such as *what, which, why, when, where*.

19.7   Ask follow-up questions

The natural course of a conversation should not be a series of unrelated questions and topics, but a thread of logically linked questions. First you ask a topic question and then you ask another question (or make a comment) related to the same topic in which you ask for more details. Here is an example:

You: So where did you go on holiday?
Them: To Berlin.
You: (1) *Follow-up*: So what did you think of the architecture?
You: (2) *Comment*: I've heard the architecture is amazing.
You: (3) *Encouragement*: So tell me all about Berlin.

19.8   Encourage your interlocutor to continue talking on the same topic

There are many ways to encourage someone to give more details on a topic that has just been initiated:

Restate part of what they have just said:

Them: But the food was terrible.
You: Terrible?
Them: Yes, in fact we had one really bad experience when . . .

Make mini summaries of what they've just said:

You: So the architecture was great, but the food was terrible.
Them: Yeah, and then we had a few problems at the hotel.

Paraphrase or agree with what they just said:

Them: Exactly. And his presentation was so boring.
You: (1) *Agree*: Yeah, really boring.
You: (2) *Paraphrase*: Yeah, a complete waste of time. I thought that the only interesting part was ...

Show interest by asking for clarification:

Them: And the hotel was not exactly cheap.
You: What do you mean by "not exactly cheap"?
Them: Well they added on a lot of extra services.
You: For example? What kind of services?
Them: And they had a disco every night.
You: So you're saying that it was very noisy? You didn't get much sleep. I had a similar experience last month in ...

Note how in the above exchanges the strategy is to use the clarification to initiate something that you want to say (e.g., *I thought that the only interesting part was ...* and *I had a similar experience last month in ...*). Basically you are showing respect for the other person by using a clarification to show interest in what they have said. This then allows you to take your "speaking turn" in the conversation. If you ask for clarification this also enables your interlocutor to make any adjustments to what they said either to help you understand better or to add details.

19.9   Make "announcements" rather than asking all the questions

If you find that you are asking all the questions, then there are two possible results. One is that you may become frustrated with the attention always being focused on your interlocutor. The other is that your interlocutor might think that you are being rather invasive.

So sometimes you need to initiate a topic yourself. If for example you have been asking question's about your interlocutor's hotel (as in 19.8 above), you can announce:

You: Well, I am staying at the Excelsior Hotel and it's not exactly cheap there either.

You: I know what you mean about the noise, where I am staying I get woken up at five every morning with people setting up their stalls at the market.

In the above examples you have directly related your experience to your interlocutor's experience. You also show that you have been listening carefully as you have repeated some of their concepts and phrases.

Other times you may want to initiate a completely new topic.

This afternoon I am giving a presentation.

Yesterday I had a look around the old town.

Tonight a group of people from my institute are going to ...

By introducing a new topic you hope that your interlocutor will ask you some questions, and thus create a more balanced exchange. However, bear in mind that if your interlocutor seems unwilling to contribute it may have nothing to do with you—they may just be having a bad day.

19.10   Offer more information than you are asked for

If you are asked a question, try to move the conversation forward by giving some extra information in your answer. For example, if you are at a conference that has been organized by your university and a foreign attendee asks you, "So are you a student here?" you could say, "Yes, I am a PhD student. I'm doing research on cross-cultural differences in first meetings." If you just replied "yes" then your questioner might perceive you as either being rude or reluctant to continue the conversation. This might be a wasted opportunity to meet a fellow researcher and discuss your field of research.

19.11   Avoid dominating the conversation

Many non-native speakers are afraid or embarrassed about not being able to follow a conversation due to poor listening skills. One strategy that some use is to try to increase the amount of time they spend speaking. Clearly the more you speak, the less you need to understand other people.

If you adopt this "talking rather than listening" strategy, continually check that your listeners are following you and are interested in what you are saying. If they are not giving you any eye contact, it probably means that either they cannot understand you or they have lost interest.

You may compromise your chances of future collaborations if you are seen to dominate conversations. The solution is to accept the fact that you will not understand everything and as a consequence let all the group of people you are with talk in equal amounts.

Below are two tactics for taking the focus off yourself.

Transfer their original question back to them:

> Them: So, are you going anywhere interesting this summer?
> You: blah blah blah. And what about you? Have you got any plans for the summer?

Ask them if they have had a similar experience:

> You: .. and during the presentation my laptop suddenly crashed.
> Them: Oh no!
> You: So I had to blah blah blah. Have you ever had any disasters like that?

19.12   Feel free to interrupt people who talk too much

In 1711, Joseph Addison, English essayist, poet, playwright, and politician, wrote,

> The English delight in Silence more than any other European Nation, if the Remarks which are made on us by Foreigners are true. Our Discourse is not kept up in Conversation, but falls into more Pauses and Intervals than in our Neighbouring Countries. To favour our Natural Taciturnity, when we are obliged to utter our Thoughts, we do it in the shortest way we are able.

Not everyone delights in silence! Some people are used to talking a lot and having a quiet audience. For you as a listener, in a social context this may not be too much of a problem. You can simply "switch off," look out of the window, and start thinking about something more interesting. However, when having a technical discussion, informal or formal, you may wish to get your own point of view across. In such situations it is perfectly legitimate to interrupt. You can say in a friendly tone:

Sorry to interrupt you but ...

Can I just make a point?

Just a minute, before I forget ...

Actually, I am quite curious to hear what Stanislav has to say about this.

19.13   Involve everyone in the conversation

There is often a tendency in a group conversation for those who speak the best English to dominate the conversation and to form a sub group. This leaves the other part of your group in silence. If your English is at a higher level than some of the others, or if you are more extrovert than them, don't use this entirely to your own advantage or as an opportunity to show off your excellent English in front of your colleagues. Instead people will appreciate it if you try and involve them. Here are some examples of how to do draw people into a conversation:

Vladimir, I think you have had a similar experience haven't you?

Monique, you were telling me earlier that ...

Bogdan, I think you and Monique must be staying at the same hotel.

Domingo I see on the program that you are doing a presentation this afternoon, what's it about exactly?

Kim, Melanie told me you are into bungee jumping.

Yoko, I read that Japan has a new government.

19.14   Avoid long silences

Different cultures have different tolerance levels for the length of periods of silence in a conversation. So don't think that you necessarily have to fill every silence. You can use the pause to think up new areas that you could talk about. Below are some tactics for re-initiating a conversation.

Return to a topic mentioned earlier or other information that you know about the person:

> So you were saying before that you had just come back from a conference. What exactly was the conference?

> I seem to remember that you once lived in London, am I right?

Introduce a new topic:

> So did you go to the social dinner last night?

> Did you hear about that hurricane in Florida?

> So do you think Brazil will win the world cup?

19.15   Avoid sounding rude

In your own language you are generally aware of when you are being impolite. You know what little phrases you can use to sound polite. The problem of not knowing such courtesy forms in English is that you might appear abrupt or rude to your interlocutors. A native speaker may be surprised by your tone because in other contexts, for example, when you are describing technical details or in writing papers / letters, you may appear to them to have a strong command of English.

The secret is to try and show some agreement with what your interlocutor is saying before you introduce your own point of view. Let's imagine two people are discussing the relative advantages and disadvantages of nuclear power. Below are some phrases that they could use in order to express their opinions without being too forceful.

> I agree with you when you say ... but nevertheless I do think that ...

> You have an interesting point there, however ...

> I quite understand what you're saying, but have you thought about ...

> Water power definitely has an important role, but did you know that it actually pollutes more than nuclear power?

> I agree with you, but I also believe that ...

The sun is certainly a safe source of energy, but ...

I know exactly what you mean, but another viewpoint / interpretation could be ...

Another typical case is when you are comparing the results of various people's research, including the people present at the discussion. Here you have to be very careful.

Professor X's results on Y are very interesting but they seem to me to be in contrast with ...

I do think your results are very interesting, but a case could be made to say that they are not quite as realistic as Professor Y's—do you think there is some truth in that?

If I could just make a comment ... I think that what these two presentations highlight is that there can be substantially different approaches to this problem. Personally, I ...

You may remember in Prof X's presentation yesterday, he gave us some results, which personally I tend to agree with. They seem to be quite different from yours, why do you think that might be?

It is not easy to be diplomatic in a foreign language, so if you do inadvertently say something that produces a bad reaction, you can say:

I am sorry, it is very difficult for me to say these things in English.

Sorry, I tend to be too direct when I speak in English.

I'm so sorry I didn't mean to sound rude.

Sometimes you need to find a way out of a discussion or at least time to pause and think.

Sorry, I just need to make a phone call.

Sorry, I just need to go to the bathroom.

Can I just think about that a second?

Just a moment. I need to think.

Sorry, I'll have to check up on that.

19.16   Express disagreement diplomatically

If your aim is to build up a relationship in a harmonious environment, then it is worth bearing the following factors in mind.

- If someone says something that you don't agree with, but the point they are making is not really important, then there is probably no benefit in contesting it
- If someone says something that is not true (but which they themselves clearly believe to be true), for example, some erroneous data, they will probably

not appreciate being confronted directly with the true facts—you will simply undermine their self-esteem

- Most people do not appreciate someone casting doubt on their opinions and beliefs, and are more likely to be even more convinced of their beliefs if these beliefs are attacked

If you decide to disagree, then try to find some aspect of what your interlocutor has said that you can agree with. State this agreement and then mention the area where you disagree. This shows that you are at least trying to understand their point of view, and that your intentions are not hostile.

> Speaker A: Your government seems to be in a complete mess at the moment.
> Speaker B: I know what you mean, and there are a lot of people in my country think so too. Some progress is being made in any case. I don't know if you've heard that ...

Note how Speaker B avoids using words like *but*, *nevertheless*, and *however* (*Some progress is being made* rather than *But some progress is being made*). Frequent use of words such as *but* may put your interlocutors on the defensive and they will simply come up with more evidence to support their initial statement. This could then lead to an embarrassing argument.

If someone says something that you believe is not true, then a good tactic is to be diplomatic and say something like:

> Oh really? I may be wrong, but I'd always thought that ...

> I didn't know that. What I heard / read was that ...

19.17   Be prepared for dealing with difficult questions

Sometimes people may ask you questions that you do not wish to answer. You can say:

> I really don't have any opinion on that.

> That's an interesting question, but I don't think I am qualified to answer it.

> That may be, I couldn't really say.

> I'm afraid I don't know anything about it.

> It's not really for me to say.

> It depends how you look at it.

> I'm sorry, I don't want to go into that.

Or alternatively you can revert the question back to the questioner:

> Why, what do you think about it?

If, on the other hand, you want to ask a question that you think might be potentially difficult or embarrassing for your interlocutor, then you can precede the question or statement by saying:

Is it OK to ask about ... ?

Do you mind me mentioning ... ?

Can I ask you what you think about ... ?

It seems that some people in your country think that ... What do you think might be the reason for that?

19.18   Direct the conversation to areas where you have a wider vocabulary or knowledge

Sometimes your ability to participate in and contribute to a conversation will depend on the vocabulary you have available on that particular topic. If you feel you don't have the vocabulary required, you could try to gently shift the conversation to an area where you know a greater number of relevant words. Of course, this shift must be to a related area rather than a totally new topic, unless there is a complete silence where it would be justified to change topic.

Food is often a subject at social dinners, regarding not only the menu of the meal itself, but also discussions about the national and typical dishes of those around the table. Discussing such dishes involves a lot of specialized vocabulary regarding ingredients and cooking techniques. However, there are other aspects of food that also have a strong cultural interest. You can inject considerable interest into a conversation about food, if you talk about the social aspects of food and eating, rather than just typical dishes. For example, you could discuss

- taboos—what foods are not acceptable to be eaten by humans (e.g., in the UK, horsemeat is rarely eaten, and cat and dog meat are never eaten)
- fasting—what foods are prohibited for religious reasons at certain times of the year
- events—what foods people eat on particular occasions (e.g., in the USA it is common to eat turkey to celebrate Christmas)
- etiquette—how guests are expected to behave (e.g., can you refuse if your host offers you more food? should you take a gift, if so what is and is not appropriate? should you take off your shoes before entering someone's house?)
- production methods—e.g., genetic engineering
- the pros and cons of being vegetarian
- food allergies

There are three ways to do this:

- Wait for a pause in the conversation and initiate a change in topic by saying: In my country at this time of year, we can't eat meat ...
- Invite others to begin a discussion by saying: I am curious to know whether anyone else is allergic to ...
- Ask a question: In your country do you have many vegetarians?

The result of this is that you will find social events more rewarding and less frustrating. Also, people will see you as someone who is able to manage a conversation and make useful contributions. These two skills are obviously also applicable outside a strictly social situation and in the context of work. Thus, you will demonstrate that you are the kind of person that is easy and efficient to work with.

19.19   Have ready excuses for ending a conversation

If you find that your interlocutor is failing to interact with you and that the situation is becoming awkward, then you might decide to end the conversation by making an excuse:

Sorry, I have just seen an old colleague of mine. I'll catch you later.

Sorry, I've just received an sms—do you mind if I just take a look?

Do you know where the bathroom is?

I just need to get a bottle of water. Maybe I'll see you at the presentation?

Even if you have not had a long conversation, try to end on a positive note and thus leave a good impression with your interlocutor. You never know when you might see them again, or what opportunities for collaboration might arise. So, smile as you say goodbye, and say:

Well, it was nice talking to you.

Well, I hope to see you at the dinner tonight.

I'll try and make sure I come to your presentation.

I'll catch up with you later.

19.20   Have ready excuses for turning down invitations for social activities

If you feel that you do not wish to participate in some social events, such as dinners or visits to clubs, then it helps if you can say something that will prevent your interlocutors from convincing you to do something against your will. If you say something like *actually, I am really tired and would like to get to bed early*, the others can simply say *well none of us are planning to be late back* or *you can sleep during tomorrow's workshop*. It is much simpler to say something like *I am sorry but I need to stay in tonight*, without giving them any further explanation. If your interlocutors carry on insisting, then just repeat the same phrase: *As I said, I need to stay in.*

However, if they do manage to persuade you, and you do decide to go, then you can say:

OK, then, I'll come.

OK you've convinced me—where are we meeting?

OK, but as long as we are not too late.

19.21   Bear in mind cultural differences

When networking or having conversations at social events, such as those organized at conferences, it is very important to bear cultural differences in mind. For example, there are many differences between the way the English and the Chinese interact with each other socially. The English say "I am sorry" or "Excuse me" very frequently, when they inadvertently touch someone, sneeze, or stop someone in the street to ask for directions. To a Chinese person such constant apologizing seems excessive. On the other hand, the Chinese are more likely to express their concern about someone's health by recommending, for example, that the person should wear more clothes or drink more water. To an English person, such suggestions would be inappropriate as by implication it seems that they are not sufficiently adult enough to make such decisions by themselves. I believe that being aware of such cultural differences is as important as learning English grammar—if not more so.

Part VI
Checking Your English

Chapter 20
Tense Usage

You will learn how to

- use the most common tenses in English
- differentiate the subtle shades of meaning between one tense and another
- avoid ambiguity and misunderstandings in misusage of tenses
- distinguish between various modal verbs

This chapter only contains those tenses, forms, and modal verbs that are most frequently used in emails, during telephone conversations, and when socializing. I have tried to explain the subtle differences between the tenses as well as the possible dangers of misusing them.

Note: The quotations on the next page do not specifically refer to English grammar, they are included for interest only.

A. Wallwork, *English for Academic Correspondence and Socializing*,
DOI 10.1007/978-1-4419-9401-1_20, © Springer Science+Business Media, LLC 2011

What the experts say

Many writers perplex their readers and hearers with mere nonsense. Their writings need sunshine. Pure and neat language I love, yet plain and customary.

Ben Jonson (1572–1637) English Renaissance dramatist, poet and actor, and contemporary of
William Shakespeare

The Latin tongue, long the vehicle used in distributing knowledge among the different nations in Europe, is daily more and more neglected; and one of the modern tongues, viz. French, seems, in point of universality, to have supplied its place. It is spoken in all the courts of Europe; and most of the literati, those even who do not speak it, have acquired knowledge of it, to enable them easily to read the books that are written in it. This gives a considerable advantage to that nation. It enables its authors to inculcate and spread through other nations, such sentiments and opinions, on important points, as are most conducive to its interests, or which may contribute to its reputation, by promoting the common interests of mankind.

Benjamin Franklin (1706–1790) American author, scientist, inventor, statesman, and diplomat

Every language ... has its own inseparable and incommunicable qualities of superiority.

Thomas de Quincey (1785–1859), English author and intellectual

The sum of human wisdom is not contained in any one language, and no single language is capable of expressing all forms and degrees of human comprehension.

Ezra Pound (1885–1972), American expatriate poet and critic

20.1 Use of the present simple

Use the present simple:

To describe states and situations that don't change.

The earth *revolves* around the sun.

The journal only *accepts* manuscripts in English.

Where *are* you from? I *come* from Ethiopia.

To talk about habits and things that are done regularly.

What *do you do*? I *study* mathematics at the University of Prague.

How often *do you go* to conferences? I *go* about twice a year.

To give a feeling of distance in formal emails, with the verbs indicated in the examples below.

I *write* to complain about the poor service I received at your hotel.

I *trust* you are keeping well.

We *wish* to inform you that ...

We *advise* you that the deadline for the manuscript expired last week.

I *regret* that we will not be able to meet your deadline.

I *appreciate* the fact / I *realize* that you must be very busy, but ...

I *acknowledge* / *confirm* receipt of your paper.

I *look forward* to hearing from you in the near future.

To describe to referees how the manuscript looks now compared to the original version.

Figure 3 now *appears* in the Appendix.

Table 6 now *contains* data on ...

The Abstract *is* now considerably shorter.

To report what others have told us.

Professor Kamatachi *sends* her kindest regards.

Kai *says* hello.

Note: Certain verbs are generally only used in the present simple rather than the present continuous (see 20.4). So, even if you are talking about something that is taking place now, you still need to use the present simple (both face to face and in emails). The present simple in such cases can be used in both formal and informal situations.

> *Do you agree* with what I am saying? Yes, I *agree*.

> I *assure* you / I *guarantee* / I *promise* I will be on time.

> I *imagine* you must have had a long journey to get here.

> I *notice* from your badge that you are from the university of ...

> I *hear / understand / gather* that you are doing a presentation this afternoon.

20.2   Non-use of the present simple

Do <u>not</u> use the present simple:

To make suggestions, ask for advice, or offer to do things. Use *shall* or *will* instead.

> *Shall I email* you to confirm the arrangements?

> *Shall we go* on the trip tomorrow?

> *Shall I open* the window?

> I *will let* you know the results of the tests tomorrow.

To react to suggestions made in an email or face to face that you are now responding to. Instead, use *will* (see 20.5).

> Sender: Please can you tell Prof Davis to contact me. Response: OK, I *will let* him now.

> Sender: If possible, could do this by Friday? Response: *I'll do* my best.

> Questioner: What would you like to drink? Response: *I'll have* a beer.

To talk about actions or situations that began in the past and continue into the present. Use the present perfect instead (see 20.9).

> I *have lived* here for six months. [Not: I live here for six months]

20.3   Use of the present continuous

Use the present continuous:

To describe an incomplete action that is going on now at this moment.

> What *is he saying*? I don't understand.

> What *are you doing*? *I'm just downloading* some photos to show you.

To talk about an incomplete action that is going on during this period of time, or a trend.

> I *am working* on a new project with Dr Huria.

> The number of people using Facebook *is growing* steadily.

To talk about a temporary event or situation.

> I usually teach at the university, but this month I *am doing* seminars at another institute.

> I have only just arrived so I *am staying* in university accommodation until I find something of my own.

To give a more friendly tone in emails and letters, particularly with verbs such as *write, enclose, attach, look forward to.*

> I *am writing* to let you know that the paper has finally been accepted.

> I *am attaching* those photos that I took at the social dinner

> I *am really looking forward* to seeing you again.

To talk about future programmed arrangements. In the question form, it does not matter whether or not you know that your interlocutor has made plans or not.

> I *am seeing* Chandra on Monday [Chandra and I have already arranged this].

> *We're flying* there on Monday. [We've already bought our plane ticket].

> What *are you doing* this weekend? *We're going* skiing.

> When *are you leaving*? I *am leaving* after my presentation this afternoon.

20.4 Non-use of continuous forms

The types of verb below are not generally used in the continuous form (i.e., present continuous, past continuous, present perfect continuous). They describe states rather than actions.

Verbs of opinion and mental state: for example, *believe, forget, gather, imagine, know, mean, notice, recognize, remember, think* (i.e., have an opinion), *understand*

> I *gather* you have been having some problems with the software.

Verbs of senses and perception: *feel, hear, see, seem, look, smell, taste*

> This fish *tastes* delicious.

Verbs that express emotions and desires: for example, *hate, hope, like, love, prefer, regret, want, wish*

> *Do you want* anymore wine?

> I *wish* my wife was here, she would love this place.

Verbs of measurement: for example, *contain, cost, hold, measure, weigh*

> This table *contains* the data on xyz.

> The recipient *holds* up to six liters.

When the above verbs refer to actions rather than states, they may be used in the continuous form. Examples:

> We *are having* dinner with the team tonight. [*have* means "eat" not "possess"]

> We *were thinking* about contacting them for a collaboration. [*think* means "consider" not "have an opinion"]

20.5   Future simple [*will*]

Use *will*:

To give a response in an email to a request by the sender. The recipient uses *will* to say what he / she plans to do to meet the request.

> Sender: Could you have a look at the doc and tell me what you think of it.
> Recipient: OK, *I'll do* it tomorrow morning.

> Sender: I was wondering whether you might be able to give me a hand with my presentation.
> Recipient: OK, *I'll have* a look at my diary when I get to the office and *I'll let* you know when will be a good time for me.

> *I'll contact* Dr Njimi and ask her to mail you.

> *I'll be* in touch soon.

To respond to a situation that presents itself at that moment.

> My mobile's ringing. *I'll just have to* answer it.

> Person A: I am having problems with this translation. Person B: *I'll help you* with it if you like.

> Person A: I don't really understand. Person B: *I'll try* to explain myself better. *I'll give* you an example.

> Person A: Would you like something to eat? Person B: No, *I'll have* something later thank you.

To refer to attachments or enclosures.

> As you *will see* from the attached copy . . .

> Below you *will find* the responses to your points re ..

> Herein you *will find* enclosed two copies of the contract.

To predict future events, based on personal intuitions.

> The number of congresses *will go* down if large-screen videoconferencing becomes possible.

> I'm pretty sure Qatar *won't win* the World Cup.

To talk about future states and events with verbs that don't take the present continuous (see 20.4)

> We *will know* tomorrow.

> She *will be* 50 next week.

To indicate formal events

> The university *will celebrate* its 500th anniversary next year.

> The next edition of the conference *will be held* in Karachi.

> The seminar *will take place* at 10.00 in Room 6.

To make requests.

> *Will you give* me a hand with this translation please?

> *Will you let* me know how you get on?

20.6 Future continuous

Use the future continuous:

To give the idea that something will happen irrespectively of your own intentions or wishes. There is a sense of inevitability—the future continuous implies that something is beyond your control.

> I'm sorry but I *won't be attending* your presentation tomorrow. [This gives the idea that the decision does not depend on you but unfortunately there are more urgent tasks that require your intention]

> *I'll be going* to the station myself so I can give you a lift there if you like. [This gives the idea that I am not doing you a personal favor by taking you to the station, as in any case I have to go there myself; it is slightly more polite than saying "I am going to the station"]

> Person A: Would you like to come with us to dinner tonight? Person B: I'm very sorry but I *will be going* with Professor Chowdry's group. [I have no choice in the matter, I have to join Chowdry's group]

In all of the above cases the use of the future simple [will] would give a very different impression. In the first example, if you say "I won't attend" it gives the idea that you do not want to attend. In the second example, "I will go" means that you make the decision now as a personal favor for your interlocutor. In the third example, "I will go" means that you spontaneously decide to go with Chowdry's group because you don't want to go with Person A.

This sense of politeness is also found with the past continuous, for example:

> I *wonder* whether you might be able to help me.

> I *was wondering* whether you might be able to me.

The past continuous is a more tentative form and thus more polite.

The future continuous is also used in the following cases too:

To talk about plans and arrangements, again when you want to give the sense that your actions do not strictly depend on you. The implication is that this is simply the way things are.

> I *will be paying* by credit card.

> My boss *will be arriving* on the 10 o'clock flight.

> As of 15 January we *will be increasing* the cost of subscription by 6%.

> We hereby inform you that from September 1 our institute *will be moving* to the address indicated below.

To give the idea that you have already been working to make something happen.

> I *will send* you the paper next week. [This sounds like you made the decision now as a reaction to your interlocutor's request]

> I *will be sending* you the paper next week. [This sounds like you had already made the decision independently of the current request by your interlocutor]

To describe some action that will be underway at a certain point in the future. In this sense it is the future equivalent to the present continuous and past continuous.

> When I get to Manchester it *will probably be raining*. [i.e., it will probably have already started to rain].

> This time next year I *will be working* in Professor Jamani's lab and *I will finally be earning* some money!

20.7   *be going to*

Use *be going to* plus the infinitive:

To refer to plans and intentions that you have already made decisions about, but for which you have not necessarily made the final arrangements:

She's going to try and get an internship somewhere. [This is her plan but she hasn't necessarily started to look yet]

Are you going to see the Sagrada Familia while you're in Barcelona? [Is this part of your planned itinerary?]

To refer to plans that indicate solitary activities that do not involve making arrangements with other people.

After the presentation I *am going to* have a long bath back at the hotel.

Tonight I *am just going to* read through my notes, then I *am going to* go to bed.

To make predictions based on present or past evidence. In some cases the evidence is already there that something is starting to happen.

Look at the sky—it looks like it *is going to* snow. [The cloud formation is such that snow can be expected]

It *is going to be* tough for students with the cuts in education that the government is planning to introduce. [Past experience shows that when spending is cut, students have difficulty paying their fees]

20.8   Past simple

Use the simple past:

To talk about completed actions in the recent past (even one second ago) or the distant past.

They *went* to the restaurant a few minutes ago. I think they *took* a taxi. But I *didn't see* Katie with them.

I *sent* the mail below to them on October 22, but have heard nothing since.

Professor Putin *called* this morning to verify ...

The University of Bologna is the oldest university in the world it *was founded* in 1088.

Even if the precise moment is not mentioned, but this moment will be clear to the recipient, use the simple past.

Regarding the data you asked for, I *forgot* to mention in my previous mail that ...

Please find attached the market report I *promised* you.

20.9   Present perfect simple

The present perfect often connects the past to the present. The action took place in the past but is not explicitly specified because we are more interested in the result than in the action itself.

Use the present perfect:

To indicate actions that took place during a period that has not yet finished.

> *I've written* more than 10 papers on the topic. [And I will probably publish more research on this topic]

> So far I *have responded* to two out of three of the referee's reports. [I still have time to reply to the third referee]

Compare:

> *Did you receive* my last email message sent on 10 March? [Precise date given]

> I just wanted to check whether you *have received* any news from Professor Shankar. [I don't know if you have received news yet]

To talk about actions took place at an indefinite or unknown time.

> I *have been* to six conferences on this subject.

> I *have been informed* that ...

> I'm sorry I *haven't replied* earlier but I *have been* out of the office all week.

To talk about actions or states that began in the past and continue into the present.

> I *have worked* for here six months. [NB Not: I work here for six months].

> We *have not made* much progress in this project so far.

Note: When talking about an action's duration use *for* if you talk about the period of time. Use *since* when you say when the action began. Examples:

> for five years, for a long time, for more than an hour

> since 2011, since January, since he joined our research team

To specify what is new and to indicate what actions have been taken.

> This is to inform you that my email address *has changed*. From now on please use:

> I *have spoken* to our administration department and they *have forwarded* your request to the head of department.

> I *have looked* at your revisions and *have just added* a few comments. Hope they help.

> A new figure *has been inserted* in Section 2.

We *have reduced* the length of the Abstract, as suggested by Reviewer 2.

We *have not made* any changes to Table 1 because we think that ...

To say *it's the first / second time* that something happened. Note: Do not use the present simple in such cases.

This is the first time I *have done* a presentation—I am very nervous.

This is the second time I *have been* to Caracas.

Do <u>not</u> use the present perfect to talk or ask about the details of the action, use the simple past. Compare:

I've seen her present twice before so I don't want to watch her again. [The consequence is more important than the precise moment when I saw her presentation]
Did you see her at the last conference or the one before? [I am now referring to a specific moment].

Have you ever bought anything from Amazon?
What exactly *did you buy*? How long *did it take* to receive them?

20.10   Present perfect continuous

Use the present perfect continuous:

To describe actions and trends that started in the past and continue in the present.

How long *have you been working* in the field of psycholinguistics?

I've been going to presentations all morning, I'm really tired.

To talk about the effect of recent events.

Why are you covered in ink? *I've been repairing* the photocopier.

He's been working for 14 hours nonstop that's why he looks so tired.

To outline problems or to introduce a topic in emails and on the telephone.

I gather you *have been experiencing* problems in downloading the conference program.

I've been talking to Jim about the fault in your computer but I can't find your email describing ...

20.11   Non-use of present perfect continuous

Do not use the present perfect continuous for completed actions or when you talk about the number of occasions that something has happened or when you specify a quantity [except in days, hours, minutes, etc.]. Use the present perfect simple or past simple instead. Compare:

We *have been writing* a lot of papers recently. [And we are likely to write some more].

We *have written* six papers in the last three years. [The next paper will be the seventh; the action of writing the first six papers is over]

I *have worked* on several projects in this field. [These several projects are now finished, but I am likely to work on similar projects in the future]

I *have been working* for three years on this project. [This project is still ongoing]

I *worked* on three projects in that field, before switching to a completely new line of research. [I now work in a different area]

He's been talking on the phone all morning. [And he is still talking now].

I've talked to him and we've resolved the matter. [The discussion is over]

Note the difference between the simple past, the present perfect, and the present perfect continuous:

I *have been trying* to call you. [And I will probably continue calling you]

I *have tried* to call you. [Probably recently, but I've stopped trying]

I *tried* to call you. [At a specific moment, for example, this morning, yesterday, at the weekend, I will not try again]

20.12   The imperative form

Use the imperative:

To tell people what you want them to do, but without seeming impolite. In any case, particularly in emails, you can make the sentence more polite and soft if you use *please*. NB there is no comma after *please*.

Let me know if you have any problems.

Say hello to Cindy for me.

Please *find* attached a copy of my paper.

Please *do not hesitate* to contact me if you need any further clarifications.

To wish people well.

> *Have* a great day.
>
> *Enjoy* your meal.
>
> *Have* a nice weekend.
>
> *Have* a great Thanksgiving!
>
> Happy Easter to everyone.
>
> A Happy Christmas to you all.

If you wish to be more formal you can say:

> I would like to take this opportunity to wish you a peaceful and prosperous New Year.

20.13   Zero and first conditional forms

The zero conditional [if + present + present] expresses general truths and scientific facts. It means "every time that" or "whenever".

> If you *mix* green and red you *get* brown.
>
> If you *work* in industry you generally *get* paid more than if you work in research.

The first conditional [if + present + will] is used to talk about real future situations, rather than general truths that are always valid.

> We wish to inform you that if we *do not receive* the revised manuscript by the end of this month, we *will be forced* to withdraw your contribution from the special issue.
>
> I *will go* on the trip tomorrow if it *doesn't* rain.

20.14   Second conditional

The second conditional [if + past simple + would] is used to refer to improbable or unreal future situations, or when making cautious requests.

> If I *had* enough money I *would* probably retire. [At the moment I don't have enough money]
>
> If my department *gave* me the funding, I *would* do my research abroad. [My department is unlikely to fund me]
>
> If I *were* you, I *would reduce* the number of slides in your presentation. [I am not you]
>
> *Would it be* OK with you, if I *delayed* sending you the revisions until next week? [I am making a cautious request]

Would you mind if we *met* in the conference bar rather than at your hotel?

If we *took* a taxi, it *would be* much quicker.

Note: Some people, particularly in the USA, use *would* in both halves of the sentence.

In replies to referees reports, the second conditional may be used to indicate the effort involved to fulfill the referee's requirements:

If we *did* as Ref. 1 suggests, this *would* entail doing several more experiments which *would* take at least six months work.

If we *removed* Figure 3, the reader *might / would not be able* to understand the significance of our data.

There is a particular form of conditional that is used almost exclusively in emails and business letters, which is when *would* [or *could*] is used in both parts of the sentence. This construction represents a form of courtesy.

I *would be* grateful if you *would send* me a copy of your paper.

If you *could get this* to me before the end of today it *would be* great.

Any information you *could give* us *would be* very much appreciated.

I *would very much appreciate* it if you *could get back* to me within the next few days.

Would is also used in polite requests:

I *would like* to inform you that ..

I *would like* to take this opportunity to ...

20.15   Third conditional

The third conditional [if + past perfect + would have + past participle] expresses how things might have been if something had (not) happened. It can be used to express regrets and hypotheses about the past, missed opportunities, and criticisms of oneself or others.

If I *had realized* how long it would take me to prepare the presentation, I *would never have offered* to do it.

I *would have come* to the airport to meet you if I *had known* that you were coming.

In conditional phrases you can change the order of the *if* clause and the main clause.

> I *will help* you if you *want*. / If you *want* I *will help* you.

> If I *had* the opportunity I *would* get a job in industry. / I *would* get a job in industry, if I *had* the opportunity

You can also mix the forms.

> If I *had not met* Professor Rossi, I *would not be* in Italy now.

20.16   Modal verbs expressing ability and possibility: *can, could, may, might*

Use *can* and *cannot* to express a general ability to do (or not be able to do) something whenever you want.

> I *can* use many different programming languages.

> I am afraid I *can't* speak English very well.

Use *can* to express certain 100% possibility and *cannot* 100% impossibility, *may [not]* for 50%.

> I *can* let you know tomorrow. [I am certain that I will be able to let you know tomorrow]

> We *cannot* cut the paper any further without losing much of the significance. [It would be impossible to make further cuts]

> I am afraid that I *cannot* attend your seminar. [It is impossible for me to come]

> I *may* go to at least one of the social events, but I am not sure I will have time. [Perhaps I will go]

You can also use *may*, *might*, and *could* to speculate about the future or talk about probability.

> You *may* remember we met last year at the EFX conference in Barcelona.

> We *may* have to abandon the project.

> They *may* not get the funding if the government keeps making cuts in education.

> Please accept our apologies for any inconvenience this *may* have caused you.

> I *could* be wrong. [But not necessarily]

> The results they obtained *could* / *might* be misleading [I am speculating]

20.17   Modal verbs expressing advice and obligation: *have to, must, need, should*

When you advise someone what to do use *should*. Alternatively, use *must* if you want to give them a very strong recommendation.

> You *should* try getting in touch with her via Facebook.

> You *must* go and see the cathedral while you're here—it is so beautiful.

Use *should* when some kind of moral or ethical issue is involved, or when you think something is likely to happen or would be a good idea.

> The government *should* spend more on research.

> I think they *should* avoid having too many parallel sessions at conferences.

> We *should* try and get to the museum early to avoid the queues.

> I sent it via DHL yesterday so you *should* get it by tomorrow at the latest.

At the end of an email *should* is often used to tell the recipient that they are free to ask further questions, etc. Note that *should* comes before the subject.

> *Should* you have any questions, please let us know.

> *Should* you need any further clarifications, do not hesitate to contact me.

Use *have to* when you talk about responsibilities (i.e., to show that an obligation probably comes from some other person, not from you). If something is not necessary or is not your responsibility, use *don't have to* or *don't need to*.

> In my country you only *have to* wear seatbelts if you are driving on a motorway.

> I *have to* catch the 6.30 train to be at work on time.

> You *have to* take your shoes off when you go in the mosque. .

> At my institute you *don't necessarily have to* always work in the lab, you can work from home if you want.

> You *don't have to* send it via fax, you can email it if you like.

Use *must* when you are making a deduction based on present circumstances.

> It appears that some mistake *must* have been made.

> Could you send your fax number again as I think I *must* have the wrong number.

> I realize you *must* be very busy at the moment but if you could spare a moment I would be most grateful.

Avoid *have to* and *must* when you are giving instructions, just use the imperative.

> To get there, just *go* out of the lobby and *turn* right, then *go* straight on for 100 meters.

> Please let me know how you *get on*.

However, if you are an authority (e.g., a conference organizer, editor of a journal), then you can use *must* in a formal situation in order to outline a procedure.

> Applications *must* be received by 30 June.

> Papers *must* be sent in both pdf and Word formats.

> The software *must* be dispatched by courier.

If you want to talk about a past obligation, the form you use will depend on whether you fulfilled the obligation or not.

> Yesterday I *had to* give a presentation—I was very nervous. [Obligation fulfilled]

> I *was supposed* to do a presentation, but in the end my prof did it for me. [Obligation not fulfilled]

> I *didn't have to* do a presentation, they let me do a poster session instead. [Potential obligation turned out not to be necessary]

> I *was going to* do a presentation, but then I decided it would be too much work. [Unfulfilled intention]

20.18   Modal verbs for offers, requests, invitations, and suggestions: *can, may, could, would, shall, will*

Use *can*, *may*, and *shall* to offer to do something. *May* is more formal.

> *May / Can / Shall* I help you?

Use *can*, *could*, *will*, and *would* to request something. *Could* and *would* are more polite.

> *Can / Could / Will / Would* you help me?

Use *would you like* to invite someone.

> *Would you like* to come out for dinner tonight?

Use *shall* to make a suggestion.

> *Shall* I open the window?

> *Shall* we go to the bar?

In emails *can* and *could* are often used to make polite requests. In that sense, they are not really questions, so many native speakers do not put a question mark at the end of the sentence.

Could you send me the doc as soon as you have a moment. Thanks.

Can you give me your feedback by the end of the week. Thanks.

You can make your request softer by preceding *could* with *do you think*. In such cases the recipient is given more chance to say "no".

Could you translate the attached document for me.

Do you think you could translate the attached document for me?

You can also make it more polite by using *please*.

Please could you tell me who I should contact regarding registering for the conference.

Questions marks are used when there is a real question, that is, when you are expecting an answer.

Can we meet up some time next week?

By the way, *can* you speak Spanish?

No questions marks are used with *may* in the following types of situations.

May I wish you a very happy new year.

May I take this opportunity to ...

May I remind you that ...

Chapter 21
Using Google to Reduce Mistakes in Your English

You will learn

- to identify typical mistakes made by non-native speakers
- the benefits and dangers of using Google Translate
- how to use Google search engines to check your English

This chapter suggests some ways of using Google Translate (hereafter GT) and the Google search engines. What I outline in this chapter is the result of my experience as a user as well as that of some colleagues in Europe and China.

Google's services are increasingly getting better, so some of the defects I have found in GT may well have been resolved by the time you read this chapter. GT is constantly updated and the way it translates something on one particular day may change the next day.

I have chosen to write about GT rather than other free automatic translation services since in my experience GT tends to work the best. GT does translations through comparisons with other translations that have already been made. To do this, it makes use of bilingual corpuses. Other automatic translators analyze the text using parsing techniques and generally produce more erratic results than GT.

I strongly recommend you do some tests using GT. You may find it performs a lot better than you had previously imagined and may save you considerable time in writing emails and other short documents.

This chapter is presented as a series of FAQs.

A. Wallwork, *English for Academic Correspondence and Socializing*,
DOI 10.1007/978-1-4419-9401-1_21, © Springer Science+Business Media, LLC 2011

Factoids

❖ Google Translate was introduced in 2007, initially with translations from French, German, and Spanish into English, and vice versa.

❖ The European Commission (EC) was one of the pioneers of machine translation and at one time their translation service produced over one million pages per year. About one-third of the officials working in the European Union's (EU) institutions were once employed in connection with interpretation and translation. The cost of translation now accounts for around 1% of the EU budget. At the time of writing, the EU has 23 official and working languages. Originally all EU documents were translated into the language of the member countries; now due to time and money constraints only a few have this privilege. According to the EC multilingualism website, the most multilingual EU citizens are those from Luxembourg, where 99% of people know at least one other foreign language, followed by Slovaks (97%) and Latvians (95%).

❖ Esperanto (meaning *one who hopes*) was a language devised by Dr Lazar Zamenhof, who was born in 1859 in Białystok, which at the time was in Russia but is now in Poland. Zamenhof felt that there could only be peace in the world if everyone spoke the same language so that no one would have a cultural advantage over anyone else. He published his work in 1887, during a period in which another 53 artificial universal languages were created. Esperanto has its own Wikipedia site—Vikipedio (eo.wikipedia.org), and Esperanto congresses are held every year. According to Wikipedia, the number of current speakers is estimated at between 250 and 5,000.

❖ One of the most infamous translations of all time was a book entitled *New Guide of the Conversation in Portuguese and English*. This book of familiar phrases had originally been published in 1836 in French and Portuguese. When an English version was produced, the services of Pedro Carilino were used. Carilino understood no English at all and merely used a French–English dictionary. The resulting book informed readers that *a relation* was for male relations (e.g., fathers, uncles) and *an relation* for female relations. In fact, he used *a* for masculine words, and *an* for feminine words throughout his guide. Carolino concluded his book by saying: *We expect then, who the little book (for the care that we wrote him, and for her typographical correction) that may be worth the acceptation of the studious persons, and especially of the Youth, at which we dedicate him particularly.*

21.1   What typical mistakes do non-native researchers make when translating into English?

To understand the benefits of GT, it helps to know what kind of mistakes you might make when translating from your language into English. You will then be able to judge how well GT does in comparison.

The abstract below was written by a PhD student of mine. She wrote directly into English but was mentally translating from Italian.

> Aim of the present paper is to present a confrontation between the syntax of the Italian language and the Inglish language. The Italian system of syntax derives form what is known in literature as the "periodical style," with many subordinate and incisive clauses, whereas the Franco-English tradition was dominated by the "european style." It was founded that, contrary to what is the commonly thought, that Italian and the English languages demonstrate a similarly complex structure. The unique difference is the fact that the English rigorously imposes that the subject be before the verb, instead in Italian can come before the verb and then the object.

The problems with the above abstract are not with the content but with the English. They are incredibly common mistakes. Most of the mistakes are influenced by what is known as mother-tongue interference, that is, the student was thinking in her own language—Italian.

- USE OF DEFINITE ARTICLE—the first word (*aim*) should be preceded by *the.* The word *aim* itself is fine, an alternative would be *purpose*
- SPELLING MISTAKES—some of these are simply wrong (*Inglish* instead of *English*), others are typos (*form* instead of *from*—see second line)
- CAPITALIZATION—*European* has an initial capital letter
- VOCABULARY / FALSE FRIENDS—*Confrontation* looks similar to the Italian word for "comparison" (*confronto*), and *periodical* (which should be *periodic*, a *periodical* is a magazine) is probably due to the fact that the author has noticed that many English words in her field end in *-ical* (e.g., *classical*, *metaphorical*). *Unique* in English has a very specific meaning, it means "like no other"—for example, a diamond can be unique. The right word would be *only*
- IRREGULAR VERB ENDINGS—the past tense of *find* is *found* not *founded* (which refers to the establishment of an institute, organization, or company)
- REDUNDANCY—the words *present* in the *present paper* and the words *the* and *language* in the phrase *the Italian language* add no value for the reader
- WORD ORDER—*in Italian can come before the subject and then the object*— this should be: *the subject can come before the object*. In English the subject must come before the verb

As a non-native speaker you will certainly make similar mistakes. How can you avoid such mistakes? Are some mistakes more "serious" than others?

Misusage of the DEFINITE ARTICLE is incredibly common. Many languages don't have definite or indefinite article, and those that do have them use them in a very different way from English. In any case, your paper will never be rejected just for a few mistakes with articles. However, if you consistently make mistakes throughout the whole paper, referees are likely to ask you to revise the English. In an email, misuse of the articles will rarely cause problems of comprehension.

Some of the SPELLING AND CAPITALIZATION mistakes, that is, *Inglish, european,* can be resolved simply by using a spell check. Typos such as *form* instead of *from* are commonly made by native speakers too; the only way to avoid them is by reading your document aloud very carefully. Poor spelling gives the idea that you were too lazy even to turn on the spell checker and that if you are not attentive to such detail in your writing the same may be said about your attention to detail in your research.

VOCABULARY problems generally regard words from general English rather than technical English. Normally, you will know the correct technical words for your field. You are more likely to make mistakes with non-technical words. Such mistakes are not incredibly serious, but can be a little confusing. For example, a confrontation generally means a face-to-face clash of ideas and has nothing to do with making a comparison. The solution here is to use a good bi-lingual dictionary.

Dealing with IRREGULAR VERBS implies that you actually know that a verb is irregular. In some cases a spell check will find the mistake simply because the word is not in its dictionary because it does not exist (e.g., *setted* or *broadcasted,* which should be *set* and *broadcast*). In other cases you simply have to know the correct form. However, problems of this kind are not likely to bother your readers.

REDUNDANCY is a major problem. Referees frequently refer to it when rejecting a paper, and in an email it may cause the recipient to stop reading.

Putting the WORDS IN THE WRONG ORDER is the most serious mistake in this abstract. For a native English speaker, if the parts of a sentence (e.g., the subject, verb, and object) appear in the wrong order it has a similar effect to a dinner where the dessert is served first, followed by the main course, and the starters come at the end.

What effect will such mistakes have on your readers? One way to understand this effect is to take a paragraph written in English and translate it literally into your own language. It will sound rather strange, even comical—well, this is the effect that your mistakes might have on your readers, particularly native speakers.

21.2   How accurate is a Google translation of a technical document?

If the author of the abstract in 21.1 had written her abstract in Italian and then used GT, she would have produced an abstract that contained far fewer mistakes, as you can see below. She might have also saved a lot of time! The differences in the correct version with respect to her original version and the Google version are highlighted in italics.

ORIGINAL VERSION	GOOGLE TRANSLATE	CORRECT VERSION
Aim of the *present* paper is to present a *confrontation* between the syntax of the Italian *language* and the *Inglish language*. The Italian system of syntax derives form what is known *in literature* as the "*periodical* style," with many subordinate and *incisive* clauses, whereas the Franco-English tradition was dominated by *the* "*european* style." It was founded that, contrary to what is the commonly thought, that Italian and the English languages demonstrate a similarly complex structure. The *unique* difference is the fact that the English *rigorously imposes* that the subject be before the verb, instead in Italian *can come before the verb and then* the object. (12 mistakes)	The purpose of this paper is to make a comparison between the syntax of Italian and English. The syntax of a sentence in the Italian system is derived from what is *called in literature magazine style*, with many subordinate *and very sharp*, while the Franco-English tradition *that has dominated call* "European style." It was found that, contrary to what is commonly thought, the Italian language and English show a similarly complex structure. The only difference is the fact that English requires that the subject comes before the verb, while in Italian *can be placed before the verb, then* the subject. (4 mistakes)	The purpose* of this paper is to make a comparison between the syntax of Italian and English. The syntax of a sentence in the Italian system is derived from what in *the* literature *is called the periodic* style, with many subordinate *clauses*, while the Franco-English tradition *was dominated by the* "European style." It was found that, contrary to what is commonly thought, *that* [the] Italian [language] and English show a similarly complex structure. The only difference is the fact that English requires that the subject comes before the verb, while in Italian *the verb* can be placed *before* the subject. * *aim* would also be correct

Of course the correct version could be further improved. For example the first sentence could be made more concise:

> The aim of this paper is to compare Italian and English syntax.

Or even more concisely:

> This paper compares Italian and English syntax.

But the above "improvements" are a question of writing style rather than accuracy with regard to English grammar or syntax.

Please note: I am absolutely NOT suggesting that you use GT and then send off your email without making any corrections. Also, I am NOT suggesting that you use GT to translate a paper. The example in the table is purely designed to show what typical mistakes non-native speakers make, and what result may be possible to achieve with GT.

You will certainly need to do a check of any emails you have translated using GT. I also suggest that you only use GT for the more technical parts of the email, and that you only use standard salutations at the beginning and end of your emails (see Chapter 22). If you use GT to work on longer documents, you will obviously have to do extensive checking and revision, but perhaps not much more than you would have had to do if you had done your own manual translation.

But if you are in a hurry, GT does have many advantages:

- in most cases it chooses the correct translation of a word—in the above example only *magazine* and *sharp* are completely wrong. Having the correct translation is particularly helpful with prepositions and conjunctions
- it does not usually make spelling mistakes. However, occasionally if the word in the source text is already in English, for some reason GT may modify its spelling
- it generally identifies the correct use of articles (including whether *the* should be omitted or not, and when *an* rather than *a* should be used) and the right prepositions
- it reduces some typical redundancies. For example, it will translate the Italian "i risultati ottenuti" (i.e., the results obtained) simply with the *results*. This generally works well but you need to make sure that GT does not inadvertently remove other words

21.3   How accurate is a Google translation of an email?

The more technical the text, the better a job GT does. GT is not as accurate with emails. I suspect that this is because fewer people submit emails to GT than they do technical documents. GT tends to make mistakes with some typical salutations, so I suggest that you refer to the useful email phrases given in Chapter 22 of this book. However, within the main body of the email, GT does a reasonable job which should allow your recipient to understand what you are trying to say with only minimal correction on your part.

You might also try my mixed mode translation, see 21.5.

21.4   What factors influence the quality of an automatic translation?

I have carried out some very limited research into using GT. From the examples I have seen, there is a huge difference from language to language. It seems to work well in the most commonly used European languages, for instance French, Italian, German, and Spanish. However, the examples I have seen from Chinese were very poor. But in the future, automatic translations will certainly continue to improve, and if they are not great in your language now, they may well be in a few years' time.

Given that you may not always be able to judge how accurate a GT translation is from your language into English, I strongly recommend that you do a few tests on a few paragraphs and get a native English speaker's opinion. If GT seems to be doing a good job, then you might consider using it with longer translations. But, let me stress again that GT is not a substitute for human intervention.

Don't be influenced by the fact that translations from English into your language may be quite poor. Far more people translate out of their own language into English than from English into their language. This means that GT gets more training into translating into English, so translations into English tend to have a much higher standard.

Another factor that influences the quality is the topic of the text. For example, GT will translate a computer manual with very high accuracy because sentences tend to be short and very standard. Also there is a great demand for the translation of such manuals, so again GT gets more training. GT generally tends to be better at technical translations rather than humanistic subjects.

Finally, the more the source text (i.e., the text to be translated) is constructed in an "English" way, the better the translation will be. So if you are originating the source text yourself, try to make it as English-like as possible by following English word order and using short, concise sentences. Put any acronyms straight into English.

21.5   Can I write in a mixture of my language and English?

I have done experiments with writing in a mixture of Italian and English within the same text and then submitting it to GT. It works well though sometimes GT gets confused and starts erroneously capitalizing words.

However, a mix of writing in your language and English could be very useful for you. This means you can write the parts you are sure of in English, and the other parts in your own language. This also helps you to follow English word order.

The result should be a more accurate translation, provided of course that the parts you write in English are not full of mistakes.

21.6   What typical mistakes does Google Translate make?

GT works considerably better on technical / scientific texts. Its error rate on humanistic texts is much higher, as they tend to be more discursive and have fewer patterns compared to technical texts. Below I have listed the most common mistakes that GT makes.

WORD ORDER

GT's main difficulty is with word order, that is, the position of nouns, verbs, adjectives, and adverbs. If in your language you put the verb before its subject, or if you put an indirect object before the direct object, then GT will not be able to create the correct English order (i.e., the reverse of the order in your language). To partially resolve this problem, see 21.7 below.

NAMES OF PEOPLE

At the time of writing, GT tends to translate people's first names and sometimes surnames. It also makes some rather unexpected translations. For example, GT sometimes translates the Italian name Adriano Rossi as Adrian Smith, or even Hadrian Smith. Clearly, Adrian is the English equivalent of the Italian Adriano. But Rossi into Smith? Well, Smith is the most common English surname just as Rossi is the most common Italian surname. GT sometimes even changes the spelling of names that exist in your language that have no equivalent in English. For example, the Italian surname Federici sometimes becomes Federico in the English version.

The issue of mistranslation of names is clearly a major problem in scientific writing, and hopefully Google will have fixed this bug by the time your read this book. If they haven't, then you need to be very careful to check that GT has not changed the names of authors that you quote in your paper or people that you refer to in an email.

ACCENTS AND SINGLE QUOTES

Does your native language use accents? If it does, then read on.

If you are, for example, French, then GT is helped considerably if you use the correct accents. Note how GT translates these two titles of a French medical paper in two ways depending on whether the accents are inserted or not. Interestingly, both translations would be possible, but one of the two might not reflect the author's real intention.

Mesurer la qualité de vie: une nécessité en thérapeutique cancérologique
GT: Measuring quality of life: a need *for therapeutic oncology*

Mesurer la qualite de vie: une necessite en therapeutique cancerologique
GT: Measuring quality of life: a need *in oncology therapeutics*

Below is the same paper title, but this time in Italian. In this case, if the accents are correctly inserted in the original text, then GT provides the correct translation. Unlike with French, GT also provides exactly the same translation if the accents are not inserted at all.

Misurare la qualità della vita: una necessità per l'oncologia terapeutiche
Misurare la qualita della vita: una necessita per l'oncologia terapeutiche
GT: Measuring the quality of life: a need for therapeutic oncology

But if the accent is placed after the final letter using a single quote (i.e., the ' character), which is a typical device used by those Italians that don't have accents on their keyboards, GT gets confused and thinks a quotation is being given.

Misurare la qualita' della vita: una necessita' per l'oncologia terapeutiche
GT: Measure the quality' of life: a necessity' for Therapeutic Oncology

Of course, words may change meaning depending on whether there is an accent or not. Here are two examples in French:

Le poisson est sale = The fish is dirty.
Le poisson est salé = The fish is salty.

Les moines aiment les jeûnes = Monks like fasting.
Les moines aiment les jeunes = Monks like young people.

The moral of the story is that if your language has accents, you need to be aware that GT may produce unusual results.

PLURAL ACRONYMS

In English, we say one CD but two CDs. Most other languages do not have a plural form for acronyms, and thus say *two CD*. GT is able to recognize this for common acronyms such as CD, DVD, and PC, but not for very technical acronyms that are only used in specific fields of research.

TENSES

GT sometimes changes the tense from the original. For example, you may use the future tense and GT will translate it into the present tense. In some cases, GT may be correct. For example, if in your language you say "I will tell him when I *will see* him," GT will correctly translate this as "I will tell him when I *see* him." This is because in a time clause, *when* takes the present and not the future. However, very occasionally GT makes mistakes when it changes tenses, so it is wise to check very carefully.

VERY SPECIALIZED VOCABULARY

GT's dictionaries are huge but do not cover absolutely every word. If GT doesn't know a word, it will normally leave it in the original language.

WORDS WITH MORE THAN ONE MEANING

This is more a problem if you use GT to translate from English into your language, as English is infamous for using the same word (e.g., *get* and *set*) to mean a multitude of different things. GT generally manages to guess the right meaning when translating into English because it looks at the surrounding words (i.e., how words are collocated together). In any case, you need to check carefully that GT has translated with the meaning you intended.

STRINGS OF WORDS USED IN COMPUTER TERMINOLOGY

If you use English phrases such as *status no-provider* in your own original language, sometimes GT will modify these when "translating" and produce, for example, *provider-no status*. Essentially, you just need to check that any English in your source text has not been altered by GT.

21.7   How can I improve the chances that Google Translate will produce a good translation?

The success level of a Google translation depends to a large extent on how similar the construction of the source language is with respect to the normal structure of English. One solution is to modify the version in your own language before you submit it to translation. This works very well with emails because it requires a lot less time than, for example, modifying an entire paper.

SYNTAX

Put the subject as near as possible to the beginning of the sentence and the main verb next to it. Put adjectives before their associated nouns. Make sure that the direct object precedes the indirect object. For the rules of English word order, see 3.6.

SENTENCE LENGTH AND PUNCTUATION

Limit the number of clauses in your sentence to one or two.

Different languages use punctuation in different ways. Before you submit your text for translation, if possible try to punctuate it in an English way. Keep the sentences short, replace semicolons with full stops, and where appropriate use commas to break up the various parts of the sentence.

USE ACTIVE RATHER THAN PASSIVE SENTENCES

The advantage of an active sentence is that it must contain a subject, and this subject must precede the verb (in English). This means that GT is likely to produce a more accurate translation.

REPLACE ANY PRONOUNS WITH THE NOUNS THAT THEY REFER TO

Pronouns in English can be very ambiguous (see 3.10) because it may not be clear for the reader what they refer to. If you replace them with the noun they refer to, GT will make a more accurate translation. This is because Google works by looking for similar sequences of words in translations that it has already done. Words such as *it*, *they*, *them*, *one* can obviously be associated with many hundreds of thousands of other words. More concrete words such as *paper*, *researchers*, *computer* will be associated with fewer other words.

DO NOT USE SYNONYMS FOR KEY WORDS

The more different words you use, the greater the chance that GT will make a mistake. So if you are a doctor, a key word may be *patient*. Try to always use *patient*, rather than finding synonyms such as *subject*, *participant*, *member*, *case*, *sufferer*. In the field of medicine, the term *patient* is more specific than the other synonyms. GT may link the other synonyms with non-medical cases, and thus choose the wrong translation.

21.8   How can I check my English using Google?

You can use a search engine to check words and phrases. For example, let's imagine that you want to check whether the phrase *these informations are* is correct English usage. Note: it is not correct*!

If you do a standard Google search and type in *"these informations are"* (note that you must put the phrase in inverted commas), you will get around three million results. This high number of results could give you a false impression by making you think that a phrase is correct when it isn't.

---

these informations are is incorrect English because *information* is uncountable in English, which means that it cannot have an *s* plural and that the words that come before and after it should be in the singular.

The correct version is *this information is*, which gives around 270 million returns, that is, 90 times more returns.

The secret is to do a more refined search. If you use Google's Advanced Search, fill in these two parts of the form:

> Find web pages that have ... this exact wording or phrase: *these informations are*
> Search within a site or domain: *.edu*

Google **Advanced Search**   Advanced Search Tips |

"these informations are" site: edu

Find web pages that have...

all these words

this exact wording or phrase: these informations are   tip

one or more of these words   OR   OR   tip

But don't show pages that have...

any of these unwanted words: tip

Need more tools?

Reading level   no reading level displayed

Results per page   10 results

Language   English

File type   any format

Search within a site or domain: .edu
                                (e.g. youtube.com, .edu)

⊞ Data, usage rights, numeric range, and more

                                                                                              Advanced Search

©2011 Google

Using these two options, Google will search for the exact phrase on all domains with the .edu tag, where .edu stands for educational sites in the USA. An alternative sites is .ac, educational domains in Great Britain. In these two domains the majority of texts are written by native English speakers.

For our example phrase, .edu returns only 60 results. On the other hand, *this information is* returns around 17 million results.

Using *google.com* search engine	"these informations are"	"this information is"
Standard Search	3,000,000	270,000,000
Advanced Search, domain: .edu	60	17,000,000
Advanced Scholar Search	2,000	2,000,000

The table above lists various searches (all numbers are rounded) conducted with google.com search engines. It highlights that

- a standard search can give misleading results—three million seems to be a high number of returns. It is a high number but given the fact that the phrase is so common, it is not high enough. This involves you making judgments as to how many returns you should expect
- using an Advanced Search with .edu specified as the domain seems (at least in this case) to give the most accurate picture of whether a phrase is likely to be correct or not

If you have any doubts, the best solution is to try alternative solutions for the same phrase, for example, to change the vocabulary, grammar, or word order within the phrase

21.9   How reliable are the prompts / suggestions given in a Google search?

When you start typing in the words used for your search, Google automatically makes suggestions before beginning to search. These prompts may already be enough for you to understand whether your English phrase is correct or not. However, the accuracy of Google's "suggestion" very much depends which Google site you use. The problem is that if you use your local site (e.g., .de, .it, .jp, .ru) you are likely to see the English errors of those who speak the same language as you. So if you decide to use this option, only use it from .com (USA).

21.10   How should I use * and "..." in a Google search?

An asterisk is a wild character, that is, a character that stands for any word or sequence of words. So for example, if you were searching for the correct preposition to use with *depend*, you could insert:

"depends * many factors"

By putting the phrase between inverted commas ("..."), you are telling Google to look for that exact phrase. If you don't put the phrase in inverted commas, Google will simply look for any occurrences of *depends* and *many* and *factors*, whether in a string or not.

This particular search gave me 12 million hits, the majority of which replaced the asterisk with either *on* or *upon*.

21.11   How should I interpret the results of a Google search?

(a) CHECK THE DOMAINS

If you are using Google to check your English, first you should look at where the results have come from. If the top three or four results do not come from native English sources (e.g., they come, instead, from language specific domains: .de, .it, .cn, .jp), then there is a very good chance that the English text that you are checking is not correct. Also, even if the domains are clearly American or British, they must also be reputable (i.e., not blogs or chatrooms).

(b) LOOK AT THE CONTEXT

Let's imagine again that you are searching for the preposition associated with the verb *to benefit*. You do not know that the correct preposition is *from*. You think it may be *of*, so you insert *benefit of*. You get 37.5 million returns and your first several thousand results clearly come from native English sources. However, you need to check because you may, in this case, get two kinds of returns:

The main *benefit of* using this system is ...

... those who will *benefit*. *Of* all the systems I have used, this is certainly the most useful.

In the first example *benefit* is not used as a verb, but as a noun, so *benefit of* is correct. In the second example, there is a punctuation boundary. Currently, Google ignores punctuation in its searches.

Note: the same word may have several different meanings, so you need to check that the hits you get contain the word or phrase with the meaning that you are checking for.

(c) CHECK THE NUMBER OF HITS

If your phrase only contains three or four words, and these three or four words are not highly technical, then a good number of returns to ensure accuracy would be several million. If you get fewer than, say, 500,000 hits, then you probably need to double-check.

If your phrase is highly technical, then you will get more accurate results using Google Scholar.

21.12   What are the benefits of Google Scholar in terms of checking my English?

In the example given in 21.8, Google Scholar did not give as reliable results as an Advanced Search using the standard Google search engine. However, Scholar does have other advantages. You can decide to search

- just titles of articles, rather than whole articles
- specific journals or all journals, and in specific fields
- articles written by specific authors
- articles written in specific years

This means that Scholar is not just useful for checking your English, but also for your literature search and to enable you to compare various styles of writing.

The fact that Google Scholar gives you the option to search for articles written by specific authors, means that you can filter out articles that have probably been written by non-native English speaking authors. You can do this by inserting the name Smith in the field 'Return articles written by'. Smith is the most common surname in the English language (over five million worldwide) and thus should give you a substantial number of returns. Other names you could try are Johnson, Williams, Brown, Jones, and Davis. But do not use these names in combination, just individually. Otherwise you will get returns where the authors of the paper were, for instance, both Smith and Johnson.

21.13   Are Google Translate and the Google Search engines accurate enough for me not to have to do any subsequent revisions?

No! You must carefully revise any translations, just as you would if you had made the translation manually by yourself. GT is not a substitute for a human translator, and an English teacher will generally give you a better answer than a Google search! However, if you use these Google tools carefully and wisely, they should help you save a lot of time and effort.

Part VII
Useful Phrases

Chapter 22
Email

Phrases that are very formal are followed by an asterisk (*).

In this section, *you* and *your* refer to the person who wrote the original email, and *recipient* refers to the person who received the writer's email.

The phrases are punctuated as follows:

(a) Where there is no punctuation at the end of the phrase, this means that typically native speakers use no punctuation. This is often the case with the initial and the final salutation. However, in these cases, it would also be possible to use a comma. So it would be possible to write both of the following:

Dear Adrian

Dear Adrian,

Some writers also use a colon after the initial salutation. Example:

Dear Adrian:

(b) A period (.) at the end of the phrase indicates that the phrase ends at this point.

(c) Three dots (...) this means that the phrase would continue.

(d) A colon (:) indicates that a list and / or comments would follow.

(e) An interrogative mark (?) indicates that this is a question. Note that often phrases that begin "Can you ..." or "Could you ..." are not considered questions when they are simply a polite way of giving someone instructions. Examples:

Could you send the file by the end of today. Thanks.

Can you let me know as soon as possible.

Examples of real questions are those where the writer is expecting a reply to his / her question:

Can you speak English?

22.1   Initial salutation

Standard

Dear Alfred

Dear Alfred Einstein

Dear Dr Einstein

Dear Professor Einstein

To group / team

Dear all

Hi all

Hi everybody

To all members of the xxx group

To someone you know well

Hi!

Hope you are keeping well.

Hope all is well.

To someone / some people whose names or job positions you don't know

Hi

Hello

Good morning

To whom it may concern * *but try to find the name of the correct person*

Dear Sir / Madam * *but try to find the name of the correct person*

22.2   Final salutation

Neutral

Best regards

Kind regards

Best wishes

Regards

Informal

All the best

Have a nice weekend and I'll write when we're back.

See you on Friday.

Hope to hear from you soon.

Speak to you soon.

Cheers

Formal

With kind regards

With best wishes

Yours sincerely

Yours faithfully

22.3   Phrase before final salutation

Very informal excuses for ending

Must go now because ...

I've got to go now.

That's all for now.

Sending regards to other people

Say hello to ...

Please send my regards to ...

Please convey my best wishes to ... *

Wishing people well

Best wishes for the holidays and the new year from all of us here at ...

Have a great Thanksgiving!

Have a nice weekend.

Happy Easter to everyone.

May I wish you a ... *

I would like to take this opportunity to wish you a peaceful and prosperous New Year. *

22.4   Giving main reason for message

To known person or group of known people

Just a quick update on ...

Just to let you know that ...

This is just a quick message to ...

This email is to inform you that ...

For your information here is ...

This is to let you know that ...

Just a quick message to ask you whether ...

I was just wondering whether ...

First contact to unknown person

I found your name in the references of X's paper on ...

I am writing to you because ...

Your address was given to me by ...

Your name was given to me by ...

Your address was given to me by ...

Making reference to previous mail / phone call / conversation

In relation to / With reference to / Regarding ...

Further to our conversation of yesterday, ...

Further to our recent meeting, ...

As requested I am sending you ...

Making reference to previous meeting at conference

You may remember we met last year ...

You may recall that we met at the conference in Bejing ...

Following up telephone call

Thanks for ringing me yesterday.

It was good to speak to you this morning.

As I said / mentioned on the phone ...

I just wanted to check that I've got the details correctly.

With reference to our phone call of ... *formal**

Re our phone call this morning ...

Further to our telephone conversation, here are the details of what we require.

Many thanks for your earlier call. As discussed, details as below:

22.5   Organizing content

Stressing main points and drawing attention to something

What I really want to stress here is ...

The important thing is ...

The key factor is ...

Can I draw your attention to ...

What I need to know is ...

It is crucial for me to ...

I cannot stress how important this is.

Indicating change in subject

One more thing ...

While I remember ...

Before I forget ...

By the way ...

Also ...

Summarizing and concluding

So, just to summarize ...

So basically I am asking you two things. First, ... And second ...

If you could answer all three of my questions I would be most grateful.

22.6   Asking favors / giving help

Asking

I found your email address on the web, and am writing to you in the hope that you may be able to help me.

Please could you ...

I was wondering if by any chance you ...

I wonder if you might be able to help me.

I would be extremely grateful if you could ...

Would you have any suggestions on how to ...

It would be very helpful for me if I could pick your brains on ...

I would like to ask your advice about ...

Showing awareness that you are taking up recipient's time

I realize you must be very busy at the moment but if you could spare a moment I would be most grateful.

If it wouldn't take up too much of your time then I would be very grateful if you could ...

Clearly, I don't want to take up too much of your time but if you could ...

Obviously, I don't expect you to .... but any help you could give me would be much appreciated.

Accepting

No problem. I'll get back to you as soon as ...

I'd be happy to help out with ...

I'd be happy to help.

Declining

I'm sorry but ...

I'd like to help but ...

Unfortunately ...

At the moment I'm afraid it's just not possible.

22.7   Invitations

Inviting

In accordance with our previous conversations, I am very glad to invite you to ... *

I sincerely hope that you will be able to accept this invitation, and look forward to hosting you in *name of town*. *

I was wondering whether you might be interested in joining the Scientific Advisory Board of ... *

I am writing to you to find out whether you would be willing to ...

Accepting

Thank you very much for your kind invitation to ... *

I would be delighted to be a member of ... *

It is very kind of you to invite me to ...

Declining

Many thanks for your kind invitation, but unfortunately ...

I am really sorry but I am going to have to turn down your invitation to ...

Thank you very much for your kind invitation. However, I am afraid that ...

Thanks very much for inviting me to ... I am really sorry but I am afraid I cannot accept.

I regret that I cannot accept your invitation at the present time because ... *

I'm sorry to inform you that I do not have sufficient expertise in *topic* to be able to review the paper. *

So it is with great regret that I am afraid that I will have to decline your invitation. *

Withdrawing acceptance

I am sorry to have to inform you that I am no longer able to ...

Due to family problems I am sorry to have to inform you that ...

I am sorry to give you such short notice and I sincerely hope that this won't cause you too much trouble.

22.8   Making inquiries

General inquiries

Hi, I have a couple of simple requests:

Could you please tell me ...

I would like to know ...

Could you possibly send me ...

I have some questions about ...

Asking to receive papers

I would like to receive a copy of your PhD Thesis "Metalanguage in Swahili."

Last week I attended the workshop on X. I was interested in your presentation on "Y." Have you by any chance written a paper on that topic? If so, I would very much appreciate it if you could email me a copy.

Ordering products, materials, chemicals, etc.

What do I need to do to order a ...?

I would like to know if I can order an xxx directly from you ...

I am looking for an xx. Do you have one in stock?

Ending an inquiry

Any information you could give me would be greatly appreciated.

Thanks in advance.

I look forward to receiving ...

Following up an inquiry

Thank you for ...

Would it be possible for you to send me a bit more information on ...

Could you please describe what is included in the ...

22.9   Replying to inquiries

Thanking

Thank you for contacting me ...

I am pleased to hear that you found my paper / presentation / report / seminar useful ...

Making reference

Regarding your queries about ...

In response to your questions:

Here is the information you requested:

As requested, I am sending you ...

Below you will find the answers to your questions ...

With reference to your request for ...

Following our telephone conversation about ...

Asking for details

Before I can answer your questions, I need further details re the following:

Before I can do anything, I need ...

Could you tell me exactly why you need x.

Adding details

Please note that ...

I would like to point out that ...

As far as I know ...

I'd also like to take this opportunity to bring to your attention ...

May I take this opportunity to ...

Telling recipients they can ask for further info

Please feel free to email, fax, or call if you have any questions.

Any questions, please ask.

Hope this is OK. Please contact Helen if you need any further details.

If you need any further details do not hesitate to contact me.

Should you have any questions please let us know.

Please do not hesitate to contact us should you need any further clarifications.

Ending

Please let me know if this helps.

I hope to be able to give you a definite answer soon.

Once again, thank you for contacting me.

22.10   Talking about the next step

Telling recipient how you want them to proceed

Could you please go through the manuscript and make any revisions you think necessary.

Please have a look at the enclosed report and let me know what you think.

If you could organize the meeting for next Tuesday, I'll send everyone the details.

Telling recipient how you will proceed

Thanks for your mail. It will take me a while to find all the answers you need but I should be able to get back to you early next week.

Re your request. I'll look into it and send you a reply by the end of the week.

I will contact you when I return.

Sorry, but I'm actually going on holiday tomorrow, so I'm afraid I won't be able to get back to you for a couple of weeks.

Asking recipient how they want you to proceed

Do you want me to ...?

Would you like me to ...?

Shall I ..?.

Do we need to ...?

Let me know whether . . .

22.11   Giving and responding to deadlines

Telling recipient by when you want a reply

I look forward to hearing from you in the near future / soon / before the end of the week.

Please could you get back to me by the end of today / this morning / as soon as possible.

I hope you can reply this morning so I can then get things moving before leaving tonight.

We would appreciate an early reply.

Please let me have your feedback by Friday so I can send you a draft schedule next week.

I know it is a very sharp deadline. So if you don't have time to answer my question, please don't worry about it.

Looking forward to your reply.

When you will reply

I should be able to send you the document tomorrow / within the next two days / first thing Thursday morning.

I'll get back to you before the end of the day.

I'm sorry but I won't be able to give you any response until ...

Saying what you will do

I will send you all the details re ... in due course.

With regard to your email dated . . ., I will talk to my colleagues and get back to you ASAP.

Saying what you've done

Given the new data that we now have available, we have ...

I have made the following changes: ...

Asking for confirmation if what you have done is acceptable

I hope that is OK—if not please raise with Mike.

Is that OK?

Asking to be kept informed

Please keep me informed of any developments.

Please keep me up to date.

Please let us know the outcome.

22.12   Chasing

Chasing your previous mail

Did you get my last message sent on ... ?

I was wondering whether you had received my email (see below).

May we remind you that we are still awaiting your reply to our message dated ... *

We would be grateful if you could reply as soon as possible.

Sorry, but given that I have not heard from you I am worried that I did not explain the situation clearly.

Empathizing with recipient

Hope this doesn't cause you any problems / too much trouble.

Sorry if this adds to your workload.

I know you must be very busy but ...

Saying when you will be able to fulfill the request

I am afraid I won't be able to start work on it until next week.

I honestly don't know when I'll be able to find the time to do it.

Excusing yourself for not having fulfilled the request yet

I am sorry, but as I am sure you are aware, I have been extremely busy doing X, so I haven't had time to do Y.

I am really sorry but I have been extremely busy.

It's been a really hectic week.

I've been snowed under with work.

22.13   Making arrangements for meetings and teleconferences

Suggesting the time

Let's arrange a call so that we can discuss it further.

Can we arrange a conference call for 15.00 on Monday 21 October?

Would it be possible for us to meet next Tuesday morning?

How about Wednesday straight after lunch?

The best days for me would be sometime between October 1 and 10, with a slight preference for early in the week of the 6th. Please let me know if that would be possible.

Informing of unavailability at that time

Would love to meet—but not this week! I can manage Nov 16 or 17, if either of those would suit you.

I am afraid I won't be available either today or tomorrow. Would Thursday 11 March suit you? Either the morning or the afternoon would be fine for me. I'd be grateful if you could let me know as soon as possible so I can make the necessary arrangements.

Sorry but I can't make it that day.

Sorry but I'll be on holiday then.

I'm afraid I have another engagement on 22 April.

Thank you for your invitation to attend your technical meeting. However, I am unlikely to be able to attend as I have a lot of engagements that day.

Declining

Unfortunately, due to limited resources I am unable to accept your invitation to come to the meeting.

I regret that I will not be able to attend the meeting.

Changing the time

Sorry, can't make the meeting at 13.00. Can we change it to 14.00? Let me know.

Re our meeting next week. I am afraid something has come up and I need to change the time. Would it be possible on Tuesday 13 at 15.00?

We were due to meet next Tuesday afternoon. Is there any chance I could move it until later in the week? Weds or Thurs perhaps?

Confirming the time

The meeting is confirmed for Friday at 10:30 am Pacific time, 12:30 pm Central time. Please send any items you want to discuss, and I will send an agenda earlier in the morning.

Responding to confirmation of the time

I look forward to seeing you on 30 November.

OK, Wednesday, March 10 at 11.00. I look forward to seeing you then.

OK, I will let the others know.

Cancelling

I am extremely sorry, but I am afraid I will not be able to participate in the teleconference that was arranged for next week.

I am sorry to leave this so late, but it looks like I won't be able to make the conference call tomorrow.

Due to family problems I will not be able to ...

22.14   Problems

Describing

Unfortunately I have a problem with your ...

There seems to be a problem with ...

I'm afraid there is a slight problem.

I am not sure I can ...

That might cause us ...

I think the server may not be working correctly.

I am not sure whether you sent me the right file.

Trying to understand the problem

I am not completely clear what the problem is.

I'm sorry but I don't seem to be able to understand the problem. If possible could you give me more details to clarify the situation.

I'm not really clear about this—please clarify.

So if I have understood correctly, the problem is ...

So you are saying that ...

Showing that you have understood

Right, I understand.

OK that's clear now.

OK I am clear now.

Fine.

Resolving

OK. I'll see what I can do.

I'm sorry about that. I will look into it immediately.

Don't worry I am sure we can sort it out.

I'll look into it and get back to you first thing tomorrow morning.

I will contact you again shortly.

Let me know if there is anything else I can do for you.

Just give me a call if you need anything else.

Saying that the problem is being resolved

I promise I'll have it back to you by the end of this week.

Rest assured that you'll have it within the next two days.

I'll do it as a matter of urgency.

I'll make it my top priority.

I'm just writing to assure you that we are working on the problem.

Explaining the cause of the problem

The reason why this happened is ...

This was due to ...

It was related to ...

22.15   Asking for and giving clarification

Asking for clarification when you don't understand

I'm not sure what you mean by ...

What exactly do you mean by ...?

Sorry, what's a "xxx"?

Giving clarification when recipient thought they understood but hadn't

Sorry, no what I meant was . . .

Sorry about the confusion, what I actually meant was ...

Sorry I obviously didn't make myself clear.

Giving clarification when reader didn't understand

What I meant by xxx is ...

My point is that ...

In other words ...

So what I'm saying is ...

So what I am asking is ...

So my question is ...

In other words ...

Checking that you've understood

I'm assuming you mean . . .

Do you mean that ...?

So are you saying that ...?

By xxx do you mean ...?

Checking whether recipient may have misunderstood

I am a bit concerned that you may have misinterpreted my email.

You sounded a little annoyed in your last mail. Maybe I had not expressed myself properly.

Acknowledging misunderstanding

OK, I'm sorry—you are right. I misunderstood.

Sorry about that, we obviously had our wires crossed!

Sorry for the confusion.

Hoping you have been clear

I hope this helps clarify the problems.

Does this all make sense now?

Have I clarified everything for you?

Do you understand what I mean now?

Replying when you have been given clarification

OK, understood.

OK, I'm clear now.

OK, but I'm still not clear about ...

22.16 Thanking

Thanking recipient for responding to your email

Many thanks for your email.

Thanks for getting back to me.

Thank you for the quick response.

Thanking in advance

Thanks in advance.

Thanks for any help you can give me.

Thank you very much for your assistance.

I thank you in advance for your cooperation.

Thanking for help already given

Thanks for your help in this matter.

Thank you for your help in solving this problem.

Many thanks for this.

Thanks once again for all your trouble.

22.17 Apologizing

For not answering mail sooner

Sorry for the delay in getting back to you.

Sorry I haven't replied sooner.

I apologize for not sending you the information you requested.

Apologies for the late reply.

Please accept our apologies for not getting back to you sooner.

For not answering mail sooner: excuses

Please accept my apologies, I was convinced that I had replied to you.

Sorry, but I have only just read your message now.

I have just got back from a conference.

I've been away for the last few days.

Sorry, but our server has been down, so we haven't been receiving any mails.

Sorry but we've been having emailing problems.

Sorry but your email must have gone into the spam.

For your email not arriving

For some reason my last email had delivery problems. So here it is again just in case you didn't get it first time round.

Please reply to the above address as our regular connection is down. Thanks very much.

For sending an incomplete email

Sorry I accidentally hit the send button.

Repeating apology at end of mail

Again sorry for the delay.

Once again, apologies for any trouble this may have caused you.

Thanks and once again sorry for not getting back to you straight away.

22.18   Sending attachments

Telling receiver about your mail

I'm attaching ...

Please find attached ...

Attached you will find ...

Here is ...

As you will see from the attached copy ...

Asking for confirmation of receipt

Please confirm / acknowledge receipt.

Let me know if you have received it.

I'd appreciate it if you could confirm your receipt via either fax or email.

Please could you acknowledge receipt of this mail as I am not sure we have your correct address.

Let me know if you can't open the file.

Giving confirmation

This is just to confirm that I received your attachment. I will get back to you by 9.00 tomorrow morning.

I confirm receipt of your attachment.

Telling sender you couldn't read the mails / attachments

Sorry I couldn't read your mail—it just has a series of strange characters.

I received your mail, but I'm afraid I can't open the attachment.

When I try to open the file the system crashes.

Telling sender they forgot to send the attachment

Thanks for your mail but I'm afraid you forgot to send the attachment.

I think you forgot to send the attachment.

I can't find the attachment.

Sending attachment again

Sorry, I just sent you an email without the attachments.
Sorry about the problems. Here's the attachment again. Let me know if you can read it.

Oops. Sorry. Here it is.

22.19   Technical problems with email, phone, and fax

Failed attempt to contact someone via phone

I have been trying to contact you over the phone but with no luck ...

I have left several messages with your secretary but ...

I am worried that I may have the wrong number. Please could you confirm that this number is correct:

Failed attempt to send / receive fax

I've tried your fax number several times but have been unable to get through.

Could you send your fax number again as I think I must have the wrong number.

Could you please send the fax again as it was too faint to read.

We only received three pages of your six-page fax.

Could you send the last two pages again please.

Asking for confirmation of arrival

I sent our order today by fax. I hope you received it successfully.

Could you just confirm that you received my email dated 10 March (see below).

Problems with Internet connection

Sorry our server has been down all morning.

Sorry but they are doing maintenance work tomorrow morning and I won't have access to my email.

My Internet service is currently not working at home, which also means I can't call out. But I should still be able to receive incoming phone calls.

22.20   Circular emails

Change of address / telephone number, etc.

Please note that as of now my email address is:

This is to inform you that as of this coming 10 September our institute will be transferring to the address given below.

We are writing to inform you of our change of telephone number. As from July 10 the initial code on all our numbers will be [0039] 50 rather than [0039] 050.

We have today moved to ...

Out of office message

Adrian Wallwork is on leave from Monday 07/08 to Wed 16/08. If you have any problems or queries please contact Anna Southern at anna.southern@virgilio.it.

I'm out of the office all day today but will get back to you tomorrow regarding any urgent messages.

If you have any urgent messages you can contact me on my mobile: [0039] 347 ...

Chapter 23
Dealing with Reviews, Referees, and Editors

23.1 Sending documents for informal revision

Explaining background

I am currently working on a paper that I would like to submit to ...

The paper is the extension of the work that I ...

The draft is still at quite an early stage.

Explaining reason for sending document to this specific person

Given your expertise, it would be great if you could take a look at ...

I would really appreciate your input on this because ...

I know that you have done a lot of research on this ...

Requesting help

When you have a moment do you think you could ... ?

Could you possibly ...

If you get a chance could you ...

Do you think you might be able to help me with ...?

I'd be grateful if you could help us with ...

Could you please check these comments and let us know if you still have any issues with ...

I hear you may be able to help out with writing the paper.

Please have a look at the enclosed report and let me know what you think.

Giving specific instructions

It would be great if you could read all of Sections 3 and 4. However, if you are short of time, please just read the last two subsections of Section 4.

Please let me know if you see any need for additions or deletions.

Don't worry about any typos at the moment or minor inconsistencies in the notation.

If you have any comments on x they would be gratefully received.

Just think about general aspects, such as whether I have missed anything vital out, or my reasoning doesn't seem to be very logical.

I'm attaching the draft in two versions: a pdf of the complete manuscript, including the graphs, and a Word file of just the text—this is so that you can write any comments directly on the file using Track Changes.

Giving deadlines

I know this is a lot to ask, but as I am already behind schedule do you think you could give me your feedback by the end of next week?

I know you must be very busy but ...

Once you have reviewed the document, please forward it to ...

A. Wallwork, *English for Academic Correspondence and Socializing*,
DOI 10.1007/978-1-4419-9401-1_23, © Springer Science+Business Media, LLC 2011

Resending documents

Sorry, but I inadvertently sent you the wrong document.

I have made a few changes to the manuscript. If you haven't already started work on it, please could you use this version instead. If you have already started, then please ignore the new version.

23.2   Receiving and commenting on documents for informal revision

Accepting to do revision

I would be pleased to read / revise your document for you.

I am happy to give you my input on the first draft.

I'd be happy to help out with editing some sections of the paper.

Thank you for sending the manuscript. I just had a quick glance at it, and it looks very promising.

Declining request to do revision

I am sorry but I am extremely busy at the moment.

I am afraid I simply don't have the time to ...

Declining a request for help after an initial acceptance

I am writing to tell you that unfortunately I no longer have the time to ...

This is because ...

Once again my sincere apologies for this.

I am extremely sorry about this and I do hope it does not put you in any difficulty.

Saying when you could begin / complete the work

In the next couple of days I will go through it and send you my comments.

I am very busy in the next few days, so I won't be able to start till Monday if that's alright with you?

I should be able to finish it by the middle of next week.

I will send you Section 3 tomorrow night, and the other sections over the weekend.

Making positive comments

First of all I think you have done a great job.

I have now had a chance to look at your manuscript, it looks very good.

I was really impressed with ...

The only comments I have to make are:

Suggesting changes

While I like the idea of ... I am not convinced that ...

I'm not sure whether ...

It might not be a bad idea to ...

Have you thought about ...?

It seems that ...

Asking for clarification

I have a few questions to ask.

Could you just clarify a couple of aspects for me:

Replying with revised version attached

I have read the manuscript carefully and made several changes and corrections.

I hope I have not changed the sense of what you wanted to say.

Attached are my comments.

I think the paper still needs some work before sending to the journal.

Please keep me up to date on the progress of this manuscript.

Let me know if you need any more help.

Please give me a call if I can be of any help.

Don't hesitate to contact me if you need any more help.

I hope this helps.

Replying to comments

Bogdan, you did a great job, thanks so much!

Thank you for your comments—they were really useful.

I completely understand what you mean when you say ... Thanks for bringing it up.

Many thanks for this. All points noted.

Yes, I see what you mean.

Thanks your comments were really helpful.

23.3   Referees reports

Making a summary of the paper

The paper deals with ...

The paper gives a good description of ...

This manuscript reports some results on the use of ...

The aim is to assess the quality of ...

This paper has many positive aspects ...

General criticisms

This paper aims to report the analysis of ... yet the author writes ...

The author needs to clarify the following points ...

Despite the title of the paper, I believe that the paper does not deal with X at all. Specifically ...

The analysis in Section 2 only covers ... Even though these are important parameters, they do not ...

Although the description of X and the samples collected seems to be detailed, accurate, and well documented, the analytical work and the discussion on Y are in need of major revision.

The manuscript does not present any improvement on the analytical procedure already described in the literature; moreover the authors fail to ...

The discussion should be reviewed since it is mainly based on results published in ...

Specific comments

Abstract: What is the real advantage of the proposed procedure with respect to ...?

page 3 line 12: The word *definite* is misspelled.

page 4: Perhaps Figure 2 could be deleted.

The following information is missing in Section 2:

There seems to be a missing reference in the bibliography.

Recommending rejection

For the above reasons, I believe that the paper is not innovative enough to be published in ...

The paper is not suitable for publication in its present form, since it does not fit the minimum requirements of originality and significance in the field covered by the Journal.

23.4   Author's reply to referees and editors

Asking for extension to deadlines

I am writing to ask whether it would be possible to extend the deadline for final submission of our paper until June 14.

The referees asked for several new experiments which will take us an extra two or three weeks to perform.

I apologize for the inconvenience caused by its late submission.

I am writing to inform you that due to unforeseen circumstances, we have to withdraw our paper.

Enclosing revised manuscript and reply to referees' reports

Attached is the revised version of our paper.

As requested, we have prepared a revised version of our manuscript, which we hope addresses the issues raised by the two reviewers.

As requested, I'm sending you the paper with the changes tracked.

Saying how your reply to the referees is organized

Below are our responses to the reviewers. The reviewers' comments are in italics, and our responses are numbered.

Rather than going through each report individually, we have organized our response under general areas.

Making positive comments about the reviewer's comments

Please extend my sincere thanks to the paper reviewers for their helpful comments.

The reviewer's suggestion is certainly helpful and ...

The reviewer is right.

These two comments made us realize that ...

Outlining changes made

We have improved the paper along the lines suggested by the Referees.

I have considered all the comments and suggestions made by reviewers of this paper, and I have incorporated most of them in the final version of this paper.

We have amended the paper addressing most of the comments provided in the referees' reports.

The tables have been enlarged and we hope they are now clearer.

The Abstract and the first sections have been improved.

We have amended the paper following the indications that you and the referees gave us.

There is now a new table (Table 1) reporting the ...

We have reduced the abstract to 150 words.

On the basis of Ref 1's first comment, we changed several parts which, as you can see, have been tracked.

Saying why some changes were not made

Reviewer 1 raised some substantial criticisms that would entail an almost completely new version of the paper.

We have tried to address the points he made but we have not been able to completely put into action all the recommendations he suggested. In order to do that, we would have gone beyond the intended scope of our paper.

Actually, this is not entirely true. In fact, ...

I understand what the referee means, however ...

The referee is absolutely right when he says .. Yet, ...

Concluding

Overall we hope we have addressed the main points raised by the reviewers.

Once again we would like to thank the reviewers for their very useful input and we also found your summary most helpful.

Chapter 24
Telephoning

The useful phrases given in this chapter do not include those used in a teleconference, see Chapter 12. The phrases in italics are responses to the phrases on the previous line / s.

There are many phrases for you to choose from. I suggest that you try to learn just the ones that are easiest for you to say. However, it is also useful for you to be aware of the other phrases, so that you will be able to recognize them when you hear them.

24.1 Introductions

Saying who you are

Good morning this is Hai Li, from the Chinese Institute of ...

Hello this is Professor Whulanza. I'm calling from the University of Indonesia.

I don't think we have actually spoken before.

No I don't think we have.

I am calling on behalf of Chandra Hurria.

Saying who you want to speak to

Could I speak to Professor Williams please?

Yes, of course, I'll just put you through.

I'm sorry but she is not available at the moment.

Well, if Professor Williams is not in, could I speak to her secretary / assistant?

Could you put me through to Dr Heinrich Muller please?

Could you give me extension 318 please?

Asking who you are speaking to

Sorry, who am I speaking to?

This is Professor William's assistant.

This is Carol on reception.

Is that Dr Abdelwahab?

Yes, speaking.

Speaking to someone you already know

Hello. This is Vladimir speaking.

Hi Vladimir, nice to hear from you, how are you doing?

Good morning. This is Vladimir Ancherbak speaking.

Good morning Dr Ancherbak, what can I do for you?

Hi Josefina, this is Ivan, how are you?

Hey, Ivan, good to hear from you. I'm fine thanks and you?

A. Wallwork, *English for Academic Correspondence and Socializing*,
DOI 10.1007/978-1-4419-9401-1_24, © Springer Science+Business Media, LLC 2011

Moving on to reason for calling

Anyway the reason I'm calling is ...

Well the reason I'm ringing you is ...

24.2   Giving background to your call

Explaining where you got their number from

Your name was given to me by Dr Bhatta-charjee, who thought you ...

I got your number from your department's website. I hope I am not disturbing you.

No, not at all, what can I do for you?

Sorry, but would you mind emailing me? I am rather busy at the moment.

If you remember we met at the conference last week and you gave me your phone number ...

Yes, of course, you were the person who asked me ... How can I help you?

Giving reason for your call

I'm calling about ...

The reason I'm ringing is to find out if you ...

I wonder if you can help me.

Could you tell me whether ... ?

I'll just check for you. What exactly do you need to know?

Do you happen to know if ... ?

No but I'll try and find out for you.

I don't know offhand—I can easily look it up for you.

I'm looking for ...

I need some information about ...

Sorry to keep you waiting. I've asked a colleague and was told that ...

Thanks for holding. I think I've got the information you were looking for.

I'm sorry I couldn't be of more help.

Explaining more about yourself to someone who does not know you

My name is Jacqueline Belchev and I am assistant professor at ...

I read your paper on ... and I was wondering whether ...

I came to your presentation on ... and I have a couple of questions to ask regarding ...

I am a PhD student at Osaka University and ...

I am currently writing a request for funds from ...

I'm in charge of a European project on ...

I will be jointly responsible for ...

I'm from the R and D lab in ...

For the last few months I've been dealing with ...

24.3   Receiving calls

Offering help

How can I help you?

Asking for name / institute / department

Could I ask the name of your institute?

Sorry, which faculty at Cairo University did you say?

Could you repeat your name please?

Who's calling please?

Sorry, who did you say you wanted to speak to?

Sorry, where are you calling from?

When you recognize who's calling

Oh good morning Ingrid, what can I do for you?

When you are the right person

Speaking.

When you're not the right person

I'm sorry but I'm not the right person, I'll put you through to someone who can help you.

I'm sorry but Professor Bergen now works at ...

Sorry but I don't think I am the right person.

I think you must have dialed the wrong number.

Are you sure you've got the right number?

When you can't talk for some reason

I'm sorry, but I'll have to call you back in five minutes.

Sorry about that. I just had to open the door for someone. Are you still there?

24.4   Person not available

Checking that person is not available

Would you check / Can you just check if he's in the lab please?

Are you sure he isn't there? I had arranged with Professor Boisseau to call him at this time.

Checking when person will be available

Can you tell me what time he'll be back?

When are you expecting her back?

Do you know when she will be in?

When will she be back from lunch?

Is there anyone else I could speak to?

Asking to be called back

Could he possibly call me back? My name is Agnès Brunel and my number is ...

Could you ask her to call me?

Could he possibly call me back as soon as he returns as it's rather urgent?

Could you just tell Dr Charnteski that I called.

She'll know why I called.

Saying when you'll call back

OK, if he's in his office this afternoon, I'll call back at around five.

Right, I'll call again next week.

24.5   Leaving a message

Asking to leave a message

This is Vassilis Akalaitis calling from the University of Athens. Could I leave a message for Karol Weber please?

Can I leave a message?

Could I leave a message with someone from administration?

Do you think I could leave a message with his secretary?

Spelling out names and numbers

Could you ask her to ring me back on 02 878 705 (zero two / eight seven eight / seven zero five).

I'm sorry but I gave you the wrong number. It's two <u>one</u> six, not two <u>three</u> six.

Shall I spell that for you?

I'll spell that again for you.

No, there is only one B in Weber not two.

That's seventeen—one seven.

No, that's Rosi with an "i" not an "a".

Yes, that's right.

Suggesting that email is the best option

Would you like me to email that to you?

It's a bit complicated isn't it? Shall I email it instead?

Asking for and giving email / website address

Could you give me your / his email address please?

Her address is: ana_regina at hotmail dot com. That's Ana with one N, A-N-A underscore regina at ...

Is that one word or two?

His address is adrianwallwork at yahoo dot com. That's adrianwallwork all one word with no dots.

The website is: e4ac.com / books, that's the letter E as in Ecuador, then the number four as a digit, then the letters A and C, then dot com, then slash "books."

Is that A as in Argentina?

Is that a forward slash?

Ending call

OK. Thanks for your help. Goodbye.

24.6 Taking a message

Asking to take a message

Would you like to leave a message?

Can I take a message?

Would you like me to give her a message?

Can I ask what it's about?

Checking

Can you spell that please?

Could I just spell that back to you?

Can I read that back to you?

So the number is 0039 050 831 2059?

So that's ...

Requesting an email

Can I confirm that by email?

I'm sorry, but would you mind emailing that to me? I'm not sure if I've got it all correctly.

Could you give me her email address please?

Concluding call

OK, I'll make sure she gets your message.

I'll refer that to him and I'll get him to call you back.

24.7   Calling someone back

When you call someone back

This is Monica Chong returning your call.

I believe you called me this morning.

Good morning Dr Wang, this is Professor Chulkin. I believe you called earlier on.

I'm sorry I wasn't in when you called but I was in a lecture.

When someone calls you back

Thanks for getting back to me.

I called you because ...

Calling someone back who you've just spoken to

Sorry to bother you again but ...

Hello, it's me again. I just wanted ...

24.8   Requests / inquiries

For someone to do something for you

Could you show it to Dr Donatis and ask her ...

No problem. / Of course.

Could you check whether I sent you ...

Could you just hold the line and I will check for you.

Can you just make sure you have received the manuscript.

Could you email me with this request as I am afraid this is not possible over the phone.

Would you mind sending it again?

I'll send it straight away.

I'll do it first thing tomorrow morning.

Request for fax / email

Could you possibly send us that by fax? Could you fax that to us?

I think you probably already have our number.

You should have our number I think.

Our fax number is the same as our phone number except for the last two digits—so it's 98 not 84.

24.9   Chasing and getting updates

Asking about progress

How's it going?

I was wondering if you had had a chance to ...

Is everything working OK?

What's the latest on ... ?

Have you got any news about ... ?

Sorry to bother you again, but I really need to know if ...

Telling someone how to proceed

Could you ring me back before 12.00 please?

I'd be grateful if you could give me an answer by this evening.

Can you get back to me first thing tomorrow?

Could you fax that to me?

Could you send me confirmation by email?

Then will you call me back and tell me ... ?

Asking how someone will proceed

Are you going to email them to me?

When can I expect your call?

Do you think you'll be able to get back to me before the end of the day?

Suggesting how someone should proceed

You could contact administration who should have the details.

The best thing to do would be to contact administration as they ...

One idea might be to contact ...

Informing your interlocutor how you will proceed

OK I'll send them to you in a few minutes.

I'll get back to you before 6.00 tonight.

I'll be in touch later today.

I'll send you the information you required first thing tomorrow.

I'll put them in the post straight away.

If you don't hear from me you can assume that everything is OK.

Asking how you should proceed

What would you like me to do with it?

What would you like me to do?

Please let me know what you'd like me to do.

Shall I ... ?

Do you want me to ... ?

24.10   Giving and asking for deadlines

Asking for a deadline

When do you need the documents back?

By when do you need an answer?

When would it suit you to have the revisions by?

Giving deadlines

Ideally I need the revised version by tomorrow night.

It would be great if you could finish it within the next three or four days.

Could you possibly send it to me by 4 o'clock?

I need them by 12 o'clock London time.

I'm really sorry but I absolutely must have them by four o'clock. The thing is ...

Responding to a deadline

OK I'll do my best.

OK I'll see what I can do.

I'll do my best but I am afraid I can't guarantee anything.

I'm really sorry but I am inundated with work, so I don't think tomorrow would be realistic. I could probably do it by Friday, would that be OK?

Confirming the deadline

OK, so I'll expect it by the end of this week.

OK, so you will get it back to me within the next few days.

24.11   Problems with understanding

Saying you can't understand

I'm sorry I didn't quite catch that.

I'm not that clear about ...

I'm sorry, what did you say?

Asking for repetition

Sorry, what did you say?

Would you mind repeating that please?

Could you say that again please?

What did you say your name was?

Your name was?

Can you repeat that last part please?

Can you go over the bit about ...?

A "what" sorry?

Can you spell that for me?

I'm still not sure what you mean by "x"?

I'm sorry I still don't understand.

Problems with the line and mobile phone reception

The line's very faint / bad.

Do you think you could call me back? I can hardly hear you.

Would you mind calling me back? The line is terrible.

I think I'd better call you back. The line is terrible.

Sorry the reception is not very good here.

Sorry you're breaking up.

Sorry I am just about to go through a tunnel so we may get cut off.

I'm so sorry we got cut off.

Problems with voice and speed

Do you think you could speak up a little, please?

Could you speak a little more slowly please?

24.12   Checking and clarifying

Checking that the other person has understood

Is there anything you're not quite clear about?

Would you like me to go over anything again?

Would you like me to repeat my name and number?

Have you got that?

Would you mind repeating that back to me?

Is that clear?

What is it that you didn't understand?

What exactly do you need to know?

Am I making myself clear?

Does that seem to make sense?

Does that sound OK to you?

Are you OK with that?

Confirming that you've understood

OK I'm with you.

Yeah, that's fine.

Yes, that sounds fine.

Yes that makes sense.

Yes, I'm clear about that.

Yes, I've got all that.

Checking that you've understood

I'm not really clear about the first and second point.

So do you mean that ... ?

Are you saying that ... ?

Confirming that other person has understood

Yes, that's right.

Exactly.

Clarifying what you've already said

What I mean is ...

What I meant by "x" was ...

Checking that you've taken everything down

Have I got everything?

Is that everything?

24.13   Apologizing

Generic apologies and responses

I'm really sorry.

Oh that's alright.

Don't worry.

Not to worry.

I'm sorry about that.

These things happen.

No problem.

I'm sorry about that. I'll get on to it straight away.

Brilliant, that would be great, thank you.

Apologizing for misunderstandings

Sorry, I didn't mean to ...

Sorry, I thought you meant ...

I meant ...

I didn't mean to offend.

Sorry I obviously didn't make myself clear.

24.14   Thanking

Thank you / Thanks very much.

You've been most / really helpful.

Thank you very much for your help.

Sorry to have troubled you.

Brilliant. Cheers.

Not at all.

You're welcome.

Don't mention it.

24.15   Leaving a voicemail

This is Professor Wallwork from the University of Pisa in Italy. It's eleven thirty in the morning our time. I've been trying to contact you all day. But I keep getting your machine. Do you think you could ring me on my mobile when you get in? This is where I'll be at until one o'clock. After that you can ring me at the office on the following number. Hope to hear you soon. Goodbye.

24.16   Talking on Skype

Can you see me OK now?

Do you want me to turn on / off the video?

I don't think you've got your microphone on properly.

I can hear you but I can't see you.

I can only see your feet / desk at the moment.

Did you add William to the conference?

Do you think you could upload the document?

I have just sent you a chat message, did you get?

Could you write that down for me and send it as a message—thanks.

Sorry, for some reason we got cut off.

Sorry, someone else seems to be trying to call me, can you just hang on a second?

24.17   Saying goodbye

OK / Right, I think that's all.

Well, I think that's everything. Goodbye.

I look forward to seeing you.

Do call if you need anything else.

Have a nice day / weekend.

You too.

Hear from you soon. Bye.

Chapter 25
Understanding Native Speakers

25.1 Requesting that the speaker modify their way of speaking

Asking the speaker to change their way of speaking

Sorry, could you speak up please?

Sorry, could you speak more slowly please?

You'll have to speak more slowly, sorry.

I don't want to sound rude but could you speak more clearly please?

Reminding speaker to change their way of speaking

Sorry, I really need you to speak up please.

Sorry, my listening skills are not very good, would you mind speaking more slowly please?

Sorry, my English is not very good, could you speak very slowly please.

25.2 Asking for repetition

Asking for repetition of the whole phrase

I'm sorry what did you say?

Could you explain that again using different words?

Sorry, could you say that again?

Sorry, I didn't catch that.

Sorry what was your question?

Identifying the part of the phrase that you did not understand

Sorry, what did you say at the beginning?

I didn't get the middle bit / last bit.

Sorry what was the last bit?

Could you say that last bit again?

Sorry I missed the bit about ...

And you did "what" sorry?

And you went "where" sorry?

You spoke to "who" sorry?

Repeating the part of the phrase up to the point where you stopped understanding

Sorry, you thought the presentation was ... ?

And then you went to ... ?

And the food was ...?

When the speaker has repeated what they said but you still cannot understand

Sorry, I still don't understand.

Sorry, do you think you could say that in another way?

A. Wallwork, *English for Academic Correspondence and Socializing,*
DOI 10.1007/978-1-4419-9401-1_25, © Springer Science+Business Media, LLC 2011

Sorry, could you say that again but much more slowly?

Sorry, could you write that word down, I can't really understand it.

When you understand the words but not the general sense

Sorry, I'm not really clear what you're saying.

Sorry I think I am missing / have missed the point.

Sorry but I am not really clear about . . .

When you didn't hear because you were distracted

Sorry, I missed that last part.

Sorry, I got distracted. What were you saying?

Sorry, I've lost track of what you were saying.

Sorry, I've forgotten the first point you made.

Sorry, I'm a bit lost.

Sorry I wasn't concentrating, what were you saying?

25.3   Clarifying

Clarifying by summarizing what other person has said

So what you're saying is . . .

So you're saying that it is true.

So if I understood you correctly, you mean . . .

Let me see if I have the big picture. You're saying that . . .

Clarifying what you have said

What I said / meant was ...

What I'm trying to say is ...

The point I'm making is ...

Let me say that in another way.

In other words, what I mean is ...

Clarifying a misunderstanding in what you said

No, that's not really what I meant.

No, actually what I meant was . . .

Well, not exactly.

What I was trying to say was ...

That's not actually what I was trying to say.

Clarifying a misunderstanding in what someone else said

I think you may have misunderstood what he said. What he meant was ...

No, I think what he was trying to say was ... Have I got that right?

If I'm not mistaken, what she was saying was ...

Checking that others are following you

Does that make sense to you?

Do you understand what I mean?

Do you understand what I'm saying?

Saying that you are or are not following someone else

Yes, I see what you're getting at.

Yes, perfectly.

Yes, I know what you are saying . . .

Yeah, yeah, yeah—I've got you.

I'm with you.

OK, I think it's clear what you are saying.

Well, no not really, could you explain it again?

When you get lost while you are speaking

Sorry, I've forgotten what I was going to say.

Sorry, I've lost track of what I was saying.

Sorry, I can see I'm not making much sense.

Sorry, I don't really know what I am talking about.

Chapter 26
Socializing

26.1 Introductions

Meeting people for the first time (previous contact via email, phone)

Hello, pleased to meet you finally.

So, finally, we meet.

I'm very glad to have the opportunity to speak to you in person.

I think we have exchanged a few email, and maybe spoken on the phone.

Meeting people for the first time (no previous contact)

Hello, I don't think we've met. I'm ...

Pleased to meet you.

Nice to meet you, too.

May I introduce myself? My name is ...

I'm responsible for / I'm in charge of ... I'm head of ...

Good morning, I'm ...

How do you do?

Here is my card.

Do you have a card?

Introducing people

Can I introduce a colleague of mine? This is Irmin Schmidt.

Hello, Pete, this is Ursula.

David, this is Olga. Olga, this is David.

I'm afraid Wolfgang cannot be with us today.

Telling people how to address you

Please call me Holger.

OK, and I'm Damo.

Fine, please call me Damo.

26.2 Meeting people who you have met before

Meeting people who you think you may have met before

Excuse me, I think we may have met before, I'm ...

Hi, have we met before?

Hi, you must be ...

Seeing people you have already met before

Hi, Tom, good to see you again, how are you doing?

Hi, how's it going? I haven't seen you for ages.

How's things?

A. Wallwork, *English for Academic Correspondence and Socializing*,
DOI 10.1007/978-1-4419-9401-1_26, © Springer Science+Business Media, LLC 2011

Great to see you.

I'm (very) pleased to see you again.

How's the new job going?

How's your husband? And the children?

How is the new project going?

Catching up

How did the trip to Africa go?

26.3   Small talk

Asking questions

Is it that the first time you have attended this conference?

Where are you staying?

Where are you from?

What did you think of the last presentation?

What presentations are you planning to see this afternoon?

What was the best presentation so far do you think?

Are you going to present something?

Had you ever seen Professor Jones present before? She's great don't you think?

Are you coming to the gala dinner?

So, you said you were doing some research into x. Do have any interesting results yet?

So you were saying your were born in x—what's it like there?

Showing interest

Oh, are you?

Oh, is it?

Oh, really?

Right.

That's interesting.

Oh, I hadn't realized.

Apologizing for something you shouldn't have said

Sorry, I didn't mean to ...

Sorry, I thought you meant ...

I meant ...

I didn't mean to offend.

Sorry I obviously didn't make myself clear.

26.4   Arranging meetings

Suggesting a time / day

Would tomorrow morning at 9.00 suit you?

Could you make it in the afternoon?

Shall we say 2.30, then?

Could you manage the day after tomorrow?

What about after the last presentation this afternoon?

Making an alternative suggestion

Tomorrow would be better for me.

If it's OK with you, I think I'd prefer to make it 3.30.

Could we make it a little later?

Responding positively

OK, that sounds like a good idea.

Yes, that's fine.

Yes, that'll be fine.

That's no problem.

Responding negatively

I'm sorry, I really don't think I will have time. I have a presentation tomorrow and I am still working on some of the slides.

I don't think I can manage tomorrow morning.

I'm not sure about what I am doing tonight, I need to check with my colleagues and then get back to you.

The problem is that I already have a series of informal meetings lined up.

Cancelling a meeting set up by the other person

Something has come up, so I'm afraid I can't come.

Sorry but the other members of my group have arranged for me to ...

Sorry but it looks as though I am going to be busy all tomorrow. The thing is I have to ...

Postponing a meeting that you set up

I'm really sorry but I can't make our meeting tomorrow morning because my professor needs me to ...

I am very sorry about this, and I am sorry I couldn't let you know sooner. I hope this has not inconvenienced you.

In any case, I was wondering whether we could rearrange for tomorrow night.

26.5   At an informal one-to-one meeting

Initiating a topic

First of all, I wanted to ask you about ...

What is your view on ... ?

Changing a topic / returning to a topic

I've just thought of something else ...

Sorry to interrupt, I just need to tell you about ...

Can I interrupt a moment?

But going back to what you said earlier ...

I've been thinking about what you said and ...

Stalling and deferring by interviewee

Could I just think about that a second?

Just a moment, I really need to think about that.

Could I get back to you on that? I'll email you the answer.

Concluding by interviewer

Well, I don't want to keep you any longer.

Well, I think that's covered everything.

I think the next session is starting in a couple of minutes, so we had better stop.

Asking for a follow up

Would it be OK if I email you with any other questions that I think of?

Would you have time to continue this conversation at lunch today?

Thanking

Thank you so much. It has been really useful.

That's great. You have told me everything I needed to know.

It was really very kind of you to ...

Thanks very much for ...

Thank you very much indeed for ...

I don't know how to thank you for ...

You've been really helpful.

Responding to thanks

You're welcome.

Don't mention it.

Not at all.

It's my pleasure.

That's alright.

26.6   General requests and offers

Inquiring

I wonder if you could help me?

Do you know where / how I could ... ?

Do you happen to know if ... ?

Excuse me, do you think you could ... ?

Responding to an inquiry

Certainly. Sure. Yes, what's the problem?

No, I'm sorry I don't actually know.

I don't actually, but if you ask that man ...

Yes, of course.

Actually, I can't I'm afraid.

Requesting help

Do you think you could give me a hand with ... ?

Would you mind helping me with ... ?

I wonder if you could help me with ... ?

Could you give me some help?

Could you do me a favor?

Accepting request for help

Sure. No problem.

Just a second and I'll be with you.

OK. Right. Where shall I start?

Declining request for help

I'm sorry but I can't just at the moment.

Sorry, but you've caught me at a bad time.

Actually, I'd rather not, if you don't mind.

Offering help

Shall I help you with ... ?

Do you want me to help you with ... ?

If you want, I could lend you hand with that.

Are you sure you don't need any help with that?

Would you like me to give you a hand with... ?

Accepting offer of help

That's really kind of you.

Great thanks.

If you're sure you can spare the time, that'd be great.

If you really don't mind, that'd be most helpful.

Declining offer of help

That's very kind of you but I think I can manage.

No, it's alright thanks.

Thanks but I really don't want to put you out.

Giving advice

Have you thought about ... ?

Don't you think perhaps you should ... ?

Perhaps it might not be a bad idea to ...

If I were you I would ...

Maybe the best thing would be to ...

Perhaps you ought to / should ...

Responding to advice

Yes, that sounds sensible.

Good thinking!

That's a good idea. Thanks.

Showing enthusiasm

That's wonderful / great / fantastic / perfect.

Well done!

Congratulations!

Good on you.

That's marvelous news. I'm so pleased for you.

Really? I can hardly believe it.

You must be so proud of yourself.

Giving condolences

Oh well, it's better than nothing.

Bad luck! Better luck next time.

Oh dear! I'm sorry to hear that.

Well, I'm sure you did everything you could.

26.7   At the bar and restaurant

Formal invitations for dinner

Would you like to have lunch next Friday?

If you are not busy tonight, would you like to ... ?

We're organizing a dinner tonight, I was wondering whether you might like to come?

I'd like to invite you to dinner.

Accepting

That's very kind of you. I'd love to come. What time are you meeting?

Thank you, I'd love to.

That sounds great.

What a nice idea.

Responding to an acceptance

Great. OK, well we could meet downstairs in the lobby.

Great. I could pass by your hotel at 7.30 if you like.

Declining

I'm afraid I can't, I'm busy on Friday.

That's very nice of you, but ...

Thanks but I have to make the final touches to my presentation.

No, I'm sorry I'm afraid I can't make it.

Unfortunately, I'm already doing something tomorrow night.

Responding to a non-acceptance

Oh that's a shame, but not to worry.

Oh well, maybe another time.

Informal invitation to go to the bar / cafe

Shall we go and have a coffee?

Would you like to go and get a coffee?

What about a coffee?

Do you know if there is a coffee machine somewhere in the building?

Offering drink / food

Can I get you anything?

What can I get you?

Would you like a coffee?

Black or white? How many sugars?

So, what would you like to drink?

Would you like some more wine?

Shall I pour it for you?

Accepting offer

I'll have a coffee please.

I think I'll have an orange juice.

No, nothing for me thanks.

Toasting

Cheers.

To your good health.

To distant friends.

Questions and answers at the bar / cafe

Do you often come to this bar?

Yes, either this one or the one across the road.

Is there a bathroom here?

Well, I think we'd better get back—the next session starts in 10 minutes.

Shall we get back?

Arriving at a restaurant

We've booked a table for 10.

Could we sit outside please?

Could we have a table in the corner / by the window?

Actually we seem to have got here a bit too early.

Are the others on their way?

Would you like something to drink / Shall we sit down at the bar while we're waiting for a table?

OK, I think we can go to our table now.

Menu

Can / May / Could I have the menu please?

Do you have a set menu / a menu with local dishes?

Do you have any vegetarian dishes?

Explaining things on the menu and asking for clarification

Shall I explain some of the things on the menu?

Well, basically these are all fish dishes.

I'd recommend it because it's really tasty and typical of this area of my country.

This is a salad made up of eggs, tuna fish, and onions.

Could you tell me what xxx is?

Making suggestions

Can I get you another drink?

Would you like anything else?

Shall I order some wine?

Would you like anything to drink? A glass of wine?

Would you like a little more wine?

Would you prefer sparkling or still water?

What are you going to have?

Are you going to have a starter?

Why don't you try some of this?

Can I tempt you to . . . ?

Would you like to try some of this? It's called xxx and is typical of this area.

What would you like for you main course?

Would you like anything for dessert? The sweets are homemade and are very good.

Saying what you are planning to order

I think I'll just have the starter and then move on to the main course.

I think I'll have fish.

I'd like a small portion of the chocolate cake.

I don't think I'll have any dessert thank you.

Requesting

Could you pass me the water please?

Could I have some butter please?

Do you think I could have some more wine?

Declining

Nothing else thanks.

Actually, I am on a diet.

Actually, I am allergic to nuts.

I've had enough thanks. It was delicious.

Being a host and encouraging guests to start

Do start.

Enjoy your meal.

Enjoy.

Tuck in.

Help yourself to the wine / salad.

Being a guest and commenting on food before beginning to eat

It smells delicious.

It looks really good.

Asking about and making comments on the food

Are you enjoying the fish?

Yes, it's very tasty.

This dish is delicious.

This wine is really good.

Ending the meal

Would you like a coffee, or something stronger?

Would anyone like anything else to eat or drink?

Paying

Could I have the bill please.

I'll get this.

That's very kind of you, but this is on me.

No, I insist on paying. You paid last time.

That's very kind of you.

Do you know if service is included?

Do people generally leave a tip?

Thanking

Thank you so much—it was a delicious meal and a great choice of restaurant.

Thanks very much. If you ever come to Berlin, let me know, there's an excellent restaurant where I would like to take you.

Thank you again, it was a lovely evening.

Replying to thanks

Not at all. It was my pleasure.

Don't mention it.

You're welcome.

26.8   At the hotel

Checking in

I have a reservation in the name of ...

The booking was confirmed by both email and fax.

Which floor is my room on?

When will it be ready?

Has anyone else from my institute arrived here already?

I will be leaving at 08.30 tomorrow morning.

Meeting someone you know by the check-in desk

Hello, I didn't know you were staying here.

How are you?

Did you have a good journey here?

Have you already checked in?

Do you want to get a drink while we wait for the others?

What room are you in?

Asking about services

Is there an Internet connection?

Is there a shuttle bus to the conference?

Can you book me a taxi?

Is there a train that goes to the airport?

What time do I have to be back to the hotel in the evening?

When is breakfast served?

How do I dial for overseas?

I'm expecting a Professor Tschaida at 7.00. Could you call me when he arrives?

Problems with the room

This key doesn't seem to work.

I have locked myself out.

My room has not been cleaned.

There are no towels.

Could I have an extra pillow please?

Would it be possible to change room, it's very noisy?

Checking out

I'd like to pay my bill.

I haven't used anything out of the minibar. But I did make one phone call.

I'll be paying by Visa.

The bill should have already been paid by my institute.

I think there is a mistake here—I didn't have anything from the bar.

Could I have my passport back?

Can I leave my luggage here and collect it later?

I left you my case with you this morning.

No it's not that one, it's got a blue stripe on it. Yes, that one.

Could you ring for a taxi for me?

26.9 Saying goodbye

Excuses for leaving

I am sorry—do you know where the bathroom is?

It was nice meeting you but sorry I just need to go to the bathroom (GB) / restroom (US).

Sorry but I just need to answer this call.

I have just remembered I need to make an urgent call.

It has been great talking to you, but I just need to make a phone call.

Sorry, I've just seen someone I know.

Sorry, but someone is waiting for me.

Listen, it has been very interesting talking to you but unfortunately I have to go ... may be we could catch up with each other tomorrow.

Using the time as an excuse for leaving

Does anyone have the correct time because I think I need to be going?

Oh, is that the time? I'm sorry but I have to go now.

Sorry, I've got to go now.

I think it's time I made a move.

Wishing well and saying goodbye (neutral)

It's been very nice talking to you.

I hope to see you again soon.

I really must be getting back.

I do hope you have a good trip.

It was a pleasure to meet you.

Please send my regards to Dr Hallamabas.

Wishing well and saying goodbye (informal)

Be seeing you.

Bye for now.

Keep in touch.

Look after yourself.

Say "hello" to Kate for me.

See you soon.

See you later.

Take care.

See you in March at the conference then.

Hope to see you before too long.

Have a safe trip home.

OK, my taxi's here.

Links and References

Further reading and resources

(1) **Referees' reports**

Excellent materials for writing and responding to referees' reports can be found on the *British Medical Journal*'s website: http://resources.bmj.com/bmj/reviewers/training-materials. On this site they have various training materials to help reviewers write their reviews. I very much recommend you read all the documents in Objective Two of their training materials.

Other suggested links:
Surviving referees' reports: http://www.bmartin.cc/pubs/08jspsrr.html
Instructions and advice for referees: http://people.bu.edu/rking/JME_files/guide_for_referees.htm
Guidelines for referees' reports:
riem.swufe.edu.cn/flv/201092512362216685.pdf and
http://www.webpondo.org/files_ene_mar04/referee.pdf

(2) **Pronunciation**

Below is the address of a pdf that explains how to use Adobe's read aloud feature.
http://www.adobe.com/designcenter/acrobat/articles/acr6araccessibility/acr6araccessibility.pdf

There are many sites on the web that are dedicated to English pronunciation, also for people with a specific mother tongue (e.g., English pronunciation for Chinese people).

For the differences between US and UK pronunciation see: http://en.wikipedia.org/wiki/American_and_British_English_pronunciation_differences

For help with listening skills:
http://www.bbc.co.uk/skillswise/words/listening/
http://www.esl-lab.com/

A. Wallwork, *English for Academic Correspondence and Socializing*,
DOI 10.1007/978-1-4419-9401-1, © Springer Science+Business Media, LLC 2011

http://www.elllo.org/

http://www.eslhome.com/esl/listen/

For more on pronunciation, see Chapter 3 *Pronunciation and Intonation* in the companion volume *English for Presentations at International Conferences.*

(3) Socializing

An excellent book to read is the classic *How to Make Friends and Influence People*, Dale Carnegie, published by Pocket Books.

Acknowledgments

Acknowledgments for the quotations in the sections entitled "What the experts say"

Thanks to Stewart Alsop (alsop-louie.com), Peter Honey (ediplc.com), and Andy Hunt (pragprog.com) for allowing me to quote them. Special thanks to the following people who agreed to write me a few lines specifically for this book: Susan Barnes, Chandler Davis, Ibrahima Diagne, Sue Fraser, Patrick Forsyth, Keith Harding, Susan Herring, Tarun Huria, Annette Kelly, Alex Lamb (www.alexlambtraining.com/index.html), Luciano Lenzini, Brian Martin, David Morand, Janice Nadler, Pierdomenico Perata Anna Southern, Richard Wiseman (http://richardwiseman.wordpress.com/tag/quirkology/), Mark Worden, Zheng Ting, and the professor in Pisa who wished to remain anonymous!

Acknowledgments for supplying me with emails and referees' reports

In addition to the people mentioned above, I would like to thank the following researchers who provided me with emails and referees' reports for this book. Also big thanks to all my PhD students who over the last 10 years have given me a constant supply of typical academic emails.

Nicola Aloia, Michele Barbera, Bernadette Batteaux, Stefania Biagioni, Silvia Brambilla, Emilia Bramanti, Francesca Bretzel, Davide Castagnetti, Shourov Keith Chatterji, Patrizia Cioni, MariaPerla Colombini, Francesca Di Donato, Marco Endrizzi, Fabrizio Falchi, Roger Fuoco, Edi Gabellieri, Valeria Galanti, Silvia Gonzali, Kamatchi Ramasamy Chandra, Stefano Lenzi, Luciano Lenzini, Leonardo Magneschi, Francesca Nicolini, Enzo Mingozzi, Elisabetta Morelli, Beatrice Pezzarossa, Marco Pardini, Roberto Pini, Emanuele Salerno, Daniel Sentenac, Paola Sgadò, Igor Spinella, Enzo Sparvoli, Pandey Sushil, Eliana Tassi, and Elisabetta Tognoni.

Sources of the Factoids

Much of the information contained in the factoids is publicly available on the Internet. Some of it was also collected from various students of mine. In particular, I would like to thank Elena Castanas, Tarun Huria, Sofia Luzgina, Daniel Sentenac, Eriko Tsuchida, and Ting Zheng for providing me with information about their countries.

Below is more information about the sources for some of the factoids, quotations, and other statistics.

Chapter 1: The second factoid is based on a statistic that claims that more than 250 billion emails are sent every day (source: Wiki Answers): the total pile would be 25,000 kilometers high, it would weigh 1,250,000 metric tonnes, and all the printed emails would have a surface area of 15,592 square kilometers The cost in euros would be around one billion. Source of third factoid: TNS "Digital Life" 10 Oct 2010.

Chapter 2: The first two factoids were provided by Dr Tarun Huria, Department of Mechanical Engineering, Indian Railways Institute of Mechanical & Electrical Engineering, India, and Dr Zheng Ting [aka Sophia Zheng], University of Shandong, Jinan, China.

Chapter 3: The statistic on people spending 40% of their time emailing comes from *I Hate People*, J Littman & M Hershon, published by Little, Brown and Company. I have been unable to locate the original source of the spell cheque poem in 13.4 (for the full version see http://www.greaterthings.com/Humor/Spelling_Chequer.htm), nor can I find the researchers involved in the Cambridge University inquiry into the phenomenal power of the human mind.

Chapter 4: The extract from Wikipedia can be found at: http://en.wikipedia.org/wiki/Emoticon. The Japanese emoticons were provided by Eriko Tsuchida.

Chapter 5: The quotation in 5.11 comes from *The Christopher Robin Birthday Book* by A.A. Milne, E.P. Dutton & Co. (1936).

Chapter 7: Factoid 1: Magda Kouřilová, Communicative characteristics of reviews of scientific papers written by non-native users of English (published in *Endocrine Regulations* Vol. 32, 107 No. 114, 1998)—www.aepress.sk/endo/full/er0298g.pdf. Factoid 2: Sweitzer BJ, Cullen DJ, How well does a journal's peer review process function? A survey of authors' opinions (*JAMA* 1994;272:152–3). Factoid 3: Juan Miguel Campanario, Have referees rejected some of the most-cited articles of all times? *Journal of the American Society for Information Science*, Volume 47 Issue 4, April 1996.

Chapter 8: Some subsections of this chapter drew ideas from the NOFOMA 2007 review guidelines.

Chapter 9: judge = assessment / review; I write = I have written, to know if = to find out whether; admitted = accepted; answer = get back to. Even after these corrections, the email would still be unacceptable in terms of content.

Chapter 12: The telephone dates come from the following sources Wikipedia, *Daily Express* (12 March 2001, article by William Harston), *The First of Everything* (by Dennis Sanders, published by Delacorte Press), *Architects of the Business Revolution* (by Des Dearlove and Stephen Coomber, published by Capstone), and my imagination. There appears to be some contrasting information with regard to when the first phone call was made and the first phones were sold.

Chapter 13: The statistics in 13.5 are reported in *Presenting with Power*, Shay McConnon, How to Books, 2002; and in *Persuasion: The Art of Influencing People*, James Borg, Pearson 2004, respectively.

Chapter 14: Factoid 1 contains information from the following sites:
http://www.gallup.com/poll/1825/about-one-four-americans-can-hold-conversation-second-language.aspx
http://www.guardian.co.uk/education/2010/aug/24/who-still-wants-learn-languages
http://www.britac.ac.uk/policy/language-matters/position-paper.cfm

Factoid 2: Talkworks at work (British Telecom), by Gerard Egan and Andrew Bailey, available for free download at: http://www.numberoneskill.com/number1skill/archive/media.ikml?PHPSESSID=0c6c664d7781ffae89e6c75332183b95

Factoid 3: Tony Buzan, *The Power of Social Intelligence*, published by Thorsons.

Factoid 4: The study is reported in D. Bone, *A Practical Guide to Efffective Listening*, Kogan Page.

Factoid 5: Native speakers' avoidance. http://scholar.lib.vt.edu/theses/available/etd-11142005-112228/unrestricted/LeeBodyMatters.pdf

Chapter 15: Factoid 1: Data taken from Sue Fraser's article "Perceptions of varieties of spoken English: implications for EIL" and reproduced by kind permission of the author.

Chapter 17: The survey mentioned in the first factoid was conducted by Professor of psychology Richard Wiseman to see what factoids are the most likely to ensure an interesting conversation at social dinners in the UK. They are contained in his wonderful book *Quirkology: The Curious Science of Everyday Lives* (Macmillan, 2007). See also his blog: http://richardwiseman.wordpress.com/tag/quirkology/. Big thanks to Andy Hunt (17.6) for giving me permission to quote from his book *Pragmatic Thinking and Learning: Refactor Your Wetware* (http://www.pragprog.com/titles/ahptl/pragmatic-thinking-and-learning).

Chapter 18: The research quoted in the introduction to this chapter: *30 Seconds to Make the Right Impression*, Eleri Sampson, published by Kogan Page. For more details on Peter Honey see: www.ediplc.com. Some of the ideas in 18.4 were based on Chapter 4, Networking, in *The Jelly Effect* by Andy Bounds, 2007, Capstone.

Chapter 19: The first three quotations in "What the experts say" come from *The Penguin International Thesaurus of Quotations*, ed. Rhoda Toma Tripp, Penguin Books. The fourth quotation is from *The Penguin Dictionary of Modern Quotations*, ed. J M and M J Cohen, Penguin Books. The fifth and sixth quotations are from the *Handbook of 20th Century Quotations*, ed Frank S Pepper, Sphere Books Ltd. The research quoted is 19.1 reported in an article for *Shape* magazine (December 1992) entitled "Are you talking to me?" and written by freelance writer Kathleen Doheny. The remarks reported in 19.2 were made by Addison in an essay written on 4 August 1711. Much of this subsection is based on a short paper entitled "Cultural differences of politeness in English and Chinese" (*Asian Social Science*, Vol. 5, No. 6, June 2009) by Dr Lu Yin, Foreign Language Department, Hebei Polytechnic University, Hebei, China. The article is available at: www.ccsenet.org/journal/index.php/ass/article/view/2492/2338

Chapter 20: The first quotations in "What the men of letters say" come from *The English Language, Essays by English & American Men of Letters 1490–1839*, ed. W.F. Bolton, 1966, Cambridge University Press. The other two quotations come from the *Handbook of 20th Century Quotations*, ed Frank S Pepper, Sphere Books Ltd.

Chapter 21: Most of Factoid 2 comes from: http://ec.europa.eu/education/languages/index_en.htm. The information in Factoid 4 comes from *English As She is Spoke*, first published in 1883 and republished in 1990 by Pryor Publications. The table in 21.8 was compiled in May 2010. If you did the same test today, you would obviously get different results.

About the Author

Since 1984 Adrian Wallwork has been editing and revising scientific papers, as well as teaching English as a foreign language. In 2000 he began specializing in training PhD students from all over the world in how to write and present their research in English. He is the author of over 20 textbooks for Springer Science+Business Media, Cambridge University Press, Oxford University Press, the BBC, and many other publishers. In 2009 he founded English for Academics (englishforacademics.com), which provides an editing and revision service for researchers.

Contact the Author

I would welcome comments on improving this book. I also hold short intensive courses for PhD students and researchers on how to write and present their research.

Please contact me at English for Academics: adrian.wallwork@e4ac.com

Index

Index by Section

Note: This index is organized by chapters and sections. Occasionally page references are given for those items that do not correspond to a section or chapter.

Index by Page Number

Note: This index is organized by pages.

Index of Names

Note: Names of people mentioned in the book, by page number.

CPSIA information can be obtained at www.ICGtesting.com
Printed in the USA
LVOW10s2210180214

374288LV00003B/63/P